The Line of Dissent

ALSO BY MARTIN DUBERMAN

Charles Francis Adams, 1807-1886

In White America

The Antislavery Vanguard: New Essays on the Abolitionists

James Russell Lowell

The Uncompleted Past

The Memory Bank

Black Mountain: An Exploration in Community

Male Armor: Selected Plays, 1968-174

Visions of Kerouac

About Time: Exploring the Gay Past

Hidden from History: Reclaiming the Gay and Lesbian Past

Paul Robeson

Cures: A Gay Man's Odyssey

Mother Earth: An Epic Play on the Life of Emma Goldman

Stonewall

The Lives of Notable Gay Men and Lesbians and *Issues in Gay and Lesbian Life (Young Adult)*

Midlife Queer

A Queer World: The Center for Gay and Lesbian Studies Reader

Queer Representations Reading Lives, Reading Cultures

Left Out: The Politics of Exclusion: Essays 1964-1999

Haymarket: A Novel

The Worlds of Lincoln Kirstein

Radical Acts: Collected Political Plays

Waiting to Land: A Political Memoir, 1985-2008

A Saving Remnant: The Radical Lives of Barbara Deming and David McReynolds

Howard Zinn: A Life on the Left

The Martin Duberman Reader

Hold Tight Gently: Michael Callen, Essex Hemphill and the Battlefield of AIDS

The Emperor Has No Clothes: Doug Ireland's Radical Voice

Jews/Queers/Germans

The Rest Of It

Has the Gay Movement Failed?

Luminous Traitor: The Just and Daring Life of Roger Casement

Naomi Weisstein: Brain Scientist, Rock Band Leader, Feminist Rebel. Her Collected Essays

Andrea Dworkin: The Feminist as Revolutionary

No One Can Silence Me: The Life of Legendary Artist and Activist Paul Robeson (Young Adult)

Reaching Ninety

Martin Duberman

The Line of Dissent

GAY OUTSIDERS
AND THE SHAPING OF HISTORY

EDITED BY

RICHARD SCHNEIDER JR.

G&LR BOOKS • BOSTON

G&LR Books
PO Box 180300
Boston, MA 20118
HGLR@aol.com
www.GLReview.org

The Line of Dissent: Gay Outsiders and the Shaping of History
Martin Duberman — 1st edition
ISBN 979-8-9888150-0-6

TO THE CURRENT GENERATION OF QUEER RADICALS

Please hurry!

Contents

Introduction

Martin Duberman's first contribution to *The G&LR—The Gay & Lesbian Review*—was in 1994, the year of our founding, which was also the 25th anniversary of the Stonewall Riots. His book on the Riots and their aftermath had recently been published, and he was kind enough to sit with me for an interview for our Stonewall issue. The resulting discussion, as insightful as it was, does not appear in this book, which includes twenty featured essays that he contributed over the years.

The title of this collection, "The Line of Dissent," suggests a common denominator to unite an unruly set of individuals—beyond the fact that all were gifted people who did great things. They were trailblazers who took on the Establishment, forging new ways of thinking and being while making important contributions to LGBTQ+ life and culture.

The first of these essays to appear, in 1997, is an in-depth profile of Edward Sagarin, author of *The Homosexual in America* (1951), a first-of-a-kind sociological study that earned him the epithet "Father of the Homophile Movement." The latest, from 2022, offers new insights into the work of sex research pioneer Alfred Kinsey, notably on his findings around homosexual behavior, plus an inside look at the work of Kinsey's acolyte C. A. Tripp, author of the explosive 1975 book *The Homosexual Matrix.*

Between these scholarly bookends came profiles of activists, poets, artists, and daredevils. A three-part series on impresario Lincoln Kirstein details how he brought ballet theater to America—but only after bringing to these shores choreographer George Balanchine, with whom he founded the New York City Ballet. An in-depth look of the Black poet Essex Hemphill examines both his radical poetry and his political activism during the AIDS crisis. And while British poet W. H. Auden was quite cautious, his lifelong partner Chester Kallman, a poet in his own right, was outspokenly gay in his poetry and his public life.

Two of Duberman's lifelong interests are the history of the American Left and that of the LGBTQ+ movement; several profiles can be found where these two concerns intersect. Barbara Deming's involvement in the gay rights movement of the 1960s and '70s was of a piece with her antiwar activism, radical feminism, and anti-racism. Sylvia "Ray" Rivera gave a speech in 1973 that set the stage for the transgender revolution years before it became a national cause. Andrea Dworkin, the controversial radical second wave feminist, was no less strenuous in her opposition to the Vietnam War.

Well outside the political arena are several profiles in dissent in ostensibly nonpolitical endeavors. Modernist artist Robert Rauschenberg is described as a "reluctant activist" who took on the art establishment by encoding his work with homoerotic imagery. Another such activist was Mary Meigs, also a Modernist-era painter, but it's her four memoirs about her life with Barbara Deming that reveal the reality of lesbian life during their era. There's even a speedboat racer in the mix, Joe Carstairs, a gender-bending woman who burst all kinds of barriers when she won major trophies in the 1920s.

Like Carstairs, *The Line of Dissent* moves quickly through a wide expanse, stopping at key moments in LGBTQ+ history to focus on a number of creative individuals who challenged the status quo and opened new channels of understanding and discovery for the generations that came next. ▪

—Richard Schneider Jr., Editor-in-Chief, The G&LR

Preface

AS FAR BACK AS THE MID-1990s, I'd now and then written a piece or sat for an interview with *The Gay & Lesbian Review*, but it's mostly in the last several years that our connection has become regularized. By then, I had retired from teaching (but not from writing), and periodically one of my archival "digs" would yield material better condensed into an article than expanded into a book. The great majority of these pieces, in modified form, initially appeared in *The Gay & Lesbian Review*; a few first appeared as chapters in one of my books or, in one case, as a piece in *The New York Times.*

Throughout these years, I want to stress, Richard Schneider, *G&LR*'s editor, has been hospitable to a fault, generous with space and wise in his councils. I very much doubt that *The Review* would have had its long and ongoing life without his gifted leadership.

It's one of history's bitter ironies that people who work for a more just society are unlikely to become its heirs. Abraham Lincoln signed his name to the Emancipation Proclamation, but it was William Lloyd Garrison's maligned crusade over the years (he was nearly lynched in Boston by a proslavery mob) that ultimately persuaded Lincoln to dip his pen in the inkwell.

Similarly, Albert Parsons, hanged by the State in 1887 for organizing against harsh working conditions, is familiar only to historians—yet his leadership in the late 19th century labor wars centrally shaped working-class consciousness and its offspring, unionization.

The Line of Dissent is "opinionated" in another sense: I've chosen subjects who I admire; the book contains no demolition jobs. The fact that my appraisals are mostly appreciative doesn't mean that I'm a shallow celebrant of anyone who challenges the status quo. I've known a fair number of mutinous types—of people regarded as outsiders—and can testify to the fact that not all rebels are insightful prophets, or even personally likeable; nor am I suggesting that every insurgent or eccentric is, by the mere fact of their oddity, a fount of insight, a guaranteed sage.

I also want to be clear that *The Line of Dissent* makes no claim to being a broad-spectrum, exhaustive account of the issues and actors central to the time period covered. I make no claim to comprehensive coverage. Any number of rebels and their causes go unacknowledged in *The Line of Dissent.* (The disability, Latino, and Native American movements are among those most notably absent, though as significant and worthy as the mere dozen I do discuss.) In our segregated society, we tend to interact—for worse, not better—primarily with those most like ourselves. Put most simply, this book is about some of the people I encountered in my own political odyssey and wanted to memorialize—people whose paths I happened to cross and whose views connected to my own.

It would be sentimental to pretend that honoring the ancestors will do *them* much good. But knowing they existed might calm the apprehension that our own struggles are merely quixotic. I had in mind, too, that their example of going against the tide might prove an antidote to today's stampede to homogenization. As Audre Lorde reminded us, you cannot transform a culture by accepting its core assumptions—like the still ingrained view that men and women are "from different planets," or the "patriotic" conviction that we're divinely entitled to invade other countries under the guise of saving them. At its inception in 1969, the Gay Liberation Front took an oppositional stance against a broad spectrum of mainstream assumptions and institutions: to the inequities of corporate capitalism, the subjection of people of color, global imperialism, and the patriarchal family. From that radical beginning, the gay movement has over the past forty years gradually shifted to the center.

The dominant strategy of its national organizations over the past few decades has been defended by its adherents as "creative assimilationism." Their focus is on joining up, on gaining access to rather than challenging, centrist institutions like marriage and the military—leaving those bastions of injustice largely intact, giving them, as it were, a clean bill of health. The gay movement's slide towards the center isn't a development I've been in sympathy with. The emphatic adherence to mainstream morality—which is to say, the values that characterize white, middle-class life—has, in my view, come at the expense of minimizing—or outright disavowing—the innovative questioning of established pieties that had characterized the gay movement at its inception.

ALTHOUGH all of the people I write about in this book were *behaviorally* part of the sexual minority, most of them were primarily involved with social injustice movements that did *not* centrally relate to their own lives. Only two of them, in fact, can be said to have invested most of their activist energy to the LGBTQ+ liberation movement (though several others *were* incidentally involved). Essex Hemphill's deepest involvement, for example, was with the *Black* struggle—he felt it was his color not his sexual orientation that centrally defined and concerned him. Similarly, Barbara Deming, a staunch advocate of nonviolence, was pre-eminently concerned with the plight of Blacks and women—all women, not just lesbians. Karl Bissinger lived with and was devoted to another man, yet his political energy went exclusively to the War Resisters League. None of the three viewed homosexuality as their "primary emergency."

Their stories provide fresh material for considering a number of interlocking questions that I raised several years ago in *Has The Gay Movement Failed?* Why has the national gay agenda over the past few decades been so insistently parochial in focusing on gaining access to mainstream institutions like marriage and the military? Why instead has the official movement shunned the more radical features of the community it purports to represent, like the practice (in contrast to the *theoretical* advocacy) of genuine partner equality, and its opposition to the "naturalness" of monogamy, lifetime pair-bonding, and binary definitions of gender? And why has the *straight* Left (like the gay mainstream) chosen to remain oblivious to the unique and subversive features of gay life—the insights it provides into gender fluidity and its skepticism about the sanctimonious insistence on combining love and sex?

A byproduct of the straight Left choosing to remain distant from all things "queer" has been the negation of any possibility of radical outsiders binding together to form a substantive alliance. Some of the individuals who appear peripherally in *The Line of Dissent*—like Christopher Lasch—inadvertently suggest why the straight Left has kept its distance from queer insights and agendas: he (and a multitude of others) insists on the view that maintaining the traditional family—dominant husband, subordinate wife, dutiful children—is the equivalent of Saving the Republic. Lasch and other straight radicals, moreover, have been unaware—or unwilling to acknowledge—that in the past, gay lefties have sometimes been involved, admittedly peripheral, in social protest movements other than their own: Sylvia Rivera's support for the Black Panther movement, Barbara Deming's early activism in anti-nuke demonstrations, Naomi Weisstein's challenge to the profound discrimination against women in science.

To a limited extent, radical gay/straight alliances did materialize in the creative decade between 1965-75, but they fell victim to the country's post-1975 mud-slide to the Right. Today, thanks to a new generation, such connections are once more emerging. Only time will tell if they're any match for the infinitely more powerful cartels that currently control economic and political life.*

Substantive social change typically originates from the margins, not the center, and those who vocally deplore "things as they are" are often derided

---

* Raina Lipsitz' *The Rise of a New Left* (Verso, 2022) is essential for understanding, and in part taking heart from, the rising tide of young radicals. Sadly, the LGBTQ+ movement is barely mentioned in Lipsitz' comprehensive account as a likely partner for a progressive coalition. Some of that implied disdain may well reflect homophobia, yet surely reflects as well the view of straight leftists that the gay movement isn't in fact notably radical.

as dangerous cranks—as peddling views and leading lives that threaten established authority or orthodox morality. Yet over time those same radical views often become both legible and persuasive to a later generation. Some even achieve majoritarian acceptance—though rarely in time to save their originators from calumny in their own day and oblivion thereafter.

—Martin Duberman

CHAPTER I

Edward Sagarin

"FATHER" OF THE HOMOPHILE MOVEMENT*

Two crucial dates frame this story: 1951 and 1973.

In 1951 a book titled *The Homosexual in America* appeared out of nowhere, its author, Donald Webster Cory, entirely unknown. The book was the first full-scale nonfiction account of gay life in the United States, and its author spoke as an insider, an avowed homosexual. In opposition to psychiatric calls for "cure" and religious demands for "repentance," Cory's message to the homosexual was to "turn inward and accept yourself...You are what you are, and what I am—a homosexual. You will not outgrow it, will not evolve in another direction, will not change on the couch of an analyst."

We jump to 1973.

The January issue of *Contemporary Sociology* carried a lengthy essay reviewing some dozen books on homosexuality published in the wake of the 1969 Stonewall riots. The author was Edward Sagarin, professor of sociology and criminology at the City University of New York, a specialist in the study of deviance, president-elect of the American Society of Criminology, and the

---

* Many of the thirty or so friends of Sagarin who agreed to talk with me did so on condition of anonymity. Since some of the quoted comments in this essay must therefore go unascribed, I've decided to omit footnotes altogether rather than offer a truncated, incomplete set.

prolific author of a slew of books and articles, including the pioneering *The Negro in American Business* (1950) and the daring (for an academic sociologist) 1962 volume, *The Anatomy of Dirty Words.* In his acid, sometimes trenchant 1973 review essay for *Contemporary Sociology*, Sagarin derided the psychoanalytic claim that homosexuals were "sick," argued against the view that "cure" was both possible and desirable, and insisted that social oppression was the primary cause of such psychopathology as existed in the gay world. Children must no longer be taught, Sagarin insisted, that "it is better to have heterosexual than homosexual patterns."

Donald Webster Cory and Edward Sagarin were one and the same person.

EDWARD SAGARIN was born in Schenectady in 1913 to Jewish Russian immigrant parents. The youngest of eight children, he lost his mother in the flu pandemic of 1918. After his father remarried, the family relocated to New York City, but Ed got along badly with his stepmother and eventually moved out. He then lived for varying lengths of time with different members of the extended Sagarin clan. His relationship with his father never recovered, and years later Ed had to be talked into showing up for his funeral.

Born with scoliosis, a lateral curvature of the spine, Ed had a noticeable hump on the right side of his back—his "posture problem," he would wryly call it as an adult. Frail, small, un-athletic, intense, and very smart, Ed grew up with taunts from his cookie-cutter schoolmates ringing regularly in his ears. Children thus stigmatized often become sensitive to the pain of others bearing marks of affliction, as well as fascinated with how they cope with the world's mean-spirited assaults. But sensitivity need not automatically manifest as compassion. It can also breed murderous disassociation—or an uneasy mix of empathy and repulsion, affinity for another outsider alternating with oddly erupting, unbidden distaste (the projection of self-disgust).

Though money was in scant supply, Ed did go to a good high school, and then somehow managed to spend more than a year in France (where he met André Gide and learned French fluently—a skill that would prove important for his future business career). On returning to the United States, Sagarin enrolled at CCNY—in the late 1920s and '30s famed for its political passion and turmoil—and became active in left-wing politics. He felt special concern over the plight of Black Americans (the concern would be lifelong); the militantly left-wing National Student League sent Sagarin and two of its other young members—one of the two would become the distinguished poet (and closeted bisexual) Muriel Rukeyser—to observe the 1933 trial in Alabama of the "Scottsboro Boys," nine Black youths falsely accused of raping two white women. After the three students were harassed by

Edward Sagarin, from the jacket of his 1974 novel A Flake of Snow. Photo: Trudi Fuller

local sheriffs, Samuel Leibowitz, chief attorney for the Scottsboro boys, felt the three students were alienating jury sympathy and appealed to them to leave town—which they agreed to do.

In 1934, approaching his twenty-first birthday, Sagarin met another young radical, Gertrude Liphshitz. A shared interest in left-wing politics initially drew the two young people together, and would always be a strong binding force between them. Their attraction to each other soon deepened beyond politics, and in 1936, they decided to marry. Gert came from a warm, caring, orthodox Jewish family—itself a powerful magnet for the love-starved young Sagarin. As was the fact that Gert's family were left-wing activists and her father a staunch union organizer.

Those who knew the couple only casually during their marriage of nearly fifty years have tended to describe Gert to me as "a Brooklyn Jewish house-wife, pleasant, levelheaded, practical," a woman who took care of the home (the couple had one child, Fred), eschewed a career, and devoted her energies to her family. But those who knew the couple well shade the relationship quite differently. They agree that Gert, on the outside, assumed a traditional house-wife's role, but insist she was far from the shyly hovering background figure described by those who saw the couple rarely and judged them superficially.

Gert, her intimates knew, had strong opinions, freely verbalized them and strenuously argued with Ed over this public issue or that paragraph in something he was writing. An emotionally centered, deeply principled woman, she was powerful ballast for her husband's comparative fragility. She also remained politically involved, and astute, all her life—active in nuclear disarmament groups like Women Strike for Peace, and later, participating in protests against the war in Vietnam.

The Sagarins' intimates also uniformly testify to the couple's mutual devotion: "Oh, the marriage hit some rough spots of course," one of their close friends told me, "but what marriage doesn't? The fact is, they adored each other." In his 1951 preface to *The Homosexual in America*, Sagarin, writing as "Donald Webster Cory," put his decision to marry in less heated terms: in "later adolescence and early manhood ... I struggled against my homosexuality; homosexual love, I told myself, is a myth. ... At the age of 25, after determining that I was capable of consummating a marriage"—in later life, Sagarin/Cory confided to a colleague that "Gertrude is the only woman I had ever had erotic feelings towards—I was wedded to a girl ... who brought deep understanding to our union and who shared many interests with me."

The tone here is cool to the point of calculation, not at all the stuff (or so we have been taught) of a successful union. The standard cultural script calls for engulfing romance and insistent feelings of sexual passion; their absence (we are told) connotes inauthenticity and foretells disaster. Add in the fact that Sagarin, even after marriage, would lead a parallel life as an active homosexual and would keep that secret from most of the world (and for a time from his wife), and we would seem to be looking at a relationship likely to fail.

But the cultural script most sexologists agree on is full of equations too glibly drawn. Sex is not the same as love (though it risks un-Americanism to say so), nor does emotional satisfaction hinge on ecstatic sexual passion, nor "honesty" guarantee a secure peace. Besides, the sexologists contradict themselves. They also tell us that the most reliable bedrock for an *enduring* union is not rapture and frank-heartedness but more prosaic (and scarcer) stuff: being a caring listener, an enjoyable companion, a reliable friend. And all of that Gert and Ed had—plus a periodic sex life as well. They viewed their marriage as a success. Should we presume to know better?

As for when, and to what extent, Gert became aware of her husband's second life, his homosexual life, she preferred in our several interviews to leave the details shrouded. One close friend of the Sagarins believes that Gert went into the marriage knowing, without ever probing for specifics, that Ed had occasional (no more than that) homosexual experiences. But other intimates believe that Gert put the pieces together at some later point—after hearing enough rumors, or receiving an anonymous letter, or herself coming upon evidence of a homosexual tryst.

What Gert was willing to tell me was that when Ed was writing The Homosexual in America in 1950 (some fourteen years into their marriage), she was well aware of the nature of the project—though not, it would seem from other sources, of the extent of "personal research" involved. Whenever it was that Gert learned the full truth, she declined to discuss (with me, at any rate) the extent, if any, of her turmoil over the knowledge, the shape of the resolutions she made, the exact measure of her accommodation. Perhaps she no longer remembers. Or ever allowed herself fully to know.

WITH THE GREAT DEPRESSION, Sagarin, like many others, had to drop out of college. He held down a variety of jobs to make ends meet, including ghost-writing and editing other people's manuscripts. He also put his fluency in French to good use, handling the European correspondence for a cosmetics firm. Gradually, he branched out into sales and management, and in the process learned a great deal about the chemistry of perfumes and the technology of their production. Born scholar that he was, Sagarin turned that knowledge into the stuff of serious, deliberative inquiry.

He published several consequential articles on the sense of smell, and then—characteristically eager to maximize whatever restricted opportunities came his way—managed to persuade Columbia University to let him teach an adjunct course on the chemistry of cosmetics. In the 1950s, he produced a massive, three-volume collection (*Cosmetics, Science and Technology*) for which he enlisted contributions from many of the country's leading specialists. Sagarin stayed active in the perfume industry in various capacities into the sixties (for a while he was involved with a firm in which Lena Horne was a partner) without ever finding in it a true vocation or ever making much more than a modest living. Martin Rieger, a Sagarin associate from those years, vividly recalls him "with his old bound briefcase, schlepping through New York City, an intelligent type who didn't fit the business at all."

Neither Ed nor Gert ever cared much about accumulating possessions or money—it was almost a matter of political principle. The woman who edited several of Sagarin's later books, and knew the couple well, put it to me this way: "Ed never knew how to take care of himself," was "hopelessly naive about money" and "an easy mark" for the assorted sharks of the academic and publishing worlds; "Gert was the more practical of the two, but they were both babes in the woods."

DONALD WEBSTER CORY believed—and most sexologists would still agree—that Alfred Kinsey's two volumes, *Sexual Behavior in the Human Male* (1948) and *Sexual Behavior in the Human Female* (1952), are unmatched for their integrity, scope, and influence. Cory made no claim that *The Homosexual in America* could "stand on the same shelf" with Kinsey's work. But he did claim—and there is no reason to doubt him—that he had "conceptualized [his own book] before I had ever heard of Kinsey." For years, Cory later wrote, "I had been impressed by the gap in the literature of homosexuality"—namely, how homosexuals "themselves felt, how they saw their lives, how they reacted to each other." Previously, penologists and psychiatrists, the self-designated experts on the subject, had used their limited clinical samples to declare homosexuality *pathological*. (The professional literature would become more majestically moralistic and denunciatory in the 60s, as psychiatric "experts" such as Edmund Bergler, Irving Bieber, and Charles Socarides joined journalists like Jess Stern (*The Sixth Man*) in painting a widely accepted portrait of homosexuality as a diseased and dangerous scourge. Hollywood would begin to confirm that image with the 1962 film *Advise and Consent*, followed by a legion of movies with simpering, vicious gay men and murderous or suicidal lesbians.

The only partial exception in the early '60s—there were none in the early '50s—were psychoanalyst Robert Lindner's several books (*Rebel Without a Cause*; *Must You Conform?*). Although Lindner refused automatically to conflate homosexuality with pathology (or nonconformity of any kind with mental illness), he also believed that more needed to be known about homosexuality—"the source of immense quantities of unhappiness and frustration"—so that it could be better "eradicated." For a less tepid and compromised view in those years, one had to look to Europe and to the sympathetic works of Magnus Hirschfeld, Edward Carpenter, and Havelock Ellis (all of whom, from today's perspective, suffer from too much pseudoscience and too many confident overgeneralizations about "third sexes," and the like).

A good deal of fiction and poetry about lesbians and gay men *had* been published before 1951—from Gertrude Stein's *Tender Buttons* in 1914 to Gore Vidal's *The City and the Pillar* in 1948. But of "insider" nonfiction, there was almost nothing before Cory's 1951 book. Not even Gide's *Corydon*, which Cory hugely admired, had fit the bill, for Gide's ambition had been to write a philosophical defense of homosexuality rather than to do what Cory hoped to do: tell how it "feels ... to be one of them—nay, one of us." But it was in honor of Gide that Sagarin chose his pseudonym: Don Cory—a reversal of *Corydon*. He added the "Webster" to avoid the possibility of another Donald Cory suing him.

Cory had no team of assistants, no foundation support, no academic legitimization—none of the perks that today are the commonplaces of research in sexology. He did have one volunteer, a footloose, financially independent young man named John Horton, who'd recently gotten his B.A. in anthropology at Columbia. Cory gave Horton two specific jobs: to look up all the laws in the 48 states that applied to homosexuality, and to write to each department of the federal government asking if they had figures on the numbers of homosexuals who worked for them. (The results are printed as appendices to *The Homosexual in America*.)

When I asked Horton why he thought Cory had turned to him for help, he replied, "Maybe because I had a black lover. Cory had had a number of affairs with black men. He used to boast of the frequency with which he was able to pick men up along the benches at Central Park West in the Seventies"—then a major gay male cruising ground. According to Horton, Cory would occasionally invite a sexual partner or friend he'd grown fond of home to dinner, but he, Horton, was "the only one Gertrude thought was homosexual" (so she told her husband, who repeated it to Horton).

In the years Cory spent preparing *The Homosexual in America*, he (as he put it in the book) "became more and more struck" by the notion that homosexuals were, like more established ethnic, racial, and subcultural groups, a distinct and legitimate minority. This became the main thesis of *The Homosexual in America*, along with the implied corollary that homosexuals were entitled to the same rights as other citizens, and that societal mistreatment—and not anything inherent in homosexuality itself—was chiefly responsible for whatever "pathology" could be found in the gay world.

Cory may not have been entitled to his claim of absolute originality in applying the minority concept to homosexuals. As early as 1921, Kurt Hiller, the left-wing German homosexual activist, had suggested something similar; and Harry Hay, the pioneering American gay radical, expressed much the same notion at much the same time Cory did. Yet it remains indisputably true that *The Homosexual in America* gave the "minority" concept wide circulation for the first time, thus laying the cornerstone for what has come to be called "identity politics."

READ TODAY, *The Homosexual in America* has its decidedly dated and conventional sections. For starters, its title: the book is not about the homosexual, it's about gay men, and the references in it to lesbian lives are perfunctory and ill-informed. Other offhanded orthodoxies dot the pages: "the sexual instinct ... is usually stronger in the male"; "a permanent relationship" is the surest guide to happiness; "promiscuity" represents a flight from intimacy; the aging homosexual is a "sad specter"; and so forth. Moreover, even as *The Homosexual in America* tries to demolish many of the reigning stereotypes about the gay world, it corroborates others. Denying the standard (and still current) view that homosexuals are more prone to depression and suicide than other people, Cory nonetheless maintains that "instability, restlessness, [and] promiscuity" are defining features of gay male life. Though he was able—far in advance of his day—to theorize a subculture based on "pretense and the mask" (and yet also deeply iconoclastic) he also negatively characterized the subculture as "fickle" and "rootless."

Yet the original, even visionary sections of *The Homosexual in America* outweigh the conventional ones and mark its true distinction. Against the current of his day, against the entrenched tradition of American sex-negativism, Cory sounded an astute—and astonishingly contemporary—note in insisting that there was nothing dishonorable about sexual pleasure; that the human animal was "basically, instinctually, and naturally" bisexual (though he added, sounding an astonishingly contemporary note, that "hard and fast categories"—homosexual, heterosexual, bisexual—are "rather meaningless oversimplification[s]); that a well-defined gay subculture existed that was all at once unassimilable to mainstream culture and "a banner-bearer in the struggle for liberalization of our sexual conventions"; that biological theories about homosexuality were mostly bad science; that "many homosexuals are, in the totality of their lives, not queer people at all, and many heterosexuals are extremely queer." Some sixty years later, such views are at the ideological heart of what is called "queer theory"—the latest and purportedly newest advance in gay self-understanding. Cory urged homosexuals "not [to] fear the group life of the gay world. ... It is a circle of protection. ... Alone, you cannot change the world, but the combined efforts of many will surely effect a beneficial change."

Who would believe it? The themes of contingency, change and fluidity being sounded in 1951, from the pen of a frail, gnome-like perfume salesman, trapped in a quixotic body, pulled in the deepest recesses of his being between anarchic Dionysian desires and the ordered virtues of Apollonian civics. The civics part ("promiscuity is a flight from intimacy," et al.) might have been less strenuously declared had Cory written in a less fearful and suffocatingly conventional time. In the early '50s, Joe McCarthy was in full, vulturous flight, political and sexual nonconformists were being purged from public and private employment alike, and not even the ACLU would lift a finger on behalf of homosexuals. When Cory, among others, tried to win the ACLU's support in 1952, the organization informed him (as he later described it) that "if we feel our rights have been denied we should go to the district attorney and to the grand jury and fight without their aid."

Cory decided that "under the circumstances" the individual homosexual had little choice but to "take refuge behind the mask." For himself at least, he couldn't justify "subjecting those close to me to possible embarrassment or injury." Yet Cory made the decision for pseudonymity ruefully, aware that he was perpetuating a vicious cycle, realizing that "until we are willing ... to identify ourselves ... we are unlikely to ... break down the barriers of shame or to change public attitudes."

Yet he hoped for the dawn of a different day, and at the close of *The Homosexual in America*, he struck a millenarian note: "In the millions who are silent and submerged, I see a potential, a reservoir of protest, a hope for a portion of mankind. And in my knowledge that our number is legion, I raise my head high and proclaim that we, the voiceless millions, are human beings, entitled to breathe the fresh air and enjoy, with all humanity, the pleasures of life and love on God's green earth."

Today—when for decades growing numbers have been coming out and joining up—such words may sound vacuous and trite. But in 1951, secrecy and fear were in the saddle, and visionary calls to arms all but unknown. A handful, like Cory, were doing *something*, however locally or anonymously, to change the oppressive climate, but most gay people, having been dutifully socialized in self-disgust, were spending their energies and exercising their willpower in concealing or denying their sexual orientation—or in trying to change it through psychotherapy. Even had the needed self-esteem and courage been in greater supply, there was, in 1951, scarcely any organized political movement to come out into.

A handful of gay men, led by Harry Hay, Rudi Gernreich (later famous as a designer), and Chuck Rowland, had just launched the tiny and secret Mattachine Society in Los Angeles—the name taken from a medieval fraternity of unmarried townsmen. That same year of 1951, the owners of a San Francisco gay bar, the Black Cat, won the landmark right from the state Supreme Court *legally* to serve gay customers. Then, in 1953, the homosexual magazine

ONE (and subsequently its corporate entity, ONE, Inc.) was launched in Los Angeles, followed two years later by the birth in San Francisco of the first lesbian organization in the United States, the Daughters of Bilitis (DOB), the name taken from Pierre Louys's erotic poem "Songs of Bilitis." These organizations comprised by the mid-fifties the minuscule "homophile" movement. The choice of the name "homophile" over "homosexual" itself illustrates the nervous hope of these pioneers that if they emphasized the non-lustful emotions (*philia* = friendship, love) they might better win sympathy and support from the antigay mainstream—not that it was aware, or cared.

WHEN *The Homosexual in America* was published, Sagarin's employer somehow found out about his double identity and fired him. As he lamented in a letter to Alfred Kinsey, "I lost my job ... directly and exclusively due to the book. It is difficult to understand how any progress can be made if economic punishment is inflicted on all who protest." (Kinsey and Cory had met briefly back in 1951 and until Kinsey's death in 1956 occasionally corresponded. By mid-1952 Sagarin used his real name when writing to Kinsey, though the level of intimacy between the two men never proceeded very far.)

Upsetting though the firing was, Sagarin soon found another job in the cosmetics industry. Besides, the book itself proved a success. It went back to press several times during the fifties, was translated into French and Spanish, and elicited 2,000 letters from readers—many of them versions of "thank you for a ray of hope." Writing to a member of ONE, Cory contentedly summarized his newfound notoriety: "my correspondence is from all over the world, in many languages, people beg me to read a manuscript, leave it on my doorstep, threaten me with a lawsuit for failing to return it, take offense when I tell them how bad it is, and would not dream of paying for the return postage. Oh well, why think of the ungrateful, when so many have written me letters that reassured me, if ever I needed it, that my work was worth undertaking!"

The Homosexual in America did prove a landmark for many, including a number of people who went on to play important roles in the pre-Stonewall gay movement. Randy Wicker, active in both the early Black and gay civil rights struggles, has told me that he considers Cory's book "the most important thing in the early gay movement. ... I was like a religious fanatic underlining passages of the Bible." For young Jim Kepner, who joined the fledgling L.A. Mattachine Society in 1952 and became an editor of *ONE* magazine, *The Homosexual in America* was "a clarion call in the dark for gays all over the country." Cory's book, Kepner told me, "gave a shot in the arm" to the newly formed Mattachine Society. He leapt with excitement one day when passing Pickwick's (the Hollywood bookstore) and saw stacks of *The Homosexual in America* displayed in the front window.

Barbara Gittings was so stirred by the book when she read it a few years after it appeared, that she wrote the publisher (Greenberg, a small press which for two decades had been issuing gay novels, bringing down a post office suit on its head) for Cory's address, then went to New York City to meet with him several times. Cory told her about Mattachine and One, Inc., and in 1956, Gittings managed a trip to the West Coast, where she also hooked up with Daughters of Bilitis (DOB); two years later, she helped found its East Coast chapter in New York City, was elected its first president, and later edited the pioneering lesbian periodical *The Ladder*.

The impact of Cory's book carried beyond gay circles. Alfred Kinsey, pressed by Cory for some sort of endorsement, managed (with Midwestern restraint) to call it "a worthwhile addition to the factual material that is available on the subject." Norman Mailer (with New York brio) hailed the book as revelatory. He even wrote an article about it for *ONE* in which he announced that "few books ... [had ever] cut so radically at my prejudices and altered my ideas so profoundly. ... I found myself thinking in effect, '*My God, homosexuals are people, too.*'"

In short order, *The Homosexual in America* became the Ur-text for the pre-Stonewall homophile movement. And Donald Webster Cory became widely regarded as its "father," an admired, celebrated figure—at least in limited circles. Sagarin gradually began to involve himself further in the embryonic public gay world—always as Cory, not Sagarin. He also set up in 1952 the Cory Book Service, using as a subscription base the large correspondence he'd received in response to *The Homosexual in America*. The book club selected for subscribers a gay-themed title each month, usually of high quality (*The Poems of Cavafy*; Angus Wilson's *Hemlock and After*; Roger Peyrefitte's *Special Friendships*).

Cory also began to give public lectures, most notably a militant speech in 1952 at the annual meeting of the International Committee for Sex Equality at the University of Frankfurt in Germany. In it, he excoriated a puritanical view of sex, lauded Kinsey's work, and acknowledged that only "a bare start had been made in enlisting friends among the medical, psychological, legal and other professions," as well as in educating homosexuals themselves away from self-condemnation and toward a realization of the necessity of struggling against social oppression—precisely the kind of work that the Mattachine Society and Daughters of Bilitis would increasingly undertake during the fifties. What had been accomplished thus far, Cory said, might appear "meager," but he stressed "the enormous importance of ... beginnings. ... This is a new cycle and a dynamic one."

When the gay magazine *ONE* made its first appearance in January 1953, Cory agreed to appear on its masthead as Contributing Editor, a position he would continue to hold for more than three years. In the most notable of the articles he wrote for *ONE*, he denounced the contempt most homosexual men felt for the effeminate among them, labeling the attitude "antifeminist, anti-woman"—a strikingly bold attitude at the time. He underscored, too, the irony of homosexuals "pleading for acceptance from the world at large" yet refusing tolerance and understanding to those within their own ranks who, in their "effeminacy" differed from the norm. Once again, Cory was expressing views uncommon at the time, ones that would continue to resonate and grow in appeal.

Cory also distinguished between effeminacy and the "very distinctive [male] homosexual method of speech" with which it was often confused; the latter, as he saw it, was a special argot, an "over-distinctive pronunciation of consonants, and lengthy pronunciation of vowels." Here, Cory was building on his earlier argument that homosexuals constituted a definable subculture—a matter still contested today—itemizing as well what he took to be a distinctive gay walk, stare and handshake. He viewed these as reflexive, not conscious, and "neither masculine nor feminine, but specifically and peculiarly homosexual."

That same year, 1953, he published his second book as Donald Webster Cory: *21 Variations on a Theme*, a collection of gay-related short stories for which he himself did new translations of de Maupassant and Verlaine and which gave Oscar Wilde's "The Priest and the Acolyte" its first publication in the U.S. By then Sagarin had become active in the Veterans' Benevolent Association (VBA), a state-chartered New York City gay male organization formed in 1948 and boasting about 100 members. Sagarin almost got Kinsey to speak to the VBA, but, pleading deadlines, Kinsey canceled out a few days before.

It was also indirectly through Kinsey that Sagarin, back in 1951 (before the publication of *The Homosexual in America*) was able to make the acquaintance of the maverick psychologist, Albert Ellis, who at the time was Chief Psychologist for New Jersey's Diagnostic Center and had just published *The Folklore of Sex*, an iconoclastic book in which he had mocked the American need to justify sexual pleasure with an overlay of romantic blather and as well made the inflammatory assertion that "society makes sick people out of 'perverts.'"

Cory had originally asked Kinsey to do the introduction to his book, but himself too busy, Kinsey had suggested Harry Benjamin, the pioneering transsexual expert ("transgender" is now the preferred term), but he too begged off, suggesting in turn Albert Ellis, who'd accepted. Meeting Ellis would prove a milestone for Cory—a liberatory one in some eyes, a disastrous one in the eyes of homophile activists.

THE SHORT INTRODUCTION Ellis wrote for *The Homosexual in America* proved to be a curious one. While applauding the book as "by far the best nonfiction picture of the American homosexual" available, and a "well-warranted indictment of our smug and sadistic heterosexual persecution of homosexuals," Ellis had disputed several of Cory's views, in particular his "pessimism concerning the possibility of adjusting homosexuals to more heterosexual modes of living."

Cory had argued that homosexuality was "involuntary though not inborn," and therefore not susceptible to "change"—through psychoanalysis or otherwise. Ellis believed that exclusive male homosexuality denoted a neurotic fear of women, and thus could and should be treated. (In these years, almost nobody thought lesbianism was frequent or important enough to be worth much discussion, let alone study.)

Ellis's treatment goal was not the standard psychoanalytic one of annihilating a male homosexual's drive, but rather aimed at adding heterosexual attraction to his repertoire of desire. He claimed a high success rate with his own patients, but never bothered to explore whether those who'd successfully "expanded their options" had actually shifted the focus of their desire or had merely changed their outward behavior—and even in terms of behavior, how many had subsequently "backslid." Similarly, nowhere in Ellis's voluminous writings, then or later, does he satisfactorily define the loaded terminology he casually employs ("neurosis," "disturbance," "inborn," etc.), nor ever question his basic assumption that some degree of heterosexuality is a prerequisite for happiness. His logic remained self-enclosed: he simply defined "exclusivity" as "neurotic," without ever offering a cogent discussion of "normalcy" as a concept, or discussing the criteria he used for recognizing it.

Ellis insisted when I talked to him that he'd never argued that all exclusively gay men were "disturbed"—merely "most." Yet in tracking his writings through the decades, it becomes clear that he admitted the *possibility* of some exclusively homosexual men being non-neurotic only in the '70s, after the modern gay movement had come into existence. Still, it remains true that as early as 1954 (in his book *The American Sexual Tragedy*), Ellis took the position—remarkable for that day, or this—that "what is scientific sauce for the goose should also be sauce for the gander ... that exclusive heterosexuality can be just as fetishistic as exclusive homosexuality."

As early as 1951, moreover, Ellis, like Sagarin, had argued that heterosexual prejudice was itself of major importance in accounting for the psychological problems found in gay people. Both he and Sagarin were also scornful of the monogamous model as "ideal" for sexual behavior, seeing it as part and parcel of a sex-negative culture; both also argued for a reevaluation of prevailing moral values that disapproved of all sexual activity not (as Sagarin put it in a 1952 article) "romantic in origin and procreative in direction."

But for several years after they first met, some distance continued to separate the two men ideologically. Their disagreements centered on the degree to which homosexuality was "curable." Following Kinsey, Sagarin agreed that "people can and do change their patterns of sexual life over a period of years," and he was willing to believe "that certain psychologists can aid certain homosexuals in accepting a bisexual pattern of life." But (doubtless thinking of himself) Sagarin continued to insist that those able to make a bisexual adjustment nonetheless went right on feeling "a major need for gratification with their own sex"—and therefore "cannot be said to be 'cured.'"

Unlike Ellis, moreover, Sagarin continued to assert in the early fifties that many if not most homosexual men could not—even when they badly wanted to, and underwent prolonged psychotherapy—simply "add" heterosexuality to their repertoire of desire. He also insisted that the typical homosexual "can only make a satisfactory adjustment when he is prepared completely to accept himself and his way of life, without regrets, misgivings, shame, or unconscious defense."

By the end of the fifties, however, Ellis and Sagarin had come to hold nearly identical views about male homosexuality, with Ellis standing ideologically pat and Sagarin shifting his views in Ellis's direction. The likely explanation for the shift is that it resulted from Sagarin entering into therapy with Ellis. Ellis denies this ("It was a case of parallel evolution that we came to hold nearly identical attitudes about homosexuality") and even denies that Sagarin was ever in formal treatment with him. "The fact is," he told me, "Sagarin and I were never more than moderately close." From time to time, in the course of discussing other matters, Sagarin would talk over some of his problems, "but he was never an actual patient of mine."

But if Ellis wants no credit for either behavioral or ideological persuasiveness, several of Sagarin's intimates insist otherwise. One of his closest friends has strongly hinted to me that Sagarin turned to Ellis as a result of family pressure at a "tumultuous" moment in the marriage—perhaps when his son Fred was born: it was time, Sagarin was told, "to get control over himself."

According to this same friend, Ellis's "repression technique"—which insists that one can learn consciously to control disruptive personal "obsessions" (what Ellis would later come to call "rational emotive therapy")—did help Sagarin curtail his homosexual "promiscuity." Sagarin believed enough in Ellis—so Ellis tells it—to send him "lots of referrals" throughout the 1950s, mostly "young men who had been his lovers."

On the other hand, we know for certain that Ellis was not Sagarin's first therapist. As he revealed in *The Homosexual in America* back in 1951, Sagarin had earlier realized that marriage had not "reduce[d] the urge for gratification with men," and "to rid" himself of it he had entered a "long analysis." To his surprise, Cory wrote in *The Homosexual in America*, the therapist had focused not on repressing or dissolving Cory's homosexuality but on overcoming his feelings of guilt about it—a goal achieved, Cory claimed in his book. His guilt did diminish and he found himself enjoying homosexual relations more than before, even while feeling fewer "fears and repugnances toward sexual union with a woman." Thereafter, as Cory completes the tale in *The Homosexual in America*, he had adopted "a temperate and disciplined indulgence in homosexual affairs," and became entirely content with his "successful marriage" and "happy home."

Ellis told me that he agreed Sagarin had a good marriage, but disputes the rest of Cory's narrative. That first "long analysis," in Ellis's view, "didn't take. ... When I met Cory he was an exceptionally promiscuous gay man." And remained so—though after their "few, informal sessions" together, according to Ellis, "Cory was able to get more pleasure from the sex he had with his wife." By 1959, in any case, after their views had become nearly identical, Ellis described Donald Webster Cory (in print) as "the best adjusted homosexual, by far, whom I have ever met."

As part of his gradual involvement in the public gay world, Cory had joined the Veterans Benevolent Association, but the organization ceased to exist in 1954 (it had "run into a little difficulty," was Cory's oblique reference to a correspondent). But the very next year saw the founding of a more overtly political organization: the New York City chapter of the Mattachine Society (MSNY). Cory had little involvement with Mattachine during its first few years of existence, despite the fact that as early as 1953, he'd praised the group's work on the West Coast as "remarkable." He'd occasionally attend one of MSNY's monthly meetings in its shabby rented loft space on West 49th Street, but it wasn't until 1957 that he agreed to be a guest speaker there. Soon after, he brought Ellis along to a meeting and before long Ellis, too, was invited to speak (this was at a time when most "experts" scornfully turned down Mattachine's invitations).

Ellis's talk at MSNY raised the hackles of at least a segment of his audience. Many members of Mattachine, though brave and unorthodox enough to join the organization or at least show up at some of its meetings, were nonetheless prone to defer to psychiatric authority and to agree with the profession's then commonplace equation of homosexuality with pathology. Yet Ellis's overbearing manner and dogmatic assertions that "fixed" homosexuality was a sign of "disturbance" and that psychotherapy should be given "a fair trial" so that "repressed" heterosexual desires could emerge, brought some angry rebuttals.

When Ellis finished speaking, "slings and arrows ... flew thick and fast" (according to the *Mattachine Newsletter*) with several members in the audience challenging Ellis's view that some degree of heterosexuality was a prerequisite for happiness. Though Ellis, as always, held his ground, he was not only invited back for additional talks but was also asked to write for the *Mattachine Review*. After all, in the context of the psychiatric profession of the day, Ellis was a decided liberal: he at least called for the decriminalization of homosexuality and was willing to testify in court against the common practice of police entrapment. By the late fifties, moreover, Ellis and Cory had joined forces to compile a comprehensive "Encyclopedia of Homosexual Behavior"—though despite several years of work and the completion of dozens of in-depth interviews, the project, due to lack of funding, was never completed nor published.

After 1957, Cory's own involvement with MSNY quickened. He never took on much of the nitty-gritty organizational work, but he did speak at the fifth annual Mattachine convention in 1958, allowed himself to be listed on the board of advisors, and was elected to the more hands-on board of directors (where, up through 1965, he compiled the highest attendance record of any director). By 1961, the New York chapter had become Mattachine's largest, and when factional infighting split the national organization, MSNY cut free and became an independent organization. It was soon after, in May 1962, that Cory finally took out formal membership. "After watching your valiant work for many years," he wrote in his application letter to Mattachine, "I have come to the conclusion that the movement for education and social justice deserves my active support. If I can be of some aid in this work, I shall feel gratified and honored."

Cory thereafter served on several committees, spoke before social and religious groups, and initiated dialogues with the YMCA on the treatment of homosexuals and with the New York Board of Health on venereal disease among the homosexual population. Randy Wicker remembers that at Mattachine meetings, he and Cory would, like competing auctioneers, try to outdo each other in exhorting members to increase their donations. By late 1962, Cory, with a touch of grandiosity, was writing Dorr Legg of California's ONE Institute, "There is a danger that the New York group might grow too dependent on me, and I do not want to exercise too much influence."

It was also in 1962 that Cory's real name became known in Mattachine for the first time. Randy Wicker remembers that when Cory's new book, *The Anatomy of Dirty Words*, was published in 1962 someone came rushing into the MSNY office one day with a copy—with author Edward Sagarin's picture prominently displayed on the back. If Sagarin (like so many other members of Mattachine) had tried to conceal his name, he'd never hidden the fact that he was married. As Frank Kameny, the pioneering Washington D.C. activist, told me, "Everyone was aware that Cory was married—[it was] known and accepted, no deal made of it. Almost nobody in Mattachine was out of the closet. People's private lives were considered their own business. Besides, Cory had short-circuited any distrust of him as a married man by having written that book" (*The Homosexual in America*).

Sagarin himself drew firm boundaries, never inviting any discussion of personal matters. Mattachine bigwig Curtis Dewees, who probably got to know Sagarin better than anyone else in the organization, was occasionally invited to the Sagarins' Brooklyn apartment—but not when Gertrude was there. Dewees and his lover, Al de Dion, also active in Mattachine, viewed Cory (in de Dion's words) as "an icon, like a Godfather." Yet even so, the members knew not to cross the line. As Dewees recalled, "My conversations with Cory were limited basically to the organization, the direction of the movement—that kind of thing; he never discussed his inner feelings with me."

Within Mattachine, Cory was regarded more with awe than affection. Not even Dewees was much drawn to him personally. "I respected the man's intelligence," he told me, "his capabilities, what he had done," but he "wasn't much fun to be around." He was too "dead serious," and when his opinion was challenged could be "thin-skinned, easily offended, aggressive."

Harry Hay, the founder of Mattachine and often called "the father of the homophile movement," actively distrusted Cory. Hay first met him (the two had corresponded earlier) when Cory went to the West Coast in 1955 to speak at the new ONE Institute of Homophile Studies. "I did not like him," Hay told me. Having himself been in the Communist Party—and "astounded" when I told him that as an undergraduate Cory had had decidedly left-wing views—Hay had grown accustomed to sniffing the air and avoiding what he sensed might be risky people or places. "I never felt safe with Cory in the room. I had the sense I was dealing with someone shifty. I remember thinking, I wish he wasn't here at ONE. Who is he really?"

Young Barry Sheer felt no such hesitation. When the famed author of *The Homosexual in America* came across the room at an MSNY meeting to introduce himself, Sheer was delighted. He'd read Cory several years earlier when, as an undergraduate at the University of Colorado in Boulder, Sheer had joined the tiny local Mattachine chapter. It was there that he'd been introduced to *The Homosexual in America*. "It was," Sheer told me, "*the* book; we would read it and discuss it all the time." Sheer flunked out of Colorado after two years, returned to the East Coast, enrolled in Farleigh-Dickinson College in New Jersey and quickly hooked up with New York Mattachine.

Sheer was a good-looking young man with a muscular body and (in his words) "an excess of testosterone." He discharged it generously into the less laden bodies of the homophile leadership, gaining a reputation (applauded by some, deplored by others) as a "star-fucker." Cory spotted Sheer at a Mattachine meeting one night in 1960 and—never a shrinking violet—invited him out for coffee. "If he hadn't written this book and been a famous person," Sheer told me, "I would have said, 'no,' because he wasn't a heck of a lot to look at. Small, with a loud, high-pitched voice, bald, somewhat deformed and walked with a limp."

Yet Sheer did quickly find himself involved in what he now calls "a 'Death in Venice' relationship. ... Cory would give me a little money and have me help him with some of his research and I would let him have sex with me. ... I couldn't be especially emotional, but he was quite happy with that, it seemed. ... He'd come and see me two or three times a week. This went on for about three years." The "comrades" in Mattachine weren't kind about Cory's relationship with Sheer. As one of them told me, "Sheer was generally regarded as predatory," and Cory was privately mocked as a John who had to pay for sex—and who then confused it with affection. Sheer soon learned that Cory's real name was Ed Sagarin, and he even met Gertrude once. He found her "a right and proper Jewish matron" and, in retrospect anyway, remains a little indignant at the way Sagarin was "two-timing" her.

Sheer enjoyed helping out with Sagarin's research, was attracted to his "powerful intellect" and enjoyed their frequent arguments about homosexuality and "the movement." By 1960, Sagarin's views had not only become indistinguishable from those of Albert Ellis, but were held no less rigidly. "We're a tree that's stunted," he would tell Sheer, "but even if a tree is stunted, does it not grow in its own way and offer shade and beauty? And shouldn't gays be treated that way?"

Sheer rejected that view as "condescending tolerance." He was part of a new generation emerging within Mattachine in the early sixties (epitomized by Frank Kameny and the militant Washington, D.C. chapter of Mattachine), insistent that there was nothing to apologize for, nothing "stunted" about homosexuals, nothing—other than society's irrational prejudice—that needed "curing." Much of which, in a more tentative, diluted version, Cory had himself argued in *The Homosexual in America*, way back in 1951, before almost anyone else, before perhaps even he was fully prepared for the radical potential in his own message. In the interim had come Albert Ellis, a ton of psychoanalytic books "proving" that homosexuality was "pathological," Cory's growing doubts about the quality of comradeship available in the homophile movement, and his growing ambition to find greater "legitimacy" as an intellectual in the straight world.

At this same time, in the early sixties, the ideological struggle was heating up in MSNY about whether homosexuality was or wasn't a "mental illness," and the emergent forces, forgetting or never knowing what Cory had once stood for, were increasingly targeting him as the epitome of the played-out Old Guard. Simultaneously, Albert Ellis, and family members as well, were encouraging Sagarin to follow his longstanding scholarly bent and formally pursue an academic career.

In 1958, at age 45, Sagarin entered an accelerated B.A. program for adults at Brooklyn College and completed his undergraduate degree in 1961—graduating in the same class as his son, Fred. He then, at age 48, entered the M.A. program in sociology and wrote his thesis on "The Anatomy of Dirty Words." Scandalized at so unorthodox a topic, Sagarin's department rejected the thesis, but Sagarin managed to get it published as a book, thumbed his nose at Brooklyn College, and enrolled in the doctoral program at NYU.

By this point he'd accumulated just enough money to put the perfume business permanently behind him. By 1966, against great odds, he emerged at age 53 with a Ph.D., an academic job, and a prolific future career as scholar, teacher, and mentor. The orphaned, taunted, physically handicapped youth, the proto-intellectual toiling away uncomplainingly for decades in a business world for which he was temperamentally unsuited, the triply deviant (disabled, homosexual, left-wing) double-lived misfit—these burdensome, knotted earlier selves would never disappear but would recede, soften, inflict less internal pain and less centrally define a life that had refocused in the legitimizing, deeply gratifying new identity of PROFESSOR Edward Sagarin. Donald Webster Cory would remain alive in print, and in a corner of Sagarin's heart—but oh, the relief of not having him constantly tugging at the sleeve, demanding to share center stage.

Sagarin's personal transition during the early to mid 1960s took place at a time when cataclysmic events—the quickening civil rights struggle at home, the escalating war in Vietnam overseas—were pummeling and reshaping American consciousness. The tug-of-war within the tiny homophile movement mirrored in miniature the larger social upheavals: the challenge to "expertise" (like those East Asian "specialists" who'd gotten us into the Vietnam war) and the new value placed on "differentness" (like the heralding of "Black is Beautiful" and SNCC's rejection of the previously hallowed goal of assimilation).

Police harassment of gay bars had long been standard, and the clientele of those bars had dutifully cowered under the cop's club. But by the mid-sixties, knee-jerk deference to authority had weakened, and when the police raided a gay bar in San Francisco in 1964, a new organization instantly sprang up—the Society for Individual Rights—to protest police harassment; by 1966, it had enrolled a thousand members, becoming the largest homophile organization in the country. That same year, a group of progressive heterosexual ministers joined with gay activists in forming the influential Council on Religion and the Homosexual to combat homophobia.

On the East Coast, too, militancy was on the rise. Under Frank Kameny's leadership, Washington, D.C. Mattachine brandished a new "Gay is Good" slogan that spelled an end to apologetics and prefigured the aggressive confrontational politics of the post-Stonewall period. At New York Mattachine, the conservatives dug in their heels and fought a rear-guard action, but the handwriting was on the wall. The Young Turks started to snicker about Cory "the closet queen," "the old auntie," "Auntie Donnie." Where once he'd been almost uniformly hailed for his pioneering role, he was now being ridiculed in *ONE* magazine as a "so-dreary goodykins."

Despite his new legion of detractors, Cory was more active in Mattachine from 1962 to 1965 than ever before, perhaps not least because he was studying it: the topic of his NYU doctoral dissertation was "Structure and Ideology in an Association of Deviants"—that is, the Mattachine Society. He sent the manuscript to Dorr Legg of One, Inc., who spent considerable time critiquing it and digging out additional source materials for Sagarin's use.

In these same years, Sagarin also began his teaching career—on the Baruch campus of the City University of New York, where he offered a course on minority groups. One of his students at Baruch was Phil Goldberg (today a novelist), who was part of the countercultural coterie on campus; he and his friends had formed a Human Rights Society, raised money for SNCC, and gone South to help with the voter campaign drive.

According to Goldberg, Ed Sagarin was one of the few faculty members sympathetic to their activities, and they were delighted when he agreed to serve as faculty adviser for the Human Rights Society. Sagarin may have begun his retreat from the homophile movement, but he remained decidedly left-leaning in his politics. Barry Sheer recalls how heatedly Sagarin would insist that "the government should take care of you and give you a good start," and if you then failed, "society should still take care of you."

One of Phil Goldberg's close friends, Eddie Zimmerman, enrolled in Sagarin's "minority groups" course. Sagarin encouraged his students to write in a non-academic, personal style (he rightly prided himself on the lucidity of his own prose), and so when it came time to do his term paper, Eddie decided to write about what it felt like to be coming out as a gay man. When he got the paper back, he saw that Sagarin had written on it, "This is very remarkable. Please see me." Eddie did drop by the office, and (as he tells the story today) Sagarin expressed "great empathy for what I'd gone through." "I've done a lot of research on this," Sagarin told him, "and I think you would benefit from knowing about a group I'm acquainted with—it's called the Mattachine Society."

Mattachine's monthly meeting, he told Eddie, was coming up, and it promised to be a lively one: the well-known writer Donald Webster Cory was scheduled to speak. Eddie decided to go to the meeting, and when he arrived was delighted to see "so many ordinary-looking, mainstream types who were gay. It was important for me." Then, with considerable fanfare, the speaker of the evening was introduced—and out from the wings strode his Professor Sagarin! As Eddie tells it, Sagarin came up to him afterward and simply said, "Look, I took a big chance inviting you here, but I thought I should. But it's our secret." They had little subsequent contact, though Eddie does remember Sagarin introducing him one day to a young, blond-haired man, who he later told Eddie was his lover.

Eddie, of course, told his friend Phil Goldberg the whole story, and the following term Phil—though not gay—decided he, too, would sign up for Sagarin's course. But he didn't much like the man ("he was strange, troll-like, put people on edge"), and he decided on a little theatrical coup of his own. For the section in the course on "the homosexual minority," Sagarin assigned reading from *The Homosexual in America*. Phil carefully rehearsed his plan for how the classroom discussion would begin. Raising his hand, smothering his glee, he boldly asked, "Mr. Cory says such and such. How do you feel about that?" Sagarin momentarily blanched, then said, "Mr. Cory and I are of one mind about it."

Sagarin's ongoing discussions with Barry Sheer had made it clear to him (as Sagarin wrote in 1963) that "I was no longer viewing the new homosexual scene from within. ... I was not of the generation that grew up after Kinsey (and Cory), the peer-oriented and other-directed youths" whose voices were beginning to be heard. Yet despite the growing disparagement of his views within Mattachine, Sagarin felt no need to adjust them. To the contrary, he decided to restate them in a new book, *The Homosexual and His Society*, and shrewdly asked young Barry Sheer to be its coauthor. (Sheer used the pseudonym "John LeRoy," under which he had earlier written articles for the gay press.)

The book appeared in 1963, and became known as "The Second Cory Report." In it, the authors argued that the homophile movement should primarily concern itself not with trying to get people to join up, but rather with "trying to ease the difficulties" of those already involved and "to enlighten the public on its attitudes." That enlightenment would begin with the acknowledgment that homosexuality was "a disturbance"—but not "antisocial in its nature."

The Homosexual and His Society bravely devoted considerable space to what was widely regarded as "unseemly" topics—like hustling and venereal disease. Moreover, the authors justified their inclusion in words that have a decidedly contemporary ring: "The hustler, the cruiser, the lonely and the distressed, the muscle-flexer, the partner-changer, the effeminate hairdresser, the closet queen who is frightened and the clothes queen who is courting social ridicule: yes, even the poor disturbed people who are caught up in the sad world of sadomasochism—they are all our brothers, and their cause is ours." This defense of outsiders of every stripe, however partial and patronizing, was complexly at odds with the fact that Sagarin was simultaneously fighting within Mattachine to hold homosexuals to a "responsible," non-confrontational appeasement of the social and psychiatric authorities of the day.

"The Second Cory Report" was immediately and angrily attacked: the reviewer in *ONE*, for example, denounced it as "pseudo-scientific" and a mere "rehash of other people's ideas." Sheer himself, in retrospect, regrets having lent his name to those portions of the book that claimed there was no such thing as a "well-adjusted homosexual," and that homosexuality originated in "a pathological situation based on fear, anxiety, or insecurity."

Yet in the counterattack Sheer and Cory published at the time in *ONE*, they gave no ground. Indeed, Cory never thereafter budged from his now formulaic views: homosexuality was not inborn, yet was a "disturbance"; the homophile movement should "accept therapy for some and adjustment within the framework of homosexuality for others"; the movement should not waste its energy either trying to argue "the utter normalcy of the homosexual" or emulating "a monogamous, romantic concept of sexuality" that derived from the official model for heterosexuality.

Cory left unaddressed most of the troubling questions a new generation of gay activists had begun to raise: By what criteria does one establish "disturbance"? Why, if there was "no such thing as a 'homosexual,'" was there any such thing as a "heterosexual"? Why should an increased capacity to have sex with someone of the opposite gender be taken as the measure of increased health—or, for that matter, an increased capacity to have sex with someone of the same gender? What was a "normal" sex life anyway? And who decided? And on the basis of which fragment of the limited and suspect "scientific" evidence? And who had the right to decide what was sexually "legitimate"?

When Frank Kameny came up from D.C. to speak at New York Mattachine in July 1964, he pulled the plug on the epistemological torture machine. "We owe apologies to no one," Kameny thundered. "Society and its official representatives owe us apologies for what they have done and are doing to us." He insisted that the homophile movement put less effort into trying to educate an indifferent heterosexual mainstream and more into direct demands for civil rights. He assailed the unproven assumptions behind the psychoanalytic model of homosexuality as a "disorder" and insisted that "the entire movement is going to stand or fall upon the question of whether homosexuality is a sickness, and upon our taking a firm stand on it."

Sagarin was in the audience the night of Kameny's speech and (according to Kameny) expressed his disagreement "courteously." But disagree Sagarin did, and proceeded to work hard against Kameny sympathizers taking over New York Mattachine. He even allowed his name to be placed in nomination for president on an opposition slate in the crucial 1965 election. Shortly before, Kameny wrote Sagarin a prophetic letter of warning: "You have gotten yourself associated with bad company ... you have become no longer the vigorous Father of the Homophile Movement, to be revered, respected and listened to, but the senile Grandfather of the Homophile Movement, to be humored and tolerated, at best; to be ignored and disregarded, usually; and to be ridiculated [sic], at worst."

The Kameny militants won the 1965 election, and most of the Old Guard within New York Mattachine, Sagarin included, left the organization immediately and for good. Sagarin tried to adopt an attitude of resigned inevitability: it is in the very nature of social movements, he counseled his allies, to turn against their founders; but "the politics of rejection would one day lead to the possibilities of rehabilitation." The Olympian tone of his abdication concealed considerable indignation and hurt. Sagarin let some of it surface when writing to Dorr Legg the following year: "the homophile movement is a hopeless mess, i.e., the biggest gang of potential blackmailers against real or alleged or ex-homosexuals in America consists of the leadership of the homophile movement. I should like to state that I regard the homophile movement as inimical to the interests of homosexuals."

During the last twenty years of Sagarin's life, much had changed. He ascended the academic ladder; reveled in the interchanges, intrigues, and joustings of the scholarly life; and approximated his long-sought dream of working in harness with a group of like-minded associates. He became an encyclopedic, adept teacher and for his favored students—mostly male—an admired mentor. And he became the proud paterfamilias: his son Fred, who had chosen to teach handicapped and autistic children as a career, married, and had three children of his own, whom Sagarin doted on.

While much changed, nothing changed. "Edward Sagarin," his new alias, added volume upon volume to the already lengthy list of writings he'd produced as "Donald Webster Cory" (none of which he'd any longer formally acknowledge as his). A few of his many books remain in print and toward the end of his life, he even got a novel published and a play produced.

Sagarin's nearly two dozen sociological works are (mostly) liberal in content and accessible in style. In his later years, he often sounded themes (as he had in 1951) with strikingly contemporary resonance: the malleability of the self, the need to historicize "expert" opinion and thus limit its claims to universality. ("Part of the changing process," Sagarin wrote in 1977, "is to believe in the possibility of change ... in the interests of freedom of choice, one must reject 'identity.'") None of his many books, however, can be seen as formative, theoretically innovative, or heretically heart-stopping. (On this, every sociologist I spoke to agreed—and every one of them requested anonymity.) Sagarin continued to champion outsiders and underdogs of various kinds (Blacks, Jews, antiwar protestors, socialists, prostitutes, alcoholics, gamblers, pornographers, schizophrenics, et al.). He fought through his writing to rescue them all from the categories of enemy, freak, or sinner, and stoutly defended their rights against the smug majoritarian morality employed against them.

And yes, he continued to defend homosexuals, that is, on the limited grounds learned at Albert Ellis's knee: homosexuality should be decriminalized, but not normalized. One should work toward alleviating the many injustices that gay people currently suffered, but "without accepting the traits that mark them as different." "In an analogy which I find striking," Sagarin wrote in a 1979 essay, "I have noted that blindness is undesirable but a blind person is not an undesirable." Homosexuality remained to him a "condition," a "pattern of adjustment" (as he put it in 1973) that represented, in essence, "a perversion of the instinctual drives." Sagarin felt no more need in the 1970s than he had in the 1950s to define the loaded, self-enclosed vocabulary that he continued to assert with such unabated confidence.

Yet his own sexuality remained unchanged—argue though he did in theory for the "malleability of the self." Barry Sheer dropped out of his life after some three or four years. Increasingly militant in the post-Stonewall years, Sheer wrote an article in 1970—"The Anti-Homosexual in America: Donald Webster Cory"—in which he cuttingly denounced his old mentor, advising the newly empowered young to forget but not to forgive him.

Sagarin always scrupulously avoided approaching any of his students sexually. But he would still—the frequency decreasing with age and declining health—do a bit of cruising here or there, have a brief encounter, or engage with the occasional Times Square hustler. One of his forays to Times Square—a premiere cruising ground in the late '60s—had particularly dire repercussions. The story centers on "Richard Stein," a young colleague of Sagarin's in the sociology department at CCNY. Stein was part of a group of New Leftist faculty whose politics had proved offensive to some of the older members of the department and who had therefore failed to get tenure. When Stein himself came up for a tenure decision, he felt that Sagarin's sponsorship would produce a positive outcome. But on the day the five-person executive committee of the department met to vote on Stein, Sagarin failed to show up and the vote, by 3 to 2, went against Stein's tenure.

What had happened? The accounts vary. According to one of his colleagues (who feels certain that his version is the accurate one), Sagarin had picked up a hustler in Times Square and gone back with him to one of the fleabag hotels that then catered to trysts and transients. The trick had turned nasty, had mugged Sagarin, and then fled. Sagarin had had a heart attack in the hotel bathroom and been taken to the hospital. His wallet gone, he couldn't be identified for a full day. However, Richard Stein, for one, doubts the accuracy of this account, primarily because he "saw no bruises of any kind" on his mentor when he visited him in the hospital.

In any case, Sagarin felt terrible about missing the crucial tenure meeting, and after he got back on his feet, he took Stein to lunch to express his deep regret. During the lunch, Sagarin spoke openly—as he almost never did—of his own homosexuality. That he did so in this instant—since the heart attack would itself have been sufficient explanation for missing the tenure meeting—suggests intense guilt and remorse, giving added credence to the narrative about the Times Square hustler. As for Stein, his career never got back on track.

By the early seventies, the "secret" of Sagarin's double identity had become known to a number of his colleagues and even to some of his students and friends. But those who were aware of Sagarin's other life, both sexual and authorial, mostly ignored it. As one of his most admiring graduate students told me, "There's a distinction between knowing and acknowledging. I felt it was impolite, not fair, nasty, to acknowledge Sagarin's homosexuality if he preferred not to discuss it." But far from everybody "knew." Robert Bierstedt, for example, who'd been chair of Sagarin's doctoral committee in 1966, was astonished when I revealed to him that Sagarin and Cory were one and the same person; Bierstedt had never, in the intervening thirty years, heard any rumor or gossip to that effect.

Sagarin himself was still not publicly owning up to the double identity. The sociologist Vern Bullough told me that after Sagarin saw galley proofs in 1975 of Bullough's forthcoming *Sexual Variance*—in which he'd said something like, "Donald Webster Cory is also known as Edward Sagarin"—Sagarin contacted the publisher, Wiley, and threatened to sue. Before Wiley would agree to go to press, they made Bullough get depositions from various individuals who'd been active in the homophile movement affirming that Sagarin and Cory were indeed one and the same person.

When the January 1973 issue of *Contemporary Sociology* appeared with a deprecatory Sagarin essay—an essay-review of a dozen recent gay liberationist books—Laud Humphreys, a professor of sociology at Pitzer College in California, hit the roof. Humphreys' own (by then notorious) 1970 book, *Tearoom Trade: Impersonal Sex in Public Places*, wasn't among those damned in the review, but Sagarin had managed glancingly to refer to Humphreys' "unconvincing" work.

The two men had some startling commonalities in their histories: both had come late to academia and sociology, both were left-wing in their politics—and both were gay men who'd married and fathered children. The parallels may have fueled Humphreys' anger; he was feeling suffocated by his own half-opened closet door and enraged at the homophobic hypocrisy of his own university, which had tried to delay his degree and also the publication of *Tearoom Trade*.

After reading Sagarin's essay, Humphreys' first reaction was to send off a rip-snorting letter of protest to the editors of *Contemporary Sociology*. He accused them of having "ordered this mass slaughter ... as a sort of 'protective reaction' strike to rid us of the troublesome 'homosexual researchers' and that embarrassing gay question all in one operation ... a whole genre of contemporary sociology, not to mention a movement for human freedom, are scheduled for clever annihilation."

When Humphreys failed to get a response that satisfied him, he decided on a second line of attack: he would speak out publicly at the 1974 annual sociology convention in Montreal. Humphreys was scheduled to appear as a discussant on a panel ("Theoretical Perspectives on Homosexuality") where Sagarin was due to give a paper surveying the recent literature. In the paper, distributed to the panelists in advance of the session, Sagarin denounced those fellow sociologists who encouraged or supported homosexuals in "coming out." In particular, he denounced the respected "pro-gay" researchers Evelyn Hooker and John Gagnon as special pleaders who'd falsified or misread their own data.

After reading Sagarin's paper, Humphreys contacted a number of sociologists who he knew to be gay and urged them to attend the panel on the following day. He then stayed up all night preparing his rebuttal. Humphreys would ever after refer to the next day's events as "Bloody Monday." Sagarin read his own paper exactly as he'd prepared it; he attacked recent "liberationist" scholarship, and, for good measure appealed to homosexuals to seek therapeutic counseling. According to *The Body Politic*, a leading gay publication of the day, Sagarin's remarks "were greeted with disbelief and laughter from attending delegates."

Laud Humphreys then rose to respond. He began by fully coming out himself for the first time as "a gay man," and then—as he'd rehearsed the night before—periodically inserted "calculated slippage" into his remarks on Sagarin's paper; that is, he'd refer one minute to "Professor Sagarin," the next to "Mr. Cory"; at one point he addressed Sagarin directly as "Mr. Cory." In all likelihood, most of the audience had never heard of Donald Webster Cory—just as today almost everyone I've mentioned the name "Cory" to, responds with a blank stare (my favorite: "Don Cory?—was he the Mafia owner of the Stonewall bar?") But Sagarin himself got decidedly rattled. When Humphreys moved in for the kill and sardonically asked, "And where did you get *your* data?" Sagarin's hands clenched and his voice choked up. "I am my data," he finally said. Tears fell from the corners of his eyes.

To no one's surprise, Sagarin was not one of the participants when, soon after the 1974 convention and in part to protest it, the Sociologists Gay Caucus was formed. Laud Humphreys served on the original steering committee.

Edward Sagarin/Donald Webster Cory died of a heart attack in 1986 at age 73. ▪

CHAPTER II

Essex Hemphill

AND ANTI-BLACK RACISM

Washington D.C. has always had a large African-American population—in 1970, it reached a peak of 70 percent of the whole, then declined to about 50 percent. It has also long been anomalous in having a high median income level alongside a poverty rate of nearly 20 percent (exceeded only by Mississippi). Blacks with college degrees have often found professional jobs in the federal government, leading to a sizeable Black middle class that stood in stark contrast to the economic insecurity felt by the majority of the city's Black population.

When Marion Barry, who'd been chair of the radical Student Nonviolent Coordinating Committee (SNCC), was elected mayor in 1978, he became the first prominent civil rights activist to become the chief executive of a major American city. Though he did start an innovative summer jobs program during his first term, he did little to improve the dilapidated housing in which a large portion of the city's Black population lived. Indeed over time, in his several terms as mayor, Barry would deeply divide D.C.'s Black community, managing to alienate *both* the churchgoing Black middle class *and* the large LGBTQ+ community (he dotted the "i" towards the end of his checkered career when he voted in 2009 against a bill that recognized same-sex marriage.) [1]

During his first term, neither Barry nor his antagonists had shown any awareness or concern for the all-but invisible Black gay men and lesbians living in their midst, often in isolation from each other. The largely hidden, unorganized world of Black gay people in D.C. stood in contrast to the visibility and assertiveness of the *white* gay community, spearheaded by the newly radicalized chapter of the pre-Stonewall Mattachine Society. Though its membership never exceeded a hundred people, with a mere dozen serving as the activist core, D.C. Mattachine had by 1980 successfully challenged the discriminatory policies of the Civil Service Commission and was continuing to put pressure on other agencies of the federal government.

D.C. Mattachine did attempt to recruit members from the African-American gay bar Nob Hill, though the effort and the response were both lukewarm. White-dominated gay organizations, even today, often fail to understand that the issue of sexual orientation has always been merely one—and not necessarily the most important—matter afflicting Black gay people on a daily, ongoing basis. Back in 1980, Washington, D.C. remained a segregated city in all but name—meaning not just its bars, but its schools, housing, medical facilities, and employment opportunities as well. For many gay people of color, race was and is the primary source of identity, with gender, class, and sexual orientation usually secondary. As the gifted young Black poet Essex Hemphill put it: "My race, even at the point of birth, was more important than my sexuality. That's going to always be the case." [2]

A Black gay presence *had* recently begun to assert itself. When preparations were being made for the first national gay march, scheduled to take place in D.C. in October 1979, a group of emerging Black artists and activists—including, prominently, Billy Jones, Delores Berry, Gil Gerald, Essex Hemphill, Michelle Parkerson, and Renee McCoy—formally incorporated as the National Coalition of Black Lesbians and Gays (NCBLG). As well, the first issue of *Blacklight* magazine, under the editorship of Sidney Brinkley, appeared.

Essex, who helped to spearhead what many were soon calling "the second black renaissance," was in 1980 still only 23 years old. Born in 1957, he was one of Mantalene and Warren Hemphill's five children. Mantalene was a strong, dignified woman who in later life held an administrative job in the copyright division of the Library of Congress. Essex came to terms with his homosexuality early on, made no effort to keep it secret and—as he later emphasized—"I exercise the same candor with my parents." The implicit agreement between many Black parents and their gay offspring often hinged on keeping the news tightly confined within the family circle. Essex would have none of that, and he and his deeply religious mother—with whom he had an intense and lasting love/anger bond—would remain at odds over the issue. [3]

Essex Hemphill
Photo courtesy Jim Marks

Essex felt quite differently about his alcoholic and abusive father, about whom he scarcely had a positive word. In his poem "Vital Signs," Essex recalled witnessing his father's violence: "I ... always see him punching and pushing, slapping and yelling." One of Essex's close friends in adulthood recalls him saying that he'd once witnessed his father stabbing his mother. His parents' stormy relationship ultimately ended in divorce.

Though small, Essex was a handsome boy, with a symmetrical face marked by intense, searching eyes and a mischievous, engaging smile. His soft, caressing voice could, when challenged, ring with implacable conviction. Essex began writing poetry when still in high school, and it would remain his most congenial medium, though he later tried his hand, unsuccessfully, at a novel. His adult essays, along with his poetry, would have a profound influence on his generation of Black writers. [4]

He was precocious, too, at sexual exploration. When Essex was fourteen, George, the forty-ish white male clerk at a convenience store near his home, kept whispering in his ear how much he wanted to suck his dick, how good he was at it. The sucking led to fucking—and went on for two years. Essex moved on to a local Black Episcopal minister who also had what Essex called "a beautiful, stimulating" mind, gave him books to read, and encouraged him to accept his sexuality as part of his intrinsic, and "blessed," personality.

In 1975, Essex enrolled as a freshman at the University of Maryland but, impatient to explore the broader world of an emerging Black gay subculture in D.C., he left after one year. Social and cultural circles in Washington were mostly divided along racial lines and for a time the best-known hangout for Black gay artists was the brownstone in Northeast D.C. of (Valerie) Papaya Mann (who'd also been a central figure in putting together the Sapphire Sapphos, Washington's first organization for African-American lesbians). By the end of the 1970s, three of the artists who first met at Papaya's brownstone, including Essex, began publishing a stunning bimonthly, *Nethula: Journal of Contemporary Literature.* That, in turn, led to heightened contact with the older generation of Black artists, including Sterling Brown and E. Ethelbert Miller. In 1980, Miller arranged for Essex and the Black lesbian poet and filmmaker Michelle Parkerson—she and Essex immediately bonded and became lifelong friends—to share a bill together at a poetry reading series at Howard University. [5]

From that point on, Essex' connections and publications proliferated. He became a founding member of the performance poetry group Station to Station, appeared on various radio shows, and self-published several poetry chapbooks. He also cofounded Cinque—named after the West African who led a successful mutiny aboard the slave ship Amistad—a trio that blended jazz, pop, and words; Essex called it "choral poetry—a kind of melodic and intelligent rap music," which performed widely and developed a loyal following.

By the early Eighties, the Coffeehouse replaced Papaya Mann's brownstone as the most prominent nurturing ground and outlet for gay Black artists in D.C., and Essex became friendly with nearly all the leading figures of what was now widely being called "the second black renaissance"—ranging from the writers Joe Beam and Assotto Saint, to the lesbian vocal duo Cassselberry and DuPree, to the members of the New York poetry collective, Other Countries. Essex was a popular figure, admired for his talent, his feisty intensity, and his bold reaction to any suggestion of racism.

One incident represents a number of others: at D.C.'s Union Station, where

Essex was on his way one day to fulfill a public engagement, a police officer stopped him simply because he was dressed in jeans, a down jacket, and a Raiders baseball cap—in other words, as Essex put it, "in the standard attire of what we will call the 'butch queer' look, the home-boy look, the look of the ghetto." When the officer tried to search him for drugs or weapons, Essex refused to cooperate, loudly accused him of harassment and told him to search the white women and men in the station first. When a white man in a suit handed Essex his business card and said he'd testify for him in court, the officer backed off.

It was a narrow, and highly atypical escape for a Black man, gay or otherwise. "You don't mess with Essex" became a byword, and not just in regard to white policemen. He had a short fuse and any attempt to censor his work, along with any hint of racism, would set it off. Yet it was well known, too, that Essex, as his close friend Wayson Jones told me, "had a very warm, gentle, and nurturing side"—a "boyish, sweet side" that some people never got to see. Or as another friend put it, "Essex is a sensitive, caring guy. [But he] ... took no crap. From anybody."

The early Eighties were a heady time. As Michelle Parkerson later described the ambiance to me: "We were beginning to put flesh on the bones of our gay identities ... our black gay identities ... and seeing those as primary voices from which we wrote, spoke, and were politicized." But this hopeful period, alas, would prove tragically short. A rising number of "inexplicable" cases of what was being called GRID (Gay-Related Immune Deficiency) began to surface among otherwise healthy gay men. And as had happened so often in the past, a link was widely drawn between "debauchery" and godly punishment (in earlier periods, it had been between "unbridled lust" and everything from leprosy to syphilis to bubonic plague). [6]

Instead of expanding the budgets for the Center for Disease Control (CDC) and the National Institutes of Health (NIH) in order to combat the growing epidemic, President Reagan did the exact opposite: he cut the budgets of both. During the first year and a half of the epidemic (soon renamed AIDS), the federal government did little—other than indulge in repetitive, homophobic speeches from congressmen like Jesse Helms and William Dannemeyer applauding the Lord's righteous punishment of homosexual immorality and repetitive calls for a quarantine program to cordon off the sinners. Self-righteous hysteria quickly mounted. One union of social workers threatened to go out on strike if forced to help AIDS patients fill out social security or welfare forms. In hospitals, nurses were garbed from head to foot in "space suits" designed for a nuclear disaster. Some refused to enter a patient's room, left them lying for hours on gurneys in the corridor, and put meal trays *outside* their door.

In the early days of the epidemic, the cities of San Francisco and New York were hardest hit. D.C. reported only 89 cases in the first wave of those afflicted—and the response was minimal. Though a thriving artistic community had arisen among Black gays in D.C., no political organizations had taken comparable root—no notable rallying points for dealing with the epidemic. Some Blacks, initially, dismissed AIDS as a white affliction, and in the early years of the epidemic the sole acknowledgments in the African-American D.C. community of the new health threat were two forums, one held at the gay bar Nob Hill, and the other at a dance club. The powerful Black religious community in D.C.—the city had no fewer than 800 congregations—reacted with what one sympathetic young pastor called "a harsh public piety unmixed with compassion." No Black church person ever matched the rhetorical viciousness of white religious leaders like Jerry Falwell, but only a handful lent a helping hand. [7]

In time, a significant number of Black leaders—including Jesse Jackson, Joseph Lowery, Coretta Scott King, Julian Bond, and David Dinkins—would become strong and public supporters of civil rights protections for gay people—and the Congressional Black Caucus would lead the fight against gay discrimination. But in the early eighties, the atmosphere was quite different. When Gil Gerard, who headed up the National Coalition of Black Lesbians and Gays (NCBLG) contacted those planning the twentieth anniversary commemoration of the 1963 March on Washington, he was greeted with uneasiness and evasion. When Gerard contacted the event's coordinator, Donna Brazile, about listing NCBLG among the endorsing organizations and to suggest Audre Lorde as one of the speakers, Brazile stopped returning his phone calls. Under pressure from the National Organization for Women (NOW), as well as half a dozen national gay organizations, it was ultimately agreed that Audre Lorde would be listed in the program as "representing the gay and lesbian community." Several other dismayingly half-hearted gestures were made. [8]

Essex wasn't yet well enough known to participate in these early confrontations; nor were he and his close circle of friends as yet overly concerned that the plague would reach widely into the Black gay community. Until 1985, Essex was mostly preoccupied with helping his friend Joe Beam put together what would be the path-breaking Black gay anthology *In the Life,* and in enjoying a live-in love affair with a naval career officer who broke it off after several years, leaving Essex sadly missing what he called "the domestic repetition of beauty that is found in caring for and being cared for by a lover." (He would later enter into another relationship of a few years duration.) Some of Essex' friends thought he made unwise choices in his lovers, that he was attracted to men who—like his father—would be likely to mistreat him. Essex thought the danger originated elsewhere and he named it powerfully in his poem, "The Tomb of Sorrow":

> *I was your man lover,*
> *gambling dangerously with my soul.*
> *I was determined to love you*
> *but you were haunted*
> *by Vietnam,*
> *taunted by demons.*
> *In my arms you dreamed*
> *of tropical jungles,*
> *of young village girls*
> *with razors embedded in their pussies,*
> *lethal chopsticks*
> *hidden in their hair,*
> *and their nipples clenched*
> *like grenade pins*
> *between your grinding teeth...*

In 1985, Essex and seven friends drove out to St. Louis in a rented car to attend NCBLG's weekend-long convention. The organization's "Statement of

Purpose" accurately reflected Essex' own values: it emphasized "Black Pride and Solidarity" and sought to create "positive attitudes between and among Black non-Gays and Black Gays." Excited at NCBLG's prospects, Essex volunteered, along with Barbara Smith and Audre Lorde, to join the publications committee of the new magazine, *Black/Out*. For Essex, racial solidarity took primacy over gay liberation but did not invalidate it or cancel it out. Many factors, he recognized—including race, class, gender, sexual orientation—contribute to forming individual "identity," their comparative importance rising and falling in response to immediate (and shifting) circumstances. Just as the NCBLG "Statement of Purpose" declared the need to work cooperatively with other lesbian and gay organizations, so too did Essex the individual acknowledge that "a lot of my recognition [as a poet] is attributable to support from the gay and lesbian community," particularly but not exclusively from the *Black* gay community. [9]

Essex did not, however, join other activists in forming the National Minority AIDS Council, which was organized "to build leadership within communities of color to address the challenges of HIV/AIDS." Both he and his close friend Joe Beam were intensely private people who avoided discussing their own health issues even with trusted friends, and only reluctantly and irregularly joined organizational efforts to fight AIDS. In the 1990s, Essex *would* occasionally speak out, openly and eloquently, about "being a person with AIDS," but earlier he rarely referenced it in his poetry. Among those few occasions was his poem "O Tell Me, Brutus," published in 1986:

> *O tell me, Brutus,*
> *With corpses decomposing*
> *In the river,*
> *Loved ones keeping fevers*
> *Quiet in city hospitals,*
> *The backrooms, locked and chained,*
> *The police with new power to seize*
> *And search our hearts, our kisses,*
> *Our mutual consents around midnight.* [10]

The attitude of New York City's pre-eminent gay publication, *The New*

York Native, towards Black gays illustrates why Essex and other people of color were reluctant to expect much understanding or help from the official, white-dominated gay movement. The Black gay community lacked the financial resources more readily available to white gays, and could have used some promotional help from the white gay press. Yet the *Native* never published a review of any of the three issues of *Blackheart* nor covered any of the frequent literary readings in the city by Black lesbians and gay men. More demeaning still was the *Native*'s hurtful policy of publishing ads in its employment section that frequently stated a preference for "WM in mid-20s."

ESSEX LIVED close to the margins. To maximize his free time to write, he settled for the occasional odd job—and the even more occasional grant. But he refused to court favor for either or to curb what one friend called his "heart-breaking honesty." He walked out of one job as a graphic artist for an electric power company when he sensed the racist bias of his boss. And when he received a grant from the Washington D.C. Mayor's Arts Awards in 1987 and its Black executive director told Essex that he'd have to remove the word "corruption"—D.C. Mayor Marion Barry was currently under investigation—from the poem he planned to read at the ceremony, Essex said he would; once onstage, though, he not only kept "corruption" in his poem but spoke openly about the attempt that had been made to censor his work. The audience responded with thunderous applause.

His rebellious spirit is manifest throughout his poetry. When the Supreme Court handed down its infamous 1987 *Bowers v. Hardwick* decision upholding a Georgia law outlawing "sodomy"—and empowering police to invade the privacy of an adult's bedroom—Essex's poem "The Occupied Territories" gave voice to the gay community's outrage:

> *You are not to touch other flesh*
> *without a police permit.*
> *You have no privacy—*
> *the State wants to seize your bed*
> *and sleep with you.*
> *The State wants to control*

> *your sexuality, your birth rate,*
> *your passion.*
> *The message is clear;*
> *your penis, your vagina,*
> *your testicles, your womb,*
> *your anus, your orgasm,*
> *these belong to the State.*
> *You are not to touch yourself*
> *or be familiar with ecstasy.*
> *The erogenous zones*
> *are not demilitarized.*

By 1987, the incidence of HIV among African Americans was twice that of whites, and Black gays and lesbians increasingly formed their own organizations to deal with the heavy toll. (GMAD—Gay Men of African Descent in New York City became particularly dynamic.) In some instances, white gay activists lent information and support—more often, it should be said, than did traditional-minded heterosexual Black leaders and organizations. As late as 1988, the Reverend Calvin Butts, executive minister of Abyssinian Baptist Church—the most prestigious church in Harlem—publicly denounced homosexuality as "against the will of God." [11]

There was a great deal less support in D.C. than in New York. Five years into the epidemic, the Reagan administration had still budgeted only meager sums for research; D.C.'s chief of police announced that he wouldn't want to be in a room with a person who had AIDS; and D.C. policemen continued to wear surgical masks and yellow gloves when dealing with AIDS patients. Yet in the mid-'80s, the Black artistic community in D.C. had continued its vibrant expansion at venues like d. c. space and the Painted Bride Art Center. At the latter, Essex, Michelle Parkerson and Wayson Jones were awarded a two week New Works Residency grant in 1987 that resulted in *Voicescapes: An Urban Mouthpiece*—an exploration of call-and-response and recitative oral traditions—and the piece was favorably reviewed in the prestigious *High Performance* magazine. They followed that success with a piece called *Dear Motherfuckin' Dreams* at the Kitchen, the well-known experimental venue in New York City.

By the late 1980s, the epidemic's tentacles had reached much deeper into the community, killing off a growing number of the creative spirits that Essex had counted among his friends. "A generation," Essex wrote, "passes before my worn out, grieving eyes. An outlaw community is being decimated without remorse. The scythe swings back and forth, back and forth, random, wild, unpredictable." Essex had known for some time that he was himself HIV-positive but had continued to feel relatively well. Before long, though, he confided to a friend that he'd begun to experience fevers and night sweats. When in 1988 his closest friend Joe Beam—just three days before his thirty-fourth birthday—succumbed to the disease, Essex put his deep grief in a poem he left unpublished in his lifetime:

> *There should have been*
> *more letters between us...*
> *There should have been*
> *more letters hastily written*
> *or carefully typed,*
> *long-winded scripts*
> *or short, cryptic messages.*
> *Volumes of letters*
> *should have gathered*
> *over time, but we leave*
> *hastily scrawled postcards,*
> *outrageous, long-distance*
> *phone bills,*
> *and in rare instances*
> *evidence that some of us*
> *were more than brothers.* [12]

By the end of 1987, AIDS had appeared in some 113 countries, and Europe had reacted with a massive educational program to inform and protect its citizens. Not so in the United States, where conservative forces continued to dominate. The right-wing anti-feminist Phyllis Schlafly, for one, offered neither sympathy nor succor; instead, she warned that gay activists were planning "grammar school sodomy classes." Back in 1976, the CDC had spent $9 million within months of the outbreak of Legionnaires' disease (which killed thirty-four people); during the first year of the AIDS epidemic, with more than two hundred people already dead, the CDC spent $1 million—while right-wingers called for quarantine and William Buckley suggested that gay men who tested positive should be tattooed on their buttocks.

The lack of government concern, let alone compassion, helped to feed a growing anger among gay people at the callous indifference to their survival. With the birth of ACT UP, militantly confrontational tactics culminated in a massive March on Washington in October 1987, and Essex, Wayson, and Michelle, the night before the march, performing two shows at d.c. space. The march itself was huge—somewhere in the neighborhood of half a million—and entirely peaceful, devoid of the kind of paramilitary drill units and rifle clubs that disfigure most large-scale parades. There was only one bunch of angry, confrontational people at the march—the Jesus freaks, carrying their hate-filled banners, screaming their violent slogans. [12]

AT THE TIME OF HIS DEATH, Joe Beam had begun work on a sequel to *In the Life,* his first anthology of Black gay male poetry and prose. His mother Dorothy became determined to fulfill her son's dream for a second volume and she turned to Essex for help. He readily agreed and even made the decision to move into the Beam home in Philadelphia to facilitate the work. Some of Dorothy's friends let it be known that they were scandalized at her having "a gay person living in your house." Dorothy—who'd been a fighter all her life, earning a master's degree at night from Temple University—minced no words: "My son's gay friends are welcome at my house any time. They hurt the same, they have the same problems. In fact they have more." [13]

Though Essex accepted without hesitation Dorothy Beam's invitation to work on the anthology, his health had in fact begun to worry him. Guarded as always about his privacy, he referred only rarely and obliquely to his symptoms: forced to cancel a performance in 1988, he told the sponsor that it was "due to circumstances related to my health. ... Believing this period of my life to be a test, I can't say I have survived it with the best qualities of my person."

With coaching from Barbara Smith—founder of the pioneering Kitchen

Table Press—about the ins-and-outs of book publishing, Essex ultimately gathered a pool of some 140 submissions for the anthology. He ended up choosing some three dozen writers, several of whom appear more than once in the book. The hefty, finished volume came to nearly three hundred pages of closely printed text, with Essex including several of his own best poems and essays. He also appended a long, vibrant—even fierce—introduction, dating it "January 1990." In it, he provided a detailed history of Black gay male literature and as well mounted an angry attack on the white gay world in general and one of its celebrities in particular: Robert Mapplethorpe, and his much-heralded series of "erotic" (Essex called them "racist") portraits of Black men.

In Essex' view, all that the AIDS crisis had succeeded in doing was to "clearly point out how significant are the cultural and economic differences" between the races in the U.S. "We are communities engaged in a fragile coexistence if we are anything at all." Mapplethorpe's photographs exemplified the difference: in Essex' view they supported the stereotype of Black men as headless, heartless creatures with monstrous phalluses, and, in doing so, reiterated the standard fantasy of Blaxploitation movies of the 1970s. "What is insulting and endangering to black men," Essex wrote, "is Mapplethorpe's *conscious* determination that the faces, the heads, and by extension, the minds and experiences of some of his black subjects are not as important as close-up shots of their cocks." Essex wanted to make sure that his critique wasn't mistaken for prudery: "I don't have any problem with erotic art. In fact, I think much of it, when rendered well, can be very beautiful and very moving." He refused, moreover, to endorse any call for censorship, and vigorously rejected the right-wing effort to prevent Mapplethorpe's work from being exhibited. [14]

To promote the completed anthology, which he titled *Brother to Brother*, Essex crisscrossed the country giving readings and interviews. In many of them, he spoke of the larger issues assailing the African-American community. He talked often and candidly about what he called "the dysfunction" of the Black intelligentsia, his special target being "assimilationist" Black academics who kept their posts, he argued, by toeing the mainstream party line. He also singled out the films of Spike Lee—*Jungle Fever* in particular—as "hostile to the black gay experience" and for reinforcing the homophobia "found in the black community." It made him all the more grateful, Essex said, for younger Black filmmakers like Michelle Parkerson, Isaac Julien, and Marlon Riggs: "there's a sincere hope there that dialogue from the marginalized and dis-empowered will be handled by people who don't have a commercial interest but a humanistic one." [15]

Brother to Brother in fact contained a number of strong pieces that held to account many leading Black intellectuals and academicians for their ongoing denunciation of homosexuality. Isaac Julian's essay, for one, centered on how the Langston Hughes estate had "disrupted the original version" of his film *Looking for Langston* by forcing him to delete several of Hughes' homoerotic poems. Marlon Riggs, in turn, contributed a piece deploring the fact that homosexuality had "been ridiculed and spoken of with absolute scorn by some of our most brilliant writers, scholars, and leaders—Amiri Baraka, Haki Madhubuti, Nathan Hare, Robert Staples, Molefi Asante and Minister Louis Farrakhan." He could have added to that list Frantz Fanon, the psychiatrist Alvin Poussaint, and Eldridge Cleaver.

The white press largely ignored *Brother to Brother. Publishers Weekly* simply dismissed the collection as "offerings of dubious literary merit." In *The New Republic,* the reviewer rather grandly expressed the wish for "a gay literature that is not merely about its own gayness" and suggested the contributors would do well to employ "the advantages of indirection" when discussing sexuality—surely a luxurious piece of advice when placed in the context of a community devastated by AIDS and desperate for succor.

In New York City, too, the AIDS crisis brought issues relating to race to a considerable boil. Allan Robinson, a Black gay member of ACT UP, scorned the white male sense of entitlement of some of its members: "They were goddamned angry. They were angry because they thought they had every-thing—trips to Brazil and Fire Island, hanging in the clubs, boyfriends, drugs, money, and living perhaps on Eighty-First Street and Central Park West. They were angry because they were being treated like everybody else. The Latino activist Moises Agosto was another prominent figure in ACT UP who ultimately became disillusioned with the organization: "The majority of people I looked up to in [the all-white Treatment and Data Committee] ... were not really that much into doing work related to access to care and treatment for disenfranchised communities." In 1992, Agosto shifted his energy to working with the National Latino Lesbian and Gay Organization. [16]

But that was not the whole story. As the proportion of Blacks rose to 33 percent of New York City's AIDS cases, a significant number of whites in ACT UP *did* focus their attention on minorities. Members of the Housing and Majority Action Committees put particular emphasis on meeting the needs of people of color and ending minority invisibility—though some white members (like Mike Callen and Jim Eigo) continued to regret that there remained "a huge gap between ACT UP rhetoric and behavior" in dealing with the realization that AIDS "disproportionately affects men and women of color." San Francisco, by way of contrast, had as early as 1986 empowered a Third World AIDS Advisory Task Force that pushed an agenda foregrounding the enormity of the needs of people of color afflicted with AIDS—who often lay beyond the outreach of AIDS organizations. [17]

Essex had always (as he himself put it) "steered clear of any heavy group involvement," with the sole exception of his longstanding membership in the National Coalition of Black Lesbians and Gays. He did participate in fundraisers for AIDS in the D.C. area and also gathered together artists, regardless of sexual identity, to do a benefit for a homeless shelter; as well, he often wove material relating to AIDS into his public performances. Though he had never expected majority white organizations like ACT UP to devote its resources to combating Black disadvantage, he could grow exceedingly angry at the opposite suggestion that Black gays relied almost exclusively on white groups for their medical needs. Yet he did acknowledge, and expressed gratitude for, the caregiving services that the white-dominated Whitman-Walker clinic in D.C. provided to people of color.

Essex wasn't naturally belligerent—that is, someone who invented or maximized slights in order to discharge their own demons. But he *was* a person of intense feeling, and when he believed that a genuine injury had been done to him, he could be vehement in confronting the offense. As someone good at meticulous detail work, he could also grow irritable when others, more slovenly and irresponsible, failed to keep their promises—and ended up damaging his own work. To avoid that pitfall, he did most of the leg work himself in publicizing *Brother to Brother*, sending out press materials to some sixty review outlets and following up with "reminder" phone calls.

When an editor at *Book World* (the *Washington Post's* review section) told him twice that no press material had arrived, Essex had the UPS shipping bill pulled—and it verified delivery. He then heard from another employee at *Book World* that the editor in question had been overheard telling someone that he wasn't interested "in reviewing gay and lesbian literature"—at which point Essex opened up with both barrels. In a blistering four page letter, he accused the editor of trading in "your integrity and credibility for lies and shabby denials in order to maintain a heterosexist hegemony that can easily find you expendable at any moment." To move that process along, he sent a copy of his letter to the editor-in-chief of *Book World*. Essex was a deeply sweet and charming man—but on some issues you'd be wise not to cross him. [18]

BOTH ESSEX and his poetry (especially his moving "A Homocide") appeared in Marlon Riggs genre-bending film *Tongues Untied*, and the two men shared a similar judgment of the standard representation of Black life featured on mainstream TV (when it treated the subject at all). Marlon's 1992 film, *Color Adjustment*, contained a sharp critique of *Roots,* the hugely popular miniseries about African American history, justifiably accusing it of minimizing the actual horrors of slavery. He and Essex also shared a negative view of the wildly successful *The Cosby Show.* They felt it insultingly avoided most of the issues that afflicted Black families, serving up instead a subliminal paean to the standard American myth that hard work and discipline are all one needs in the U.S. to reach the pinnacles of success (translation: racism was an insignificant obstacle to black advancement).

After working along steadily on producing a collection of his own selected poems and essays, Essex published in 1992 the volume *Ceremonies.* Thematically, the collection centered on his life as a Black gay man, belittled or condemned by the straight Black world (even though sharing its racial indignities), and ignored or patronized by the white gay world. His voice throughout the book was anguished and angry, intensely proud and independent even as he maintained his forlorn search, in a bleak and ominous landscape, for sustained connection:

> *I plunder every bit of love*
> *in my possession.*
> *I am looking for an answer*
> *to drugs and corruption.*
> *I enter the diminishing*
> *circumstance of prayer.*
> *Inside a homemade Baptist church*
> *perched on the edge*
> *of the voodoo ghetto,*
> *the murmurs of believers*
> *rise and fall, exhaled*
> *from a single spotted lung.*
> *The congregation sings*
> *to an out-of-tune piano*
> *while death is rioting,*
> *splashing blood about*
> *like gasoline.*

Although *Ceremonies* won the National Library Association's New Authors in Poetry Award and reached the gay bestseller lists, it was largely ignored by both white and Black mainstream media outlets. Yet over the next eighteen months, Essex received numerous invitations to speak, and travelled widely. When asked about his health, he responded along the lines of "it's pretty good. I've had mild disturbances, but I've been fortunate so far, and that is the qualifier: so far." His indefatigable agent Frances Goldin secured a two-book contract for him with the conglomerate publishing house of NAL/ Dutton/Penguin—one was for a projected anthology of short fiction by Black gay men, and the other for his tentatively titled novel in progress, "Standing in the Gap." [19]

When he completed a first draft of the novel, Essex sent copies both to Goldin and to Peter Borland, the acquisitions editor at Penguin. Their verdict, though couched in encouraging language about the book's potential, was decidedly negative. Goldin felt there was "far too much unconvincing dialog and too much lecturing," and Borland suggested a radical revision that included a shift from an omnipotent third person voice to a first-person narration.

Essex' response was receptive and gracious; he even declared enthusiasm for moving ahead with a major overhaul on the novel. He was at the moment in a good space, having won a yearlong residency as a visiting scholar at the prestigious Getty Center for the History of Art and the Humanities in California. He was given a splendid apartment, along with an assistant, and his opening presentation about his current projects was, by his own account, "very well attended by scholars and staff." But midpoint in the yearlong residency, Essex' health took a turn for the worse, and the doctors confirmed that his T cell count—the prime indicator of the health of the immune system—had fallen to the dangerously low level of 23. He wrote Frances Goldin that he was "not too frightened, but simply stated ... all is a mess right now." He had all along been determined to maintain what he called "a positive way of living," but there was no gainsaying the fact that by the end of his stay at the Getty he had little energy, and his spirits were only "fair." He put work on the pending anthology and novel on hold and used his limited energy towards finishing a new series of poems, including a major one he would call "Vital Signs."

Returning to the East Coast, Essex laid low, husbanding his strength for writing. Like so many others, he listened intently for word that some new, effective treatment for AIDS had been discovered and would soon be released. But 1993 came and went without any medical breakthrough. The only relatively new development was a somewhat more sympathetic change in public opinion. Hollywood released its big-budget film, *Philadelphia*, with Tom Hanks playing an estimable gay lawyer—and it earned $125 million at the box office. Elton John came out, and soon after that, the multiple gold medal swimmer Greg Louganis revealed that he, too, was HIV-positive. Yet the early nineties also saw a 30 percent *upswing* in hate crimes against gay people. The dragon of homophobia had not been slain, and the disease of AIDS had ballooned into a global phenomenon (in sub-Saharan Africa alone,

15 million people had become infected by the early nineties).

By now, Essex was receiving periodic blood transfusions, which for a time did boost his strength somewhat. Mostly he stayed home, listened to music—which had always been important to him—and occasionally attempted to write, finally finishing "Vital Signs." On reaching the close of the poem, he turned from poetry to prose:

> *Some of the T cells I am without are not here through my own fault. I didn't lose all of them foolishly, and I didn't lose all of them erotically. Some of the missing T cells were lost to racism, a well-known transmittable disease. Some were lost to poverty because there was no money to do something about the plumbing before the pipes burst and the room flooded. Homophobia killed quite a few, but so did my rage and my pointed furies, so did the wars at home and the wars within, so did the drugs I took to remain calm, cool, collected. ... Actually, there are T cells scattered all about me at doorways where I was denied entrance because I was a faggot or a nigga or too poor or too black. There are T cells spilling out of my ashtrays from the cigarettes I have anxiously smoked. There are T cells all over the floors of several bathhouses, coast to coast, and halfway around the world, and in numerous parks, and in countless bars, and in places I am forgetting to make room for other memories. My T cells are strewn about like the leaves of a mighty tree, like the fallen hair of an old man, like the stars of a collapsing universe.* [20]

Essex had written his own gallant, sorrowful elegy. There were still occasional days in 1994 when he had enough energy to write, and he did manage a trip to see his mother and siblings (though it proved "exhausting"). Increasingly, though, he withdrew—"to deal with my stuff," he wrote enigmatically to Barbara Smith. He tried to sustain his lifelong ability to focus on the positive: "I just remember to say 'thank you' for every day I am able to have. I don't really desire too many things other than the chance to keep creating."

He continued to keep the details of his illness even from close friends. That had been typical of how he'd handled AIDS all along: he'd simply gone about his business as best he could, neither clarifying nor lamenting—and certainly never exaggerating—his condition. After a bout with the dreaded PCP pneumonia, he spent most of his time alone in his apartment, dealing with fevers, night sweats, and painful neuropathy—and becoming ever thinner. What little writing he was able to do was later privately printed in a nineteen-page limited edition entitled *Domestic Life.* [21]

By 1995, he was frequently in and out of the hospital, and then, when no longer able to take care of himself, entered the University of Pennsylvania Hospital in Philadelphia. Very few visitors were allowed to see him. When one close friend, Ron Simmons, was granted a visit, he reported back to other friends that "Essex is no longer able to speak, he could only point and a horrible rattle came from his throat." He died, age 38, on November 5, 1995.

One month later, the FDA approved the release of Saquinavir, the first of a new class of drugs called protease inhibitors which in the years ahead would convert AIDS from a death sentence to a manageable disease. Essex was one of the unlucky ones who narrowly missed the "miracle." But if HIV finally became treatable, homophobia and racism continued their tenacious hold on the national psyche. If one disease had been contained, the other two still ran riot. That was made clear when, a mere two years after Essex' death, a new book, *America in Black and White*, appeared authored by two prominent white academicians, Stephen and Abigail Thernstrom.

The Thernstroms confidently presented themselves as "anti-racist," but their book told another story—one of blind self-deception. *America in Black and White* was in fact balm for the growing number of whites announcing themselves weary of "the race question." In a chilly tone of dispassion that bordered on disdain, the Thernstroms provided a lethal rationale for justifying white complacency: on the one hand, they grossly overestimated the progress of racial equality to date, and, on the other, argued that further advances hinged on Blacks getting their act together. Fatigued white hearts sighed in grateful unison.

Early on in their book, and repetitively, the Thernstroms equated moral urgency with civil disorder. They simplistically dismissed Huey Newton as a man who "led a life of serious crime," and disposed of Congressman John Conyers Jr. in three words: "sarcastic and abrasive." Militancy, the Thernstroms warned, led to riots, and riots marked "the end of hope." Meaning: the hope of winning or retaining white sympathy. They offered the 1965 Watts riot as a case in point, describing it as a "seemingly gleeful" mob overreacting to "an ordinary police action." In doing so, they managed simultaneously to reduce the LAPD's longstanding record for brutality to the equivalent of a feather duster, and Black rage to a childish pout.

All of which I took, with the memory of Essex' righteous intransigence in mind, as a personal affront and, as a commentary on race relations, shockingly smug. And I said so, in a blistering review of *America in Black and White* in the *Los Angeles Times.* In response to the Thernstroms stern insistence that Blacks must "properly" engage the political system, must cease talking about the "specialness" of Black culture or demanding preferential treatment, I pointed out that if Blacks had historically placed their hopes on convincing whites of their "individual merit" rather than on collective struggle against a racism that stigmatized on the basis of group membership, there would never have been a civil rights movement.

In insisting, moreover, that the practice of "set-asides" had "failed miserably," the Thernstroms had expressed moral outrage (an attitude they'd denounced when coming from Blacks) at the bribes, kickbacks, and assorted other corrupt practices that became part of the system of "set-asides." They never probed deep enough to raise the question "what else could one expect in an economic system based on greed and corruption?"—the kind of corruption that had long allowed racism to systematically exclude Black bids in the construction industry. (Atlanta, before the election of a black mayor in 1974, with a population half Black, awarded exactly .5% of city contracts to Black firms.) If the presence of periodic dishonesty was an argument for dismantling a policy of affirmative action or set-asides, then the Thernstroms might have better expended their energy warring against market capitalism.

They instead invested it on persuading us that white racism had declined to the point that it was no longer a significant factor in accounting for the ongoing plight of many African Americans. They announced, for example, that "naked discrimination" among real estate agents was a thing of the past; what bias remained was, the Thernstroms claimed, the unwillingness of African

Americans to live in areas that have only a handful of Black residents—an argument that amounted to an inventive new way of blaming the victim. Besides, the prevalence of Black poverty militated against affording the high rents of many white neighborhoods. The Thernstroms had an answer for that argument too: "Black poverty is not due to curtailed opportunities but to the disintegration of 'intact, two-parent families' in the Black community." The Thernstroms never entertained the view that single parents, supplemented by a kinship network, can provide a viable, and nurturing, environment.

Instead, they insisted that "there is work available—even in inner city neighborhoods," though "unmotivated" (a word unnervingly close to "shiftless") Blacks had failed to avail themselves of the jobs. We hear nothing from the Thernstroms about the wretched, dead-end nature of the available work; nor the accumulated rage over forever starting, and remaining, at the bottom-line entry level; nor the multiplicity of everyday slights that African-Americans suffer. For the Thernstroms, such arguments amount to misplaced empathy. They prefer the Calvinist lecture: Blacks must learn basic literacy skills, "good diction, how to dress appropriately, wake up to an alarm, arrive at work on time, and listen to direction and criticism once there."

These platitudinous harangues take the place of acknowledging (let alone deploring) the corrosive history of stereotyping that Blacks face, along with the stultifying assumptions about Black intellectual inferiority. The Thernstroms are tone deaf to the burdens of history, to the inculcation of inferiority, generation after generation that Blacks have been subjected to—and often risen above, or circumvented through a highly sophisticated culture of their own. Like most Americans, the Thernstroms obsess about the here-and-now and have only a scant awareness of how past experience influences present behavior.

AN IDLE THOUGHT: what if the Thernstroms had gotten to know Essex Hemphill? Perhaps then they might have been able to shed their threadbare empathy, reevaluate their odd negation of entrenched racism, and begun to fathom the value of differentness. I doubt it though. The rot has gone too deep. ▪

NOTES

1. David K. Johnson, *The Lavender Scare: The Cold War Persecution of Gays and Lesbians in the Federal Government*, Univ. of Chicago Press, 193-94, 211-14. This essay is a much condensed, re-written version of material in Duberman, *Hold Tight Gently,* The New Press, 2014. Additionally, I'm indebted to Frances Goldin, Essex' literary agent (and at the time, my own), who located Essex' early poems for me in her back files, as well as the manuscript of his long-lost novel, "Standing in the Gap."

2. For this and the following paragraph: Sidney Brinkley, "Making History," in *Smash the Church, Smash the State*, ed. Tommi Avicolli Mecca, City Lights, 2009; Cathy J. Cohen, *The Boundaries of Blackness: AIDS* and *the Breakdown of Black Politics,* Univ. of Chicago Press, 1999.

3. Hemphill, "Miss Emily's Grandson Won't Hush His Mouth," *Outweek,* Aug. 8, 1990; "Where We Live: A Conversation with Essex Hemphill and Isaac Julien," in *[speak my name] Black Men on Masculinity and the American Dream*, ed. Don Belton, Beacon, 1995; interview with Wayson Jones, May 2009; Wayson Jones to me, April 15, 2013.

4. See Hemphill's chapbooks: *Diamonds Was in the Kitty; Some of the People We Love Are Terrorists; Earth Life;* and the best known of them: *Conditions.* See also Hemphill, *Ceremonies,* Cleis, 1992.

5. Interviews with Miller, Ron Simmons, Chris Prince, Wayson Jones, and Michelle Parkerson, May 2009.

6. Interview with Michelle Parkerson, May 2009. For the historical dimension, see Peter Lewis Allen's fine study, *The Wages of Sin: Sex and Disease, Past and Present,* Univ. of Chicago Press, 2000.

7. Eric Brandt, *Dangerous Liaisons: Blacks, Gays, and the Struggle* for *Equality,* The New Press, 1999; Cathy J. Cohen, *The Boundaries* of *Blackness, Ch. 4;* Elinor Burkett, *The Gravest Show on Earth: America in the Age* of *AIDS,* Houghton Mifflin, 1995.

8. Jennifer Brier, *Infectious Ideas: U.S. Political Responses to the AIDS Crisis,* Univ. of North Carolina Press, 2009; JohnManuel Andriote, *Victory Deferred*, rev. ed. (2011).

9. Beam to Hemphill, Aug. 11, 1985, Hemphill to Beam, Dec. 5, 1985, Feb. 18 [1986?], Joe Beam Papers, the Schomburg Center for Research in Black Culture, New York Public Library. The NCBLG Statement of Purpose is printed in *Black/Out* 1, nos. 3-4 (1987).

10. Hemphill, "O Tell Me, Brutus" initially appeared in his 1986 chapbook *Conditions* and was then reprinted in *Ceremonies,* 168. In mid-1993, Essex appeared on a panel, "AIDS: Images and Analysis in the Arts and Media" (WRicketts@aol.com, November 7, 1995) in the Gay, Lesbian, and Bisexual People of Color list GLBPOC "Tribute."

11. Cohen, *Boundaries,* 95-102.

12. Hemphill, Domestic Life, private edition, 1994, courtesy Wayson Jones. Amin Ghaziani, *The Dividends* of *Dissent: How Conflict and Culture Work in Lesbian and Gay Marches on Washington,* Univ. of Chicago Press, 2008.

13. archivistssociety.wordpress.com; Hemphill to Barbara Smith, Aug. 1, 1989, courtesy Smith.

14. Hemphill, ed., *Brother to Brother: New Writings by Black Gay* Men, conceived by Joe Beam, project managed by Dorothy Beam, Alyson, 1991; "Black Talk: A Personal Interview with Essex Hemphill..." *Au Courant,* July 29, 1991.

15. For this and the following paragraph: Frank Broderick interview with Hemphill, n.d., Joe Beam Papers, Schomburg Library; *Publishers Weekly,* May 10, 1991; *Windy City Times,* March 21, 1991; *Lambda Book Report,* May-June 1991; Hemphill, "If Freud Had Been a Neurotic Colored Woman," *Gay Community News,* Feb. 25-March 3, 1991. In *Brother to Brother,* see "Looking for Langston:

An Interview with Isaac Julian," Ron Simmons, "Tongues Untied: An Interview with Marlon Riggs," and Marlon Riggs, "Black Macho Revisited: Reflections of a Snap! Queen."

16. As quoted in Andriote, *Victory Deferred,* 195, and Brier, *Infectious Ideas,* 163-71, 184 (Agosto).

17. Deborah B. Gould, *Moving Politics: Emotion* and *ACT UP's Fight Against AIDS,* Univ. of Chicago Press, 2009, Ch. 4; Harlon L. Dalton, "AIDS in Blackface," *Daedalus,* Summer 1989.

18. Hemphill to Barbara Smith, Aug. 27, 1991, enclosing the exchange of letters regarding the *Book World* controversy, courtesy of Smith.

19. For this and the following three paragraphs: Michelle Parkerson to me, April 8, 2013; Hemphill to Assotto Saint, June 10, 1993, Assotto Saint (Yves Lubin) Papers, Schomburg Library; Goldin to Hemphill, Sept. 1, 1992, Jan. 13, 1993; Goldin to Peter Borland (NAL), Nov. 4, 1992; Hemphill to Goldin, Dec. 21, 1992, Feb. 16, July 28, Sept. 1993—all courtesy Goldin. I discovered the draft manuscript of Essex' novel in the files of the Goldin Agency. My own assessment of the novel agrees with that of Goldin and Borland.

20. For this and the following paragraph: Hemphill, "Vital Signs," in *Life Sentences,* edited and with an introduction by Thomas Avena, 21-57, Mercury House, 1994; Hemphill to Barbara Smith, Dec. 12, 1994, May 15, 1995, courtesy Smith.

21. For this and the following paragraph: Hemphill, *"Domestic Life",* courtesy Wayson Jones; interviews with Jones, Chris Prince, and Ron Simmons, May 2009.

Sylvia 'Ray' Rivera

BEFORE TRANSGENDER

Before I met Sylvia, I first saw her in action. The year was 1973, the place Washington Square in New York City where I was seated on the ground with several thousand others listening to an assortment of speakers congratulate us on completion of the fourth annual Stonewall march. Thus far in the proceedings several gay honchos had exhorted us to keep up the good fight, interspersed with what one might generously call "entertainment"—including an electric guitarist who between inept strumming complained bitterly about his inability to find a distributor for his homosexual love songs. "You can guess why?" he yelled out to the crowd. "Yeah," one wag shouted back, "because they're talentless!" [1]

Despite that exchange, the mood of the day had been festive and self-congratulatory. Then suddenly—I happened to be sitting fairly close to the front and got an early sense of an abrupt shift in the atmosphere—some sort of angry commotion erupted from the back of the stage. As the volume increased, it became clear that a somewhat "effeminate" and decidedly upset young man, was trying to push his way to the microphone. It was Sylvia. Sylvia Ray Rivera Mendoza, already well-known as Sylvia Rivera to those involved with GLF (Gay Liberation Front) and GAA (Gay Activists Alliance)—the two gay rights organizations that had sprung up in the aftermath of the 1969 Stonewall riots. The flamboyant, fearless Sylvia, we knew, was a force to be reckoned with. Or as she later put it to me after I got to know her: "I don't take no shit from nobody." [2]

On that June day in 1973, Sylvia was determined to get ahold of the microphone to let the crowd of mostly young white males, have a piece of her mind. During that period in her life, she was periodically shooting up heroin, alternating with speed ("black beauties"). She was determined to give the crowd a piece—an enraged piece—of her mind. And, briefly, she succeeded.

Gaining hold of the mike, she let the audience have it between the eyes: "How many of you white, middle-class motherfuckers have been in jail? Been raped? Had your noses broken? Well, *I* have, honey. And so have plenty of your sisters. And they're still in jail, and still being raped. And what are you doing about it? *Nothing!*"

The term "sisters" in those years loosely alternated with "transvestites," "transsexuals," and "drag queens," as the dominant terms used by and for nonbinary people, some of whom would—in a later period, when descriptive categories had shifted—have probably referred to themselves instead as trans (or perhaps "gender fluid," "genderqueer," "nonbinary," etc.). In 1973, queer theory and "gender as performance" were not yet in the air. In later years when the term "trans" had become widely used and embraced various expressions of gender nonconformity, Sylvia increasingly adopted it for herself—to the point where today those who reject binary notions of gender often claim Sylvia as "the mother" of the movement. [3]

But back in 1990-91, when I asked Sylvia directly if she thought of herself as "transsexual," she scoffed, "Honey, you crazy? I *love* my cock, love usin' it! I just want to be me. I want to be Sylvia Rivera. I like pretending. I like to have the role. I like to dress up and pretend, and let the world think about what I am. Is he, or isn't he? That's what I enjoy. I don't want to be a woman. Why? That means I can't fuck nobody up the ass. Two holes? No, no, no. That ain't going to get it. No, no, no." She *did*, at one point think she might want a sexchange operation, but soon decided that (as she put it to me) "I don't want to be a woman. I want to be Sylvia Rivera." Simply "Sylvia"—or as she summed it up, "a man with a penis who likes to dress up as a woman." [4]

The term she most frequently used to describe herself was "drag queen" or simply "queen." But she was never one who cared about clear-cut definitions—which may well be one central reason why she subsequently emerged as a radical figure. Unlike most of us, who refuse to acknowledge the evidence from our unruly nighttime dreams of the wildness of our fantasy lives, Sylvia disliked any attempt to categorize her too rigidly, to cast her fixedly in any one mold, preferring to let her random, sometimes contradictory impulses exist side by side.

As she put it, "I like to pull some shit out of the closet, throw on some female attire, a blouse or whatever—not complete drag—paint or a little makeup—and hit the streets." The community she identified with most consistently was the world of drag queens: "The drag queens have a strong bond with each other and we make our own little family because we have to, because nobody else is there." With me, anyway, Sylvia consistently used the female pronoun, often wore makeup, mixed and matched her clothing, rarely dressed in full drag, and was never a drag queen stage performer—except briefly, later in life, when living upstate in Tarrytown.

Going back to the raucous Gay Pride rally in 1973, Sylvia's appearance that day was androgynous, though her vocabulary ("sisters," "bitches") was mostly binary. Curiously, the Radicalesbian spokeswoman who emerged that day as Sylvia's chief antagonist on the platform, wresting the microphone away from her, was herself garbed in a lumberjack shirt, dungarees and boots—male drag in the early Seventies that was commonplace in the lesbian community. Yet the Radicalesbian spokeswoman saw no irony in her lambasting Sylvia, and by implication all drag queens, for aping and perpetuating traditionally stereotypic versions of "femininity." By way of furious response, Lee Brewster, the editor of *DRAG* magazine who'd done a number of drag shows as benefits for The Mattachine Society, and was that day resplendent in a floor length green gown and platinum wig, angrily threw her tiara into the crowd, shouting "farewell, my sometime friends." Sobbing, she left the stage—to a chorus of boos.

Sylvia felt deeply hurt at the mockery and jeers of her purported comrades;

she quit the movement that same day and fell into a deep depression. She felt the years she'd given to the "middle-class white club" were "a waste" and swore she'd "never forgive the movement for what they've done to my people." Yet she'd reappear every year—she missed only twice—from then on until her death in 2002 to march in drag in the annual Gay Pride Parade. "I did it out of spite," she told me, "because I knew they didn't want me there." [5]

My own sympathies back on that day in 1973 were with Sylvia. As I wrote in my diary, "I thought the point of gay lib was 'vive la difference.' Vive our difference, much of the crowd seemed to be saying today. And 'our,' moreover, is defined by numbers and power—the same majoritarian tyranny the movement protests in the society at large. Thus prejudice and oppression, the targets of protest, get reproduced in the ranks of the protesters. And the oppressor rests comfortable in the knowledge that the oppressed will take over the function of denouncing each other."

WHO WAS SYLVIA RIVERA? What was her background, where did she come from? What ingredients formed her flamboyantly defiant style? Was she some sort of drugged-out kook, as her detractors claimed? Or was she the herald of an emerging new resistance to traditional gender norms, as her admirers—multiple now, few back then—insist?

Her story as it has come down to us is full of blanks and contradictions, and as well, dependent on who is telling it—a sympathizer or an antagonist. I count myself among the sympathizers—which needs acknowledgement up front, in the name of forewarning the reader. The Sylvia I knew was brave, canny, and astonishingly resourceful; "street-wise," if you like, though with "street" standing in for a nervy, tough disdain for the "respectable" postures of mainstream morality.

Born in 1951 to Hispanic parents (Venezuela on his mother's side, Puerto Rico on his father's), Ray was three when his mother, having divorced her drug-dealing husband (Ray's stepfather) after he threatened to kill her, instead took on the job herself and decided to take Ray with her. Purchasing a bottle of "J.O. Rat Poison," she put down a glass of it in front of Ray and when he complained of the taste, kept adding sugar.

Only 23, his mother proceeded to drink most of the bottle herself, wandered into her neighbor's apartment—had she changed her mind?—and was rushed to the hospital, where she lingered for three days. The doctors managed to pump out Ray's stomach and—his father having disappeared years earlier—was released to the care of his grandmother (his younger sister was turned over to his stepfather).

Ray always referred to his grandmother as "Viejita" (an affec-

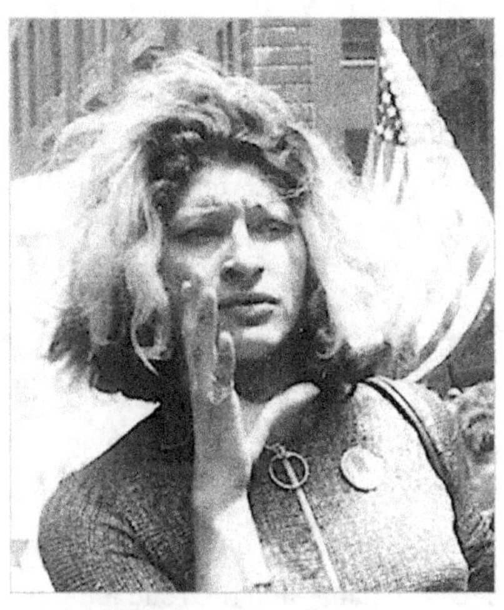

Sylvia Rivera, Christopher Street Liberation Day March in New York City, June 24, 1973.
Photo: Leonard Fink, courtesy LGBTQ+ Community Center National History Archive

tionate term for "Old Lady"), but she was far from benign: "I only wanted your sister, not *you*" she'd regularly tell him. Deciding early on that her grandson was a "troublemaker," Viejita routinely beat him for assorted infractions. "She loved me in her own way," Ray wistfully recalled, "but I never really felt that love. A hard-working woman employed as a pieceworker at the Pickwick Mills factory in Brooklyn, Viejita paid neighbors to watch Ray during her absence. She sent him to the local public school for the first and second grades, then when he was six shipped him upstate to board at the St. Agnes Catholic school. [6]

When after a time the nuns told her that "he doesn't belong here, he needs a home," Viejita reluctantly took him back. But only to farm him out again soon after, this time to Sarah, another of her daughters, who lived on Long Island and had no children of her own. With Sarah, Ray did feel able "to talk to her and tell her my feelings." Yet like Viejita, Sarah felt he was "born trouble," and could be a harsh taskmaster. "I never really caused that much of a problem," Sylvia told me many years later, "I was cleaning the house, learning how to cook, learning how to iron," but when Sylvia "got into one of her moods ... she used to beat my fucking ass for no reason at all"—sometimes substituting a two by four for a belt. One day when she was hitting him, Ray snapped, and fought back. Soon after he ran away.

Viejita took him back, but not happily. By then, Sylvia was eleven. In the fourth grade, he started occasionally to wear face makeup. By the fifth, he'd been seduced by his teacher, a married man with eight children, and by the sixth, his insistence on skipping rope with the girls resulted in his being commonly ridiculed as a "faggot." When Viejita was at work, Ray would rifle through her clothes and experiment with her makeup. One day he decided to shave his eyebrows but bungled the job and ran for help to a sympathetic neighbor's apartment. She told him not to worry and promptly painted on new eyebrows for him. That night, not thinking, he took a bath, washed his face and hair—and then suddenly realized he'd accidentally washed off the paint. "Where are your eyebrows?!" Viejita demanded. "Oh, they must have fallen off and went down the sink. Let me see if I can catch them," was the panicky Ray's *non sequitur* reply. Viejita grabbed him—and the eyebrow pencil—and painted the brows back on.

It was a loving gesture, which Sylvia still fondly remembered years later—though at the time, in a fit of shame, he swallowed a bottle of Viejeta's medication in an effort to kill himself. Viejita rushed him off to Bellevue, where they pumped out his stomach and told Viejita that he might not make it. When he did start to wake up, it was to discover that Viejita was in the process of removing his mother's cross from around his neck. When he resisted, she screamed: "You're gonna die!" Never at a loss for words, Ray shot back: "Then I should have it!"

He didn't die, but they kept him at Bellevue for several months, long enough for him to get friendly with "Danny," another patient, who told him about the hustling scene at Times Square. At age seven, Ray had already had his first sexual experience (with a cousin), and his second at age ten; both times he was "completely thrilled ... just started going out and having sex with all these boys." And no sooner was he released from Bellevue than he was up at 42nd Street where, he later remembered, "I bumped into queens, real fucking queens—oh wow! There really are more of them!" Before long, he ran away from home wearing full face makeup and met his first lover, a fellow hustler named Gary. Sylvia was eleven, Gary eighteen.

For $25 a week, they were able to rent a room *with* bath at the Hotel Aristo (since torn down) on Sixth Avenue in the Forties; remarkably, they stayed together as a couple for seven years. Sylvia had learned to cook as a child, and to make the apartment homier she hooked up a hot plate. Before long, their hotel room became something of a drop-in center for the area's street kids. "I got to learn a lot from Gary," Sylvia later told me, "and not just hustling. Every weekend we'd go to his family's house in Flushing. They were very understanding; it was like having a family, even though it was someone else's. We went through a whole lot of changes, you know. We beat the shit out of each other, but he did help my mind, he was there when I really needed him. I guess that's why I'll always love him. Gary was a good guy." He later married and had children—and named his daughter "Sylvia." The two stayed in touch for a while, but as Sylvia later put it, "I said to myself, 'don't bother him.' Leave him alone, he's happy, he's married." [7]

TIMES SQUARE had long been a center of gay hustling (and would continue to be until its recent transformation into a glitzy eyesore). In 1948, the popular pulp magazine *Salute* published an article entitled "Nightmare Alley, USA" that lamented the "sad decline" of a neighborhood that until the 1920s had been seen as "the glamorous heartbeat" of the theater world. Of late, according to *Salute,* the Times Square area had become the "horrifying" scene of "dozens of twisted, money-mad kids, aged ten to eighteen, daily offer[ing] themselves to homosexuals." [8]

Ray, for his part, was elated with his new home at the Aristo. Like most of the young hustlers who worked Times Square, he renamed himself; he chose "Sylvia Lee Rivera," a ritual ceremony was held, and she soon had something like the equivalent of an extended family. Chief among her new friends were "Bambi," "Andorra," "Bubbles," "Miss June"—and above all "Miss Marsha P. Johnson" (alias Malcolm Michaels, Jr.), a Black queen some five years older than Sylvia, who assumed the big sister role, coaching Sylvia in the stratagems of survival, even getting her a part-time messenger job. Among the wisdom Marsha imparted was how to behave when the police performed one of their routine "arrests," loading a bevy of queens into the paddy wagon, carting them off for an overnight stay in the Tombs—and then returning them to 42nd Street the next morning. Marsha operated on the basis of intuition, and Sylvia learned to trust it.

Forty-Second street was safer in the 1960s than it subsequently became. "I never had a lot of trouble," Sylvia told me, "the boys would stay on 42nd, the queens on Eighth Avenue." Sylvia made quick, shrewd judgments of people, and though on one level fearless, she wasn't foolhardy—except, that is, when totally stoned. She rarely said yes to a client until she'd had a few minutes to size him up. But nobody's instincts are infallible. Sylvia only hustled in drag for a few months, but that brief period marked the one time she got into serious trouble. "When we were in bed my dick fell out," she told me, "the customer called me a 'lousy fag,' hit me and threatened me. So I pulled out the gun I sometimes carried and shot him, though not badly. He brought me to trial but I beat the rap."

Yet Sylvia seems in retrospect to have underplayed the occasional danger she faced. In words that contradict her "one time" account of trouble, she also told me that now and then she'd find herself in a hotel room with a guy who somehow hadn't seen through the face makeup and thought he'd picked up a genuine female. That's when the threat of danger was most likely to loom. The words "*What the fuck?!—you're a guy!*" usually signaled the onset of violence, and she did have guns pulled on her several times. "I never had a lot of trouble," she insisted, yet having had *so much* trouble in her life, she was prone to minimize a mere threat or holdup. She in fact recounted *in the plural* the number of times johns or other hustlers had tried to rip her off; she learned to sew her money in a hidden pocket—that way, when held up, she would hold out her purse—"Here, take my bag"—knowing full well that it was empty.

By the mid-1960s, the issue of homosexuality had increasingly surfaced as a topic of public discussion and even as the occasional site of militant resistance to oppression (exemplified by the Washington D.C. chapter of the Mattachine Society). The blossoming counterculture broadly contested traditional norms and institutions, and the Black civil rights struggle, along with the escalating protest against the war in Vietnam, had begun the challenge to orthodoxy that emboldened other outsiders, including feminists and gay rights advocates, to mount liberation movements of their own. In the buildup to Stonewall, an increasing resistance had developed to the longstanding view that homosexuality was a pathological disorder and that sexual orientation was the product of inauspicious parenting (dominant mother, absent or angry father)—an orientation, its "victims" were assured, that could be cured through psychiatric intervention. Anger over this longstanding consensus view of homosexuality had not yet reached a critical mass, nor had a militant determination to overturn it as yet solidified. But within a very few years, all that would change.

Sylvia had always been markedly "different" from the prescribed norm and already had behind her a lifetime of suffering. She turned to drugs to ease the pain, and for a period of roughly five years, she switched back and forth on a mixed cocktail of heroin, cocaine, "black beauties" (speed), and alcohol. Her tolerance for heroin was huge. One night, after her connection warned her that the current batch was super-strong, Sylvia ignored him, shot up the full dose—and woke up in a snow bank. At the height of her addiction, she was shooting up two hundred dollars' worth a day (or so she insists). Needing simultaneously to pay for the hormone shots she'd started (and abandoned), she rifled more than a few wallets of her clients. Yet later, when her close friend "Miss June" died of an overdose, Sylvia would finally decide to kick drugs—though not alcohol—cold turkey. ("It was hard," she told me, "but I didn't want to die like that.")

At the close of the tumultuous 1960s, left-wing agitation escalated and—particularly to conservatives—the country seemed to be coming apart at the seams. The Tet offensive in Vietnam mocked the power elite's claim that an American victory would be inevitable, swift, and uncompromising. The assassinations of Martin Luther King Jr. and Robert Kennedy cast serious doubt on any hope of peaceful reform and sparked riots in dozens of cities.

College students across the country took over campus buildings, defying the legitimacy of the government—and the university. By the fall of 1968, there was a sharp rise in the number of SDS (Students for a Democratic

Society) chapters, and across the country shocking events became everyday news reports, with the Oakland police murdering Black Panthers in their beds, the Berkeley police sealing off People's Park, and the National Guard confronting protesters and wounding about a hundred people.

Then, in June 1969, gay liberation explosively announced its newfound militancy in five days of rioting resulting from an otherwise standard police raid of the gay bar Stonewall. Sylvia and her friends had never frequented Stonewall; they considered it generally unfriendly to street queens, with only a few favored ones, like Tiffany and Tammy Novak, even allowed to enter Stonewall. As Sylvia would later put it, "Stonewall was basically like a taboo place for a lot of drag queens or effeminate gay men who liked to wear makeup and be like outrageous." Their own bar of choice was Washington Square on Broadway and Third Street which *opened* at three in the morning and catered to transvestites. [9]

But on June 27, the night of the first riot, Sylvia and her lover Gary just happened to be at Stonewall. They'd returned that very evening from D.C. where, short of cash, they'd been (as Sylvia put it) "doing bad paper." They were supposed to go to a party for Marsha P. Johnson's birthday, but the death of Judy Garland that same day had put Sylvia in a funk: "it was like your childhood actually ended when she passed, because I thought she was the greatest singer and the greatest actress of my childhood. ... Who else was there to look up to? I was feeling her death. ... I was hysterical, fucked up on black beauties and coke."

The Mafia-owned Stonewall bar had long made regular payoffs to the local Sixth Precinct and not wanting to close down a cash cow, police raids, though common, had in the past tended to be strictly *pro forma*. If the raid followed its usual pattern, the police would stride arrogantly through, push a few patrons against a wall, and make either no or few arrests, mostly booking those who lacked an ID or weren't wearing the requisite three pieces of clothing "appropriate" to their gender (which, absurdly, was an actual law at the time).

The raid on June 27th was different. The Mafia owners had *not* been notified in advance, which had been customary; eight detectives from the

First Division, *not* the Sixth Precinct, led the officers; and some of the lower-level Mafia employees were among those arrested. Sylvia and Gary were inside the bar and as they were being ushered out by the police, one of the cops stopped Sylvia, who had on makeup but wasn't in drag, and she spat out, "I'm a *boy*!" As she later told me, "I just didn't want to be bothered any more and would probably have swung at the cop if Gary hadn't been there. Once outside, "people just started throwing coins at the cops, then rocks and bricks and bottles. ... I thought, there's going to be a change in the world. ... I never went home. ... Gary just couldn't take me away from the area. [10]

When a patrol van pulled up in front of Stonewall and the police started to load prisoners, a crowd quickly gathered in front of the bar, and efforts by the police to disperse it—previously a simple task—drew boos and shouts instead. Gary tried to persuade Sylvia that they should leave before the situation got uglier, but Sylvia was having none of it. "Are you nuts?" she yelled. "I'm not missing a minute of this—it's the *revolution*!" And in a real sense it was. As the crowd swelled and grew increasingly raucous, the police retreated back inside the bar. Then someone managed to uproot a loose parking meter and used it as a battering ram against the Stonewall's door. At the same time someone squirted lighter fluid through the shattered glass window on the bar's façade, tossing in matches along with bottles. A shard of glass cut one of the officers near his eye, alarming the police still further. A few of them lunged out into the crowd trying to pull prisoners back into the bar with them, but that enflamed the protest still further. When one of the matches finally caught fire, igniting a whoosh of flames, the police sent out the emergency signal 10-41—a call for help to the fearsome Tactical Patrol Force.

The full-blown confrontation lasted until three-thirty a.m., and in the upshot four police officers were injured and thirteen protestors arrested, seven of them Stonewall employees. Even then Sylvia refused to go home; fueled by black beauties, she kept walking the streets, setting garbage cans on fire, venting her pent-up rage. As she later put it, "I wanted to do everything destructive I could think of to pay back those who'd hurt us over the years ... we weren't going to take their fucking bullshit anymore." The rioting went on, sporadically, for four more days.

IN THE MONTHS that followed, the radical Gay Liberation Front (GLF) emerged; its agenda was centered on gay rights but included a broad range of social issues, from feminism and anti-capitalism to declarations of support for Castro and the Black Panthers. The range was *too* broad to suit those activists who wanted to concentrate *solely* on winning civil rights for gay people; to that end, the Gay Activists Alliance came into being about a year later. Sylvia made her presence known at both organizations, and soon discovered that even among progressive gays, "the sisters" weren't entirely welcome. Street people frightened some of the young gay rebels, many of whom had middle-class backgrounds or aspirations. Sylvia and her friends embodied Otherness: they were from the wrong ethnic groups, the wrong side of the tracks, wore the wrong clothes, spoke the wrong languages or the right language the wrong way (fractured and furious). [11]

Before attending her first GAA meeting, Sylvia called in advance to ask if "queens were welcome as members." She was told "yes," but when she and her friend Josie showed up, they were told to sit in the back of the room. It was there that Sylvia first met Bebe Scarpi, the only other queen sitting in their area; she and Sylvia would remain longtime friends (and Bebe would serve on the founding board in 1973 of the National Gay and Lesbian Task Force). Despite the qualified acceptance, Sylvia became an active GAA member and participated in a number of the group's confrontational "zaps."

She was particularly active in GAA's petition drive to get a gay rights bill passed through the City Council. She decided to park herself at night right in the middle of 42nd Street between Seventh and Eighth Avenues, yelling out raspily, demandingly, for passersby to sign her petition: "Excuse me! Excuse me! Could you please sign this petition to stop discrimination against homosexuals in housing and jobs?" Her street-hustling friends stood around gaping at "the sister's" audacity ("This is the butchest thing you ever done, girl!"). [12]

The police let her be for three or four nights but then brusquely told her to "move on," that she didn't have a permit. Sylvia held her ground: "I'm not movin!," she told the cops, "I got my constitutional rights. I got my free speech to change the law!" The cops thought otherwise and before long a police cruiser pulled up behind her, unceremoniously dumped her inside and took her to the Fourteenth Precinct station. At the time, Sylvia was working an eleven p.m. shift in an A&P warehouse in New Jersey and feared that if she didn't show up, she'd lose the job (she didn't). At the hearing the next morning, a cadre of members from GLF and GAA showed up to cheer her on, and the well-known gay journalist Arthur Bell wrote an article about her in *The Village Voice.* She was on her way to becoming something of a movement celebrity, or, as she put it: "I could just snap my fingers and everyone would come running." Legal Aid got her out of jail, and the next night she was back at her station on Forty-Second. The cops left her alone. One of them signed her petition and wished her "best of luck."

GLF's raucous meetings and its broad attack on social injustice were closer to Sylvia's style than GAA; many in GLF shared her rude anarchism and her blanket denunciation of established authority. "I was getting more and more radical," Sylvia told me, "and I wanted to go and do more." In her view, GAA was getting more middle-class, with a sizeable contingent insistent that drag queens were "genital males," and therefore outside the movement. She never formally left GAA (her friend Bebe would continue to pay Sylvia's annual dues), but came to believe—at least for a time—that only GLF "backed me to the hilt."

She increasingly involved herself in GLF "actions." When the NYU authorities in the summer of 1970 banned any further gay dances in Weinstein Hall, Sylvia played a prominent role in the four-day sit-in that followed. She also went to Philadelphia, along with others from GLF, to attend the huge Panthers' Revolutionary People's Constitutional Convention. When GLF sent money to the Panthers, Eldridge Cleaver sent it back, but Huey Newton was more sympathetic; from the stage of the Revolutionary Convention he urged acceptance of gay and lesbian people "as part of the Revolution." He was all but alone: the Panthers were not only deeply homophobic but also reluctant to heed feminist calls for leadership roles. Sylvia, though, got a special charge from the Convention when, turning down the corridor, she came face to face with Huey; he promptly greeted her with "Yeah, you're the queen from New York—you're Sylvia." As she later told me, "I stood there and cried. It was a great moving moment." [13]

Yet before long, she began to feel ignored or rejected in GLF—more like a mascot than an equal. And she continued to make some people nervous. A number of its members—though fewer than in GAA—regarded her as a shrieking harridan, an out-of-control druggy, a harpy, hysterical and unreliable. Though she made some people decidedly nervous, Sylvia never physically attacked or stole from anyone in the movement; she essentially viewed the people in both GLF and GAA as comrades, exempt from the raw backstabbing of the streets. She was ferocious in her loyalty to "the revolution," and for a time thought she'd found a home within its ranks. But when she upped the ante and began to agitate for the rights of "our part of the community," she found at best tolerance, not comradeship.

She got the message. It hurt, but didn't surprise her.

Rejection was an old familiar. She decided to turn her energy toward helping her own people, to focus on the plight of "the sisters," the "youngsters," the underage street queens (she herself was by now all of nineteen) who needed some respite, some refuge from the dangerous threats of daily life. At first, Sylvia believed that GLF would help her in setting up a place, a center of some kind, where "the kids" (several of whom were older than Sylvia) could catch their breath, unwind, find emotional support, maybe even learn enough skills to be employable, to start a new kind of life.

The first person she talked to about "getting a place for the young sisters" was her old friend Marsha P. ("pay it no mind") Johnson. Marsha sometimes had trouble staying focused in conversation—some people claimed that drugs had made her a permanent space cadet; others that she was "a free spirit" who took a thought and let it wander until coming to a natural pause. Years later, Sylvia acknowledged that Marsha could "travel in her mind" but insisted that the two of them had "*lots* of political talks and Marsha helped me to analyze, instead of me jumping off the gun. Marsha's got a good head. I would do anything for Marsha. She has helped a whole lot of people."[14]

Sylvia's idea for setting up a refuge for street queens concentrated Marsha's mind wonderfully. She was immediately excited, eager to help. Sylvia had decided in advance to make Marsha president of any group they succeeded in forming, but Marsha, sensibly, wouldn't hear of it. "You stay on one thought when you speak, with anything you do," she told Sylvia. "I go off in all directions. You'll be president. I'll be vice president."

They quickly hit on a name for the group: Street Transvestites Actual Revolutionaries (STAR), then decided to change "Actual" to "Action." The first "housing" they managed to secure was the back of a trailer truck that had been abandoned in a Greenwich Village outdoor parking area. It wasn't much—but it beat sleeping in doorways. In no time at all, they managed to round up some two dozen young street queens grateful to know they could sleep in the same place more than one night. Sylvia set only one ground rule: though nobody *had* to go out and hustle, when they *did* they had to kick back a percentage to help keep "STAR House" going. Marsha and Sylvia took it upon themselves to do more hustling than usual in order to spare "the children" and to ensure that they could earn enough to return to the truck each morning with breakfast food for everyone.

For a while, everything went according to plan. Then one morning as Sylvia and Marsha rounded Christopher Street, their arms loaded with groceries, they stopped dead in their tracks. The truck was *moving*! Apparently it had not been abandoned and the owner had come to reclaim it—not dreaming that twenty young queens were asleep in the back. The startup noise, fortunately, woke almost all of them, and one by one they started to jump from the back of the truck. "We're standing there like two *yentas*," Sylvia later told me. "I mean, we're talking about two crazy women: 'Oh my God, the kids, the kids! Oh Lord Jesus, please don't take the children!'" In the upshot only one youngster remained in the van as it pulled away. Stoned on downers, she woke up several days later—on her way to California.

Bubbles Rose Marie, one of the queens who'd been living in the truck, suggested to Sylvia that she go talk to Michael Umbers, a well-known Mafia figure in the Village who owned a building on Second Street that was more or less empty. Sylvia took up the idea and Umbers, for whatever reasons of his own, agreed to a small amount of rental money up front and firm deadlines for subsequent payments. Delighted, Sylvia and Marsha encouraged all the sisters to "hustle their asses off" in order to meet the down payment.

The building had no electricity or plumbing, a broken boiler and (in

Sylvia's words) a bunch of queens "that don't know shit about nothing, we're looking at the tools, we're looking at each other. We just started taking things apart, putting them back together, and the next thing we knew, the motherfucker boiler was working!" With guaranteed heat, they formally named the place STAR House, and set about trying to make it livable. Sylvia got a number of members from both GLF and GAA to promise they'd come by and help fix the place up. A few GAAers did show up to help paint, to clean up the rubbish strewn all over the yard, and to install some primitive plumbing. Several of them happened to be teachers, and Sylvia's long-range hope was that she could enlist them to help turn the top floor of the building into a kind of school, teaching those young queens who were illiterate how to read and write. (Sylvia herself had only a sixth-grade education, yet would later manage to get hired for three different managerial jobs in food services.)

To raise additional funds, Sylvia persuaded GLF to front her enough money to buy beer and setups for a benefit dance. GAA balked at letting Sylvia borrow their stereo set, but she somehow managed to procure equipment elsewhere. The dance came off in style. What Sylvia called her "STAR House Kids" decorated the hall with Christmas bulbs and spangled reflectors and outdid each other in sewing together elaborate costumes. Sylvia, exhausted from a string of sleepless nights, settled for a simple outfit of pants and blouse. Throughout the evening she foreswore dancing and sat resolutely at the door making sure that everybody paid to get in. At midnight she briefly stopped the music and dancing and delivered a touching little speech: "This dance is for the people of the streets who are part of our gay community. Let's give them a better chance than I had when I came out. I don't know if any of you ever lived on the streets. Many transvestites who make up STAR do. We are asking you for money tonight. Winter is coming and we need money for clothes and rent. Please dig into your pockets and help STAR." To her great surprise, a few of the young queens abruptly interrupted by presenting Sylvia with a huge bouquet of red roses. According to one account, she "wept buckets."

With some actual money in hand, STAR House seemed to have a fighting chance. Sylvia started to cook big dinners every night, sternly admonishing "the children" that they "don't have to live off that candy shit." Before anyone left for an evening of hustling, she insisted on a ritual—though no one was forced to participate—that she called "working with the saints." Devoted from childhood to Santeria (thanks to the influence of her grandmother, Viejeta) and having chosen St. Barbara as the "patron saint of gay Hispanics," Sylvia set up an altar, complete with incense and candles; gathered the sisters around it and offered up a prayer: "I know we're doing wrong, but we gotta survive, so please help us."

And for a while St. Barbara complied. Then one day as Sylvia was crossing Christopher Street, she found Mike Umbers blocking her path. Not a welcome sight. Umbers was big, and Umbers was angry. "Where the hell is my money?! I warned ya about firm deadlines, right? I'm not gonna warn ya again." Sylvia was genuinely confused. Bubbles Rose Marie, Sylvia's initial contact with Umbers, had been handling the monthly payments and Sylvia had regularly given Bubbles $300 a month for Mike, as she told him that day on Christopher Street. All Umbers knew was that he hadn't been paid in three months, and he wanted it *now*. Sylvia raced back to Second Street and confronted Bubbles, who was unconvincingly mumbling something about the cost of repairs, when Umbers himself arrived. He told Bubbles flat out that unless he got his money, she was as good as dead.

Enraged at the threat, Sylvia turned from yelling at Bubbles and lit into Umbers instead, screaming that if anything happened to Bubbles she, Sylvia, would go straight to the police. "For chrissake," she yelled, "it's only money! Don't kill somebody for money, for chrissake. So the bitch fucked up. Fine. So kick her ass. But don't *kill* her! You can take her outside right now and I won't stop you. Or make the bitch get out on the corner."

"The bitch is fat," Umbers grunted. "That bitch can't make no money." Wheeling on Sylvia, he yelled, "You've always been a fuckin' bitch!"—and stormed out.

The next thing Sylvia knew, Bubbles had skipped town ("like she always does when she gets in hot water"). Sylvia tried to save STAR House with a last-ditch appeal to GAA for a loan. They turned her down but told her she could leave a box at the front table soliciting donations. She did, but collected only a few dollars. It was probably time to pack it in, Sylvia thought. It wasn't as if Bubbles and the rent were the only problems. Two of the queens were regularly getting into fist fights whenever they got high, and Marsha had become overwhelmed with problems. Her fifth husband, Candy, who was heavily into drugs, made the mistake of trying to rob a plainclothesman—and got his head blown off. Marsha said she "couldn't hardly stand it" and had to see a doctor for her "bad nerves." [15]

If there was any chance of getting things back on an even keel at STAR House, Mike Umbers killed it. Instead of violence, he simply called the city marshals and had Sylvia and her brood evicted for non-payment of rent. With no way to pay off the money owed Umbers nor of persuading him to give them additional breathing space, Sylvia had no choice but to throw in the towel. But she and the kids had revenge of a sort: they busted up all the repairs they'd put into the building and for good measure threw the refrigerator out the back window. "That's the type of we fuck you over right back."

SYLVIA REMAINED ACTIVE in the movement a while longer, but being forcibly escorted off the stage at the 1973 Gay Pride celebration in Washington Square Park hurt her deeply. She no longer felt wanted. By that point, GAA had already tried to cut a deal with the City Council to drop the "extreme" elements of the gay community (transvestites and drag queens) from the anti-discrimination ordinance in return for passage of the bill. The Council rejected the deal, but the attempt alone left Sylvia feeling understandably betrayed. A week after the Washington Square incident, her depression deepened to the point where she tried to cut herself, and was hospitalized. "They fucked everything I believed in the gay community," she told me years later. "It would be too hard for me to get re-involved because I'm not going to forget what they did to me on that fourth anniversary of Stonewall. I feel the community owes me more than I owe them."

Sylvia announced that she was quitting the movement. She meant it, too. Offered a job in food services with the Marriott Corporation in Tarrytown, New York, she left the city, re-appearing only to march in the annual Gay Pride Parade. During that period, I traveled back and forth to Tarrytown to do interviews with her, and each time she would have to consume the better part of a quart of alcohol before she felt able to talk freely.

The point came when substance abuse cost her the job with Marriott. As a matter of survival, she returned to New York in the early nineties and lived on the Christopher Street piers, mostly in a "community" of some 30 homeless people huddled in crumbled cardboard huts. The low point came during a bitterly cold winter evening when Sylvia aggressively demanded that the Gay and Lesbian Community Center on 13th Street in Manhattan allow her and other homeless gay people to sleep inside, and was refused. Her humiliation was complete when in 1995 the city bulldozed the Piers preparatory to its reclamation of the waterfront; in sadness and rage, Sylvia ripped apart her own "house" before the bulldozer could get to it. Soon after, she thought seriously of suicide but turned to the bottle instead.

"Yeah, I'm crazy because the world has made me crazy," she told someone attempting to interview her. Left alone, she stared out across the Hudson, tears in her eyes: "Well Marsha," she whispered, "we tried, that's all I can say ... we tried." [16]

Yet against all odds, a fourth act still lay ahead. Things initially picked up a bit when she became an active member of the Metropolitan Community Church and helped to administer the MCC's food pantry. They improved still more when she found a home at Transy House, the shelter that a few transgender people had created for themselves in Brooklyn. There, Sylvia discovered more than a place to live: she found acknowledgement of her proud history and a platform from which to reclaim a public voice. It allowed her to kick alcohol—cold turkey. And it allowed her to speak her mind. She became particularly active in denouncing the Human Rights Campaign (HRC), the most powerful and prosperous of the national gay organizations, after they decided not to include "transgender" as a protected category in the Employment Non-Discrimination Act that they presented to Congress. Sylvia bitterly denounced HRC's abandonment of the trans community: "I'm tired of sitting on the back of the bumper. It's not even the back of the bus anymore—it's the back of the bumper. The bitch on wheels is back."

During the last five years of Sylvia's life, appreciation of her contribution to "liberation" gradually increased. She again began to get invitations to speak and, true to her fabulist temperament and her theatrical penchant for exaggeration, did so in a varying script of sometimes baffling contradiction. Towards the end of her life she even tried, unsuccessfully, to re-activate STAR House and as well, joined in organizing the New York State Transgender Coalition. The culmination of her restoration as an icon of transgender liberation came in 2000, when she was invited to Rome to participate in the Millennium March, and heard herself acclaimed as "the mother of all gay people." In response, she rapturously told the huge crowd, "I didn't think thirty years ago that I would have so many children."

Sylvia died of liver cancer in February 2002. ▪

Addendum

IN HIS BOOK, *Stonewall* (St. Martins Press, 2004), David Carter omitted any mention of Sylvia. He made clear why in a subsequent interview, in which he insisted that "Sylvia's account of her being there [at Stonewall] on the first night was a fabrication." Carter cites as his chief source Sylvia's friend Marsha P. Johnson, who has said that Sylvia on the first night of the riots was "asleep in Bryant Park after taking heroin." Carter also charges that in her various accounts of the riots Sylvia showed "a real inconsistency." Inconsistent memory, of course, is not a rare human trait. Sylvia, to be sure, *was* a fabulist. And I agree with Carter that she could be wildly inconsistent. Still, in the many tapes Sylvia and I made in 1990-1991, I came to believe that her testimony as a witness to the riots was basically sound, even while recognizing her powers of invention. (I'd hardly be shocked if evidence does eventually surface that Sylvia got the multiple nights of rioting mixed up, and *wasn't* present on the first night.)

Large questions regarding memory in general are pertinent here, in particular the groundbreaking research of Elizabeth Loftus, who's been called "the most influential female psychologist of the twentieth century." Her work has led to a paradigm shift that regards even the best of memories as "reconstructed, not replayed." "Our representation of the past," she's argued, "takes on a living, shifting reality. It is not fixed and immutable, not a place way back there that is preserved in stone, but a living thing that changes shape, expands, shrinks, and expands again, an amoeba-like creature." What Loftus describes as "the flimsy curtain that separates our imagination and our memory" applies alike to Marsha and to Sylvia—both of whom had *very* large powers of imagination.

NOTES

1. In regard to current unsettled pronoun usage, I've uneasily decided to shift from "him" to "her" at the point in the narrative when Ray adopts the name Sylvia for herself.

2. The 1973 confrontation was captured on film and Vito Russo screened it for me shortly before his death from AIDS. The narrative of Sylvia's life that follows is primarily based on the tapes she and I did in 1990 to '91 when I was researching my 1993 book, *Stonewall* (reissued by Penguin in 2019). This version derives from my portrait of Sylvia in *Stonewall,* though I've included considerably more material from the tapes. The tapes are themselves available in the Martin Duberman papers at The New York Public Library (henceforth Rivera tapes/Duberman papers, NYPL). To avoid disrupting the narrative too frequently, I'll cite specific tape numbers only when a given quotation is particularly full or controversial.

One other point: Sylvia and I remained in touch until her death in 2002, and I spoke at her memorial service. A few of her comments in this chapter are from our periodic and untaped conversations during the 1992 to 2002 period.

3. For a fine discussion of the variants in terminology, see David Valentine, *Imagining Transgender,* Duke University Press, 2007. See also, https://zcomm.org/zmagazine/sylvia-rivera-1951-2002-by-michael-bronski.

4. For this and the following two paragraphs: Rivera tape 02888/Duberman papers, NYPL.

5. Rivera tapes 02887-02891/Duberman papers, NYPL. Also, "The Death and Life of Marsha P. Johnson" (Netflix, David France producer).

6. For this and following two paragraphs: Rivera tape 02887/Duberman papers, NYPL.

7. Rivera tape 02887/Duberman papers, NYPL.

8. Selwyn James, "Nightmare Alley USA," *Salute,* March 1949, in Duberman, *About Time: Exploring the Gay Past.* Seahorse Press: 1986, revised and reprinted by Meridian, 1991. In the same volume, see "Boys and Boy-Loving."

9. For this and the following paragraph: Rivera tapes 02888-02891/Duberman papers, NYPL.

10. For this and the following two paragraphs: Howard Smith, "Full Moon over Stonewall," *The Village Voice,* July 3, 1969; "Queen Power: Fags Against Police in Stonewall Bust," *RAT,* July 1969; Lucian Truscott IV, "Gay Power Comes to Sheridan Square," *The Village Voice,* July 3, 1969; Marty Robinson, "I Remember Stonewall," *San Francisco Examiner,* June 4, 1989; Maida Tilchen, "Mythologizing Stonewall," *Gay Community News,* June 23, 1979. For a view that emphasizes the "inconsistencies" in Sylvia's account of her role at Stonewall, see https: www.gaycitynews.nyc/stories/2019/15/David-carter-stonewall-2019-06-27-gcn.html. See also the Addendum at the

close of this essay—a call for additional discussion of the variant interpretations.

11. Jim Kepner, *Our Movement Since Stonewall,* IGLA, 1992; Toby Marotta, *The Politics of Homosexuality,* Houghton, 1981; Arthur Bell, *Dancing the Gay Lib Blues,* Simon & Schuster, 1971; Dennis Altman, *Homosexual Oppression and Liberation,* Dutton, 1971; Arnie Kantrowitz, *Under the Rainbow,* Morrow, 1977; Lois Hart, "Some News and a Whole Lot of Opinion," *Come Out!,* Times Change Press, 1970; Marcia Gallo, *Different Daughters,* Carroll & Graf, 2006.

12. For this and the following two paragraphs: Rivera tapes 02888-02889/Duberman papers, NYPL.

13. For Weinstein: *Gay Flames,* no. 5; John Murray, *Homosexual Liberation,* Praeger, 1971, 119-123; Arthur Bell, *Dancing the Gay Lib Blues,* 110-119; Duberman, *Stonewall,* Dutton 1993, 308-319; Arthur Bell Papers and GAA Papers (box 15), in IGIC Papers, NYPL.

14. Rivera tape 02888/Duberman papers, NYPL.

15. For this and the following two paragraphs: Rivera tapes 02888, 02889/Duberman papers, NYPL. In 1992 Marsha's body washed up at the Piers. The police called it a suicide, but never followed up. When the Anti-Violence Project tried to investigate it was told "the case file is missing" ("The Death and Life of Marsha P. Johnson," Netflix). Marsha's death devastated Sylvia.

16. Randy Wicker Interviews Sylvia Rivera on the Pier (https://vimeo.com/35975275); "The Death and Life of Marsha P. Johnson" (Netflix); Jessi Gan, "Still at the Back of the Bus" (http://redalyc.uaemex.mx/redalyc/pdf/377/37719107.pdf).

17. gaytoday.com/interview/070104in.asp [Carter]; Rachel Aviv, "How Elizabeth Loftus Changed The Meaning of Memory," *The New Yorker,* April 5, 2021.

CHAPTER IV

Barbara Deming

AND DIRECT ACTION NONVIOLENCE

Born in 1917 into an upper-middle class Manhattan family that was largely traditional in its habits and opinions, Barbara felt closer to her "caring and principled" father than to her self-absorbed mother. Among her father's concerns as his daughter approached adulthood was that she should focus her attention on finding "a good man to marry." Though a dutiful daughter, Barbara surprised herself at age 16 by falling in love instead with Norma Millay, a neighbor at the family's New City country home and the sister of Edna St. Vincent Millay. The passionate affair was broken off only when Barbara left for Bennington College in 1934. [1]

At Bennington, her studies focused on English literature, and she herself grew into a strikingly attractive woman, tall and willowy, with straight black hair and bangs. She eschewed makeup and dressed simply, slept with men and women, and had one serious if intermittent affair with an older student, Dorothy ("Casey") Case. It was not a matter of rebelling against her father's wishes or setting out to displease him; she simply was drawn to women more than to men.

On graduating from Bennington, she worked for several years in the theater as low-level staff, picked up a master's degree in drama, and again fell in love with a woman—who ended up leaving her to marry Barbara's brother. Initially stunned, she accepted the shift in sentiments and remained friendly with the new couple. In her view, "if love is really love, it cannot stop being what it is—though it can stop seeking. ... Then it changes, certainly; but it does not expire. Even when one falls in love again." [2]

Emotionally and professionally unsettled for roughly the next decade, Barbara had enough income from a family bequest to travel widely. In Turin, she had a brief affair with "Pete," a man she'd met earlier in the States, but when he announced "I'm *fucking* you!" during intercourse, Barbara's "whole self," as she later put it, flinched "as if slapped by his words." No, she recognized with a jolt, "he never will know me and I never will know him. For this penis has been taught to think itself Lord and Master. And I am not the one to unteach it this inanity. ... My spirit stands still—absolutely attentive at last. ... I am this self that I am. I affirm it. Yes. I am. And I will not be robbed." [3]

Her sexuality affirmed, Barbara and Mary Meigs, a gifted painter and writer, fell in love in 1954. Mary came from a wealthy, socially prominent family (one ancestor had been a signer of the Constitution) who lived in D.C. in the five-story redbrick house previously owned by Alice Roosevelt Longworth. Yet the Meigses were something of an anomaly: they shunned ostentation and supported the Democratic Party. Mary herself had been well-educated, was outspoken and candid, and shared Barbara's preference for living rather austerely and close to nature. The two women took a house together in the town of Wellfleet on Cape Cod.

Their nearby neighbors were the novelist Mary McCarthy and her ex-husband, the well-known critic Edmund Wilson, who was very much drawn to Meigs—even to feeling at one point that he might be falling in love with her. He asked her directly if she was a lesbian and Mary, startled, hedged in replying ("well, yes—sort of"). This was after all the 1950s when it was nearly universally assumed that homosexuality was an illness—a pathological one. It was a time when, despite the existence of an incipient gay movement, most homosexuals bent their energies

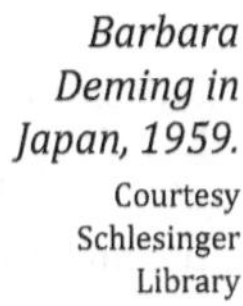

Barbara Deming in Japan, 1959.
Courtesy Schlesinger Library

to remaining hidden. As Mary once put it, she and Barbara lived in "the shadowy world of denial and pretense," though openly living together; "We lead double lives ... [our] beautiful and loving experiences ... have to be kept secret; and the lives we live make us wary and cold." Edmund Wilson's attitude didn't help. Mary recorded his words to the effect that "homosexuality is in contravention of some immutable law ... lesbians are faintly ridiculous." [4]

Barbara's acceptance of her lesbianism evolved in parallel to her political convictions. During the Korean War, she'd accepted the U.S. assertion that the conflict was inevitable—essential to the "national interest." By the 1952 presidential election two years later, she'd progressed to handing out buttons for the Democratic candidate Adlai Stevenson. By the late '50s, she and Mary set off on a prolonged series of travels that moved her much further along on the left-wing spectrum. In Israel, Barbara somehow got to spend a whole evening alone with Martin Buber discussing nonviolence; in India, she read Gandhi more deeply than before; and in Cuba, she formed the firm conviction that under Castro the island had finally "gained its independence from us"—and that was "as it should be." But she did regret Castro's resort to violence, and in 1960, back in the States, she became involved with the Committee for Non-Violent Action

(CNVA) as well as, more generally, the issues of racism, civil defense, and nuclear disarmament.

From that point on, her commitment to nonviolence deepened, though she never rigidly dismissed "for all people at all times and places methods of violent and armed struggle"—after all, it had been central to the success of the American revolution. Barbara also believed that it was "crucial to establish women's *right* to violent self-defense when under attack." Mary admired Barbara's growing sense of mission and her bravery in pursuing it, but she herself abhorred participating in a plethora of meetings and demonstrations, let alone the prospect of going to jail. She decided that *her* true path was her art—that, and "caring about the life around me ... being attentive to my own rhythms, to the messages that I received when I kept very still." By the early '60s, she and Barbara began to move steadily in different directions. [5]

In 1962, Barbara joined a small group of signatories to call for national demonstrations against President Kennedy's eight-week resumption of nuclear bomb tests in the Pacific; she also championed *unilateral* nuclear disarmament. Soon after, she added the struggle for racial equality to her political agenda and then, by the end of the decade, radical feminism and lesbian rights had also become essential ingredients in what she called "the struggle to claim my life as my own." Regardless of which issue took momentary prominence on her activist agenda, she never simply dropped her other concerns; nor did she waver from what had become a consistent commitment to the strategy of direct-action nonviolent protest. She had come to believe strongly that nonviolence was an inherent feature of androgyny—that it encouraged in every individual both self-assertion (traditionally associated with "masculinity") and empathy (traditionally assigned to "femininity"). As Barbara put it, "One asserts one's rights as a human being, but asserts them with consideration for the other."

Before she began to participate in direct action events, she signed on to a sixteen-day training program sponsored by the radical Peacemakers and was enthralled with the diverse group of fellow trainees: "The candor and innocence of their actions give to these people," Barbara wrote, "an extraordinary spontaneity—the sense that an individual can act and *has* weight. If no one else will do it, then do it yourself."

Following the training, Barbara joined a CNVA-sponsored series of peace walks and vigils against the submarines currently being built in Connecticut shipyards and equipped with Polaris missiles (each with the capacity to carry a hydrogen-bomb warhead). The following year, in demonstration of her growing conviction that the power of arms had to be supplanted by the power of persuasion, she spent a week on the road with the San Francisco-to-Moscow Walk for Peace. When she asked her fellow walkers if they felt there was really any hope for such a shift, she got variations of the same answer; "I don't operate on the basis of hope. I simply ask myself what is right and what is wrong." Barbara was impressed; Mary Meigs was not. She didn't believe that everyone had a conscience, buried or otherwise. She equated conscience with guilt originating from the hierarchical structure of the family. By 1962-63, as Barbara's political involvement escalated, the two women, after ten years of living together, drew increasingly apart. [6]

Barbara became convinced that the issues of disarmament and Black civil rights were two parts of one struggle; both were committed to non-violence, both insisted that the country live up to the Declaration of Independence's promise of inalienable rights, and both shared a strategy of "firmness with friendliness." And she believed that the peace movement was also a "freedom" movement—freedom from alignment with repressive regimes and from the pessimistic certainty of a nuclear war. Some of her radical associates, especially those primarily involved in the peace movement, disagreed. They argued that a considerable number of Southern whites otherwise sympathetic to the peace movement would shy away if Blacks became involved. Others insisted that an alliance would be a disservice to Blacks themselves by handing their opponents ammunition to denounce them as "unpatriotic." [7]

By 1963, Barbara had pretty much become a fulltime activist, increasingly known and admired in radical circles. In that year she accompanied A. J. Muste, the leading figure in the War Resisters League, to a five-day international conference—55 people from thirteen countries—in the hill town of Boummana, Lebanon to plan a World Peace Brigade for Nonviolent Action (it had been Gandhi who'd first called for such a meeting shortly before his assassination). The Brigade's first project was a march into Northern Rhodesia (which in 1964 became Zambia) to protest the racist white government; the British halted the marchers at the border. Lacking resources, the Brigade thereafter became inactive, though it would be reincarnated as Peace Brigades International in 1981.

By 1963, Barbara's priorities had shifted. The urgency of the Black struggle had come to occupy most of her energy. In Birmingham, she was arrested and jailed while demonstrating with a sign around her neck reading "All Men Are Brothers." (The condition of women was still on the back burner, on the cusp of breaking out into a political movement.) Released six days later from the Birmingham jail, Barbara upped the ante, attending a lengthening string of meetings and demonstrations. She felt a special thrill hearing Martin Luther King Jr. tell one gathering that "we have a weapon that they can't handle. They don't know what to do with us when we are nonviolent. ... You don't need to strike them in return, or curse them in return. Just keep going. Just keep presenting your body as a witness." [8]

And Barbara did. On a march through Albany, Georgia, she was again arrested and this time jailed for a full month. Crowded into a small cell, she was forced to sleep on the floor—though the constant noise made rest fleeting in any case. Over the month-long incarceration, her vitality—though not her commitment—gradually ebbed away. Allowed a brief visit to her, A. J. Muste thought she looked as if "made of paper." Her stomach rebelled against the repetitive diet of grits, bitter turnips, and black-eyed peas; combined with the lack of exercise, her bowels seized up for several weeks and she finally required a series of enemas. Yet through it all—and "unutterably tired of being in here"—she held firm. Her determination was fueled by a particular view of human nature, one commonly shared by those who seriously committed themselves to movements for radical social change in the 1960s: namely, that human beings are *naturally* drawn to affiliation and cooperation rather than aggression and enmity. It was a view widely shared in the '60s, as exemplified in the movement for non-coercive "free" schools and exemplified in the work of such champions of "non-coercive" education as A. S. Neill, John Holt, and Paolo Freire—and reflected as well in a number of bestselling works by a new breed of anthropologists and primatologists. [9]

Finally released from prison, Barbara, along with others who'd marched beside her, rested up at Koinonia Farm, a haven for racial egalitarians, then headed back to Wellfleet, where she sat for weeks and weeks "able to do little more than stare at the birds and the bushes." Yet turmoil was again around the corner, this time domestic in nature. Mary Meigs had fallen in love with Marie-Claire Blais, a twenty-three-year-old French-Canadian writer whom Edmund Wilson had taken under his wing. Mary offered "M-C" (as she was often called) the use of a small house on her Wellfleet property, and before long, Marie-Claire was taking her meals with Mary and Barbara. For a time Barbara thought that she herself might be falling in love with M-C, and their relationship did briefly become sexual. (In a letter to a close friend, M-C claimed that Barbara had "imposed" herself.) Similarly, she initially pretended to admire Barbara's political activities, but that later gave way to increasing annoyance: she told Mary that Barbara was "terrorizing" her—which given Barbara's gentle temperament seems highly unlikely. [10]

By then, Edmund Wilson had become openly negative about M-C, calling her "that little bitch," and he predicted to Barbara that *she* would be the one who ended up being "left out in the cold." Fortunately for Barbara, she ran into a woman, Jane Verlaine, who she'd distantly known at Bennington and they became increasingly involved. By the time Mary dissolved the Wellfleet household several years later to go off with M-C to live in Brittany, Barbara and Jane had formed (as Barbara put it) a "permanent and unshakeable" bond and found their own place in Monticello, New York. [11]

Throughout this period of domestic turmoil, Barbara had maintained her political activism—especially in regard to the escalating war in Vietnam. In April 1966, she joined a six-person group, including A. J. Muste, that travelled to Saigon, though to do so she had to overcome her terror of flying. The trip convinced her that she could handle fear—and convinced her too that more people had to move from "words of dissent to acts of disobedience." In December–January 1966-67, she took part in a peace delegation to North Vietnam which lasted for eleven days—and left her horrified at the firsthand view of American destruction. She saw clear and abundant evidence everywhere of the destruction wrought by U.S. bombing on nonmilitary targets like schools, churches, hospitals, and homes. The U.S., she became convinced, was waging a deliberate "war of terror against the civilian population."

Returning to the States, she spent the winter of 1967 on a cross-country speaking tour to share her experiences while in Vietnam and her fear "that we Americans are on our way to becoming the *world's* bullies," all the while "confident in our hearts that we are a well-intentioned people and therefore incapable of atrocities." On a second lecture tour, she described to her audiences the widespread devastation she'd seen, urging them to take some form of action—to stop paying taxes, to refuse purchase of government bonds, to boycott companies like Dow Chemical that manufactured napalm and other weapons of destruction. [12]

Barbara herself joined the planners for a massive demonstration on October 21, 1967 in front of the Pentagon. In the upshot, some hundred thousand people turned out—the largest antiwar protest to date. Further emboldened, Barbara took part six months later in the Poor People's Campaign that Martin Luther King Jr. had initiated. She joined the campaign at its starting point at the Lorraine Motel in Memphis, where King had been murdered, and walked from there to the encampment in Resurrection City, where she stayed for a full three weeks. The experience was grim. It rained so often that the plywood shelters leaked, mud was omnipresent, garbage went uncollected, water was scarce, and food was primarily confined to bologna sandwiches. The police randomly attacked the encampment with Mace, sometimes blinding and choking people for long periods. The public address system loudly amplified garbled instructions, and civility took a rapid nose dive. The federal government finally ordered the encampment closed down, and the residents were too demoralized to put up a fight. [13]

Reflecting on the "lessons" of Resurrection City in a powerful and influential essay, "On Revolution and Equilibrium," Barbara placed the experience in a larger context. If, she asked, nonviolent campaigns had to date produced only slight gains for Blacks, did that mean nonviolent tactics were the wrong ones? "Was an appeal to conscience an impotent illusion? Would resort to violence have brought greater gains?" Barbara refused to judge those who, increasingly frustrated, were currently arguing that counterviolence was the only effective way to combat the violence employed against Blacks or the Vietnamese people. She agreed with the defectors from non-violence that the peace movement had too often confined itself to petition and relied too glibly on a demeaning appeal to their opponents "to love one's fellow human beings." [14]

Yet nonviolence, Barbara insisted, need not be either humble or meek in its appeal to conscience. What was needed was a firm refusal to do another's will, to *firmly* exert nonviolent force: "one doesn't just say 'I don't believe in this war' but refuses to put on a uniform. One doesn't just say 'the use of napalm is atrocious' but refuses to fund it by refusing to pay one's taxes, and so on ." What differentiated this kind of force from traditional violence was the refusal "to injure the antagonist ... it is quite possible to frustrate another's action without doing him injury. ... We can put more pressure on the antagonist for whom we show human concern. ... It is precisely solicitude for his person *in combination with* a stubborn interference with his actions"—the synergy of love and truthfulness—that produces uniquely effective pressure.

Barbara was aware that her formulation was subject to challenge. In asserting, for example, that "the antagonist cannot take the interference with his actions personally because his person is not threatened," the concept of *personhood* is porous. Wouldn't a confirmed segregationist, convinced that God had created Blacks as inferior beings, feel that in assaulting the very basis of his belief system, his *person* was being violated? The issue, as Barbara herself put it, was "infinitely complex."

THE FAST-MOVING EVENTS of the late Sixties in the U.S. was akin to an automatic rifle going off at a firing range. Martin Luther King Jr.'s assassination in April 1968 sparked enraged rioting throughout the country. Two months later, Robert Kennedy was shot dead at the Ambassador Hotel in Los Angeles, followed by the Chicago police bloodily assaulting protesters at the 1968 Democratic Party convention (and then a "conspiracy" trial of the so-called Chicago Eight that was itself a parody of justice). Then in December 1969 came the police murder of Black Panther leaders Fred Hampton and Mark Clark, and the killing during an antiwar protest of four students at Kent State University. A nonviolent solution to the country's ills seemed to some mere wishful thinking. But Barbara held to her views and continued to participate in a variety of actions (though the many adjustments involved in shifting partners and homes inescapably absorbed some of her energy).

No sooner had her personal life settled down than she was in a car accident that very nearly took her life. Hospitalized for four months with multiple injuries and in agonizing discomfort, she was subsequently invalided at home for nearly a year (including months in a body cast). Inactivity being contrary to her nature, the long days of convalescence were "dark and painful"—though she complained little.

It wasn't until mid-August 1972 that she was able, to a limited extent, to resume political activity. At the time, debate was raging on the Left about whether or not the antiwar movement's confrontational tactics should be put on hold in the name of working for the election of the Democratic candidate George McGovern to the presidency. Barbara took the position that resistance activities *had* to continue in case McGovern reneged on or diluted his promise to end the Vietnam war. But others—including the prominent activist Dave Dellinger—refused to endorse McGovern, calling for the Left to stop playing "the electoral game." To which Barbara, who'd never been a true ideologue, forcefully replied, "I say damn all those labels! I say DAMN what we may have decided about all elections before this. If there is at least a significant opportunity here to end the war ... let us try to seize it." [15]

When McGovern lost in a landslide, Barbara feared that Nixon would choose to regard his victory as a mandate to reject peace negotiations and to further escalate the bombing raids; she thought he might even prove capable of using atomic weaponry. Though a temperamental optimist, Barbara was the kind "who is never surprised when things go wrong." Nixon's victory frightened but did not stop her. Nor did she turn away from mainstream channels of protest that *might* yield results: along with many others, she went to the Capitol to try and persuade individual congressmen to vote to cut off funding for the war. She also resurrected her earlier idea of recruiting hundreds of American women to live and work in scattered Vietnam villages in the hope that their presence might stay the U.S. government's hand. Neither effort bore fruit.

As the war dragged on, Barbara's mounting interest in the burgeoning feminist movement began to absorb some of her frustrated energy. During her year of invalidism, she'd read much of the emerging new literature—ranking highest Shulamith Firestone's *The Dialectic of Sex* and theologian Mary Daly's *The Church* and *the Second Sex*—and she gradually became friendly with some of the movement's leading figures, including Adrienne Rich, Robin Morgan, Ti-Grace Atkinson, and Andrea Dworkin. She also began writing more about feminist issues and several of her articles became widely known, especially "Two Perspectives on Women's Struggles" and "On Anger." Adrienne Rich was particularly affected by Barbara's essays and wrote her to say that "your work has meant a great deal to me." [16]

Barbara's richly provocative essay "On Anger" became particularly influential. In it, she argued that one kind of anger was healthy—"the concentration of one's whole being in the determination: this must change." Neither agitation nor confrontation were necessary components of that determination: it respects oneself and the other. Barbara was aware that many pacifists in fact harbored repressed anger they found difficult to acknowledge—as she put it: "we discover in ourselves murderers." Yet it was precisely when repressed anger surfaced, Barbara believed, that a movement for social change begins to show signs of life. What one did with the anger was all important. If one acknowledged and disciplined it—took the "murder" out of it—it could facilitate unification with others comparably oppressed: the anger would be utilized not to destroy the oppressor but to change one's subservient status through conscious solidarity with those similarly tyrannized over.

One needed to recognize as well, in Barbara's view, that "we are members one of another, that nobody, nothing is strictly *Other*." Men, for example, can learn connectedness—"we have to insist they can." To destroy "maleness" and "femaleness" as we currently know them, it was necessary to insist, she argued, that the qualities traditionally defining them as polar opposites were in fact potentially present in all. *"Won't we always be men's prey,"* she asked, "until they come to acknowledge that in each one of *them* is what Adrienne [Rich] beautifully calls a 'ghostly woman' ?" Adrienne herself was less convinced. She was aware that some of the greatest apostles of nonviolence—Gandhi for one—"perpetuated psychic violence on women." She felt too that women were wholly entitled to defend themselves violently from male assault and rape (on that point Barbara agreed).

The resistance of male leftists to feminist insights greatly disturbed Barbara. She became convinced that "until the left becomes feminist, it is flawed, can't make real revolution." Yet most of the men she approached responded defensively, even though her message was gently phrased. Still, she felt that "so many of us [are] changing so fast these days that I think it a mistake to count any of us who *are* changing hopeless." And on a personal level enough men—she pointed, for example, to the prominent civil rights lawyer Arthur Kinoy—did respond positively to the feminist message to give her hope.

Barbara had never fully recovered from her car accident and by 1976, she fell ill again and again. Though only sixty, she tired quickly, had to restrict travel, and felt that she could no longer take the bitter northern winters. Though she acknowledged the move as a "drastic step," she and Jane decided to relocate to Florida. They bought a small house on Sugar-loaf Key, which was about 20 miles north of Key West and moved there in the spring of 1977. It was "a great tearing away" from friends, family, and movement work, yet necessary for survival. A slow adjustment began.

OVER TIME a few women began to join Barbara and Jane at Sugarloaf and it became a small lesbian community. At its height, about a dozen women were in residence, though most stayed for only a few years. Nonetheless, Sugarloaf came to mean a great deal to Barbara, even if she sometimes felt "starved" for solitude, especially when "too much communal living" stood in the way of getting some writing done. Still, she never withdrew from politics, whether local or global. She joined the unsuccessful fight to get the Equal Rights Amendment passed in Florida—one of thirteen states to vote against ratification and to keep the amendment to this day from becoming part of the Constitution.

On the national level, too, she continued to raise her voice. A longtime advocate of nuclear disarmament, she wrote and distributed a statement that included these telling lines: "Our politicians tell us that we have to be strong" but "we had better ask ourselves what the word means. Are we strong if we show that we are capable of destroying all life on this earth?" In regard to the national debate then current about women serving in the military, Barbara raised an unorthodox point about the dubious merits of being part of the armed forces: the military "train you not to ask why the war is being waged, why these particular people should be killed—just do as you're told, kill when you're told to. Mindlessly." As for the then common consensus that women would not be sent into combat, Barbara challenged the rationale: "the powers-that-be feel women shouldn't be subjected to violence. If they felt this, they would give battered women and rape victims help they don't give. No, the [powers-that-be] ... want to assure the men they're ordering around that dealing-out violence is reserved for them—and somehow proves that they are more than women are." [17]

Barbara continued to feel that most men on the Left were *not* true comrades—and certainly not feminists. If they were perhaps more gentle than other men, Barbara believed that they too "need to hold on to power over others, to treat others as owned." And she let them know how she felt about it. When her old antiwar "comrade" Father Daniel Berrigan publicly compared abortion clinics to the Pentagon ("war is also an abortion, and abortion is also a war"), Barbara indignantly wrote him to say that he was simply playing with words—"and playing with the deepest feelings of women. Women do not have abortions in the spirit of war! ... to insist that women bear children that they don't want to bear—Dan, isn't this *making war* on women?" Berrigan was unpersuaded and sent Barbara a muddled response that adhered to the teachings of his Catholic faith.

Barbara found men on the left also untrustworthy allies on the question of gay rights. The War Resisters League, non-Marxist and secular, was somewhat of an exception among organizations on the Left. Its founder, A. J. Muste, had himself been profoundly homophobic—after Bayard Rustin was arrested on a "morals charge," Muste opposed hiring him as a staff member. But Muste had in that instance been overruled, and the organization as a whole continued to be uncommonly welcoming of gay people to its ranks. As early as 1969, almost immediately after the Stonewall riots, the War Resistance League's magazine *Win* put out a gay liberation issue. The League even had two gay men—David McReynolds and Igal Roodenko—and one bisexual man, Karl Bissinger, on its small staff (though none of the three became active in the struggle for gay rights).

If Barbara was unhappy about the disconnect between the male left and feminism, she was no less concerned about the seeming disinterest of feminists in the principle of nonviolence. At the start of second-wave feminism, she'd taken it for granted that feminists "would see nonviolence as an obviously natural approach for them." She explained their indifference as a function of the need most women felt to express their long-buried anger, to refuse to any longer be "the ones to suffer." They were unable, as Barbara saw it, to feel any "bond with the oppressor"—though that principle was to her at the heart of a true understanding of nonviolence. Women, she decided, still felt "too vulnerable to be able to deal with the fact of kinship with, and likeness to men."

In the early years of living at Sugarloaf, Barbara would occasionally undertake trips north—in 1982, for example, to the National Women's Studies Association meetings, and, in 1983, to the Seneca Women's Encampment at Romulus, New York. At Seneca she joined the demonstration against the planned deployment of NATO first-strike Cruise and Pershing II missiles to Europe from the nearby Army Depot. The local citizenry responded angrily to the demonstration, denouncing "these outsiders disgracing our community" and shouting out "Nuke the Dykes!" and "Lesbian-Communists go home!" [18]

A significant number of women remained at Seneca for several months but Barbara, after three weeks, and feeling frail and exhausted, had to take herself back to Sugarloaf. Soon after returning, she came down with flu-like symptoms that refused to abate. She and Jane finally decided to fly to New York City to consult with Barbara's brother, a physician. He hospitalized her for tests and in March 1984, the verdict came down: Barbara had ovarian cancer. She underwent chemotherapy for several months, but the doctors told her that the cancer was too far advanced to hope for a cure. She and Jane returned to Sugarloaf. [19]

Barbara was determined "to give to her dying the same passion" with which she'd lived and loved, but by the end of July, she'd wasted away to skin and bones. Jane wrote in her diary that "I've always seen her snap back. ... Now I am scared that she won't ... this time is it & I am in great distress ... disabling distress, not helpful tears relieving emotional tension." [20]

Within days, Barbara's pain rose to excruciating levels, and she started taking a higher level of morphine, which made her sleep a great deal. She soon slipped into a coma, and two days later, at age sixty-seven, she died. Bereft, Jane tried to sum up in her diary Barbara's unique qualities, describing her "innate shyness" and "self-deprecation," her "physical spiritual beauty," her "passionate, attentive quality. She paid attention. She listened. She answered." ∎

NOTES

1. This portrait is drawn primarily from the Barbara Deming Papers at the Schlesinger Library (BDSL) and appeared in *The Gay & Lesbian Review,* May-June 2020. A much fuller version is in Duberman, *A Saving Remnant,* The New Press, 2011. Unless otherwise specified, all quotations come from BDSL; for a full listing of citations, see the "Notes" that conclude *A Saving Remnant.*

2. Deming, *A Humming Under My Feet,* Women's Press, 1985, 228-229.

3. Deming, *A Humming,* passim.

4. Mary Meigs, *Lily Briscoe: A Self-Portrait,* Talonbooks, 1981, 13-15, 24-27, 39-40, 111; Edmund Wilson journals, *The Fifties,* ed. Leon Edel, Farrar, Straus & Giroux, 1986, 518-519, 551-561, and *The Sixties,* ed. Lewis M. Dabney, Farrar, Straus & Giroux, 1993; Martin Duberman, "Prelude to a Mary Meigs Biography?," *The Gay & Lesbian Review,* Sept.-Oct. 2021, 25-30.

5. For this and following two paragraphs: Leah Fritz interview with Deming, *Ms.,* Nov. 1978; Meigs, *Lily Briscoe,* 96-103.

6. Deming, "San Francisco-Moscow: Why They Walk," *Nation,* July 15, 1961, and her follow-up piece, "New Mission to Moscow," *Nation,* Dec. 23, 1961; Mary Meigs, *Lily Briscoe,* 84-103.

7. Jane Meyerding, ed. *We Are All Part of One Another: A Barbara Deming Reader.* New Society, 1984, 77-80.

8. Deming, "In the Birmingham Jail," *Nation,* May 25, 1963; Deming, "Notes After Birmingham," *Liberation,* Summer 1963.

9. On radical education: A.S. Neill, *Summerhill;* Paulo Freire, *The Pedagogy* of *the Oppressed;* Jonathan Kozol, *Death at an Early Age;* John Holt, *How Children Fail and How Children Learn.* For anthropology and primatology: Oren Harman, *The Price of Altruism;* Matt Ridley, *The Origins of Virtue;* Robert Sapolsky, *The Trouble with Testosterone*—and anything by the anthropologist Frans de Waal.

10. Duberman, "Prelude to a Mary Meigs Biography?," *The Gay & Lesbian Review,* Sept.-Oct. 2021, 25-30.

11. Blais to Lapointe, Apr. [1966?]; postcard Oct. 22, 1967; letter Jan. 24, 1969, Marie-Claire Blais Papers, Bibliothèque et Archives, Montréal, Canada; Marie-Claire Blais, *American Notebooks,* Talonbooks, 1996; Mary Meigs Papers, Bryn Mawr College; Wilson, *The Sixties,* ed. Dabney, 407-8, 455-56.

12. Deming, "The Temptations of Power—Report on a Visit to North Vietnam," reprinted in Deming, *Revolution* and *Equilibrium,* Grossman, 1971.

13. Deming, "Mud City." *Liberation.* Sept. 1968.

14. Deming, "Revolution and Equilibrium." *Liberation,* Feb. 1968.

15. David Dellinger, *From Yale to Jail,* 405-8. See also, Andrew Hunt, *David Dellinger;* John D'Emilio, *Lost Prophet;* Scott H. Bennet, *Radical Pacifism;* Marilyn B. Young, *The Vietnam Wars 1945-1990;* Deming, *We Cannot Live Without Our Lives.*

16. The quotes in this and the following two paragraphs are from "Two Perspectives" and "On Anger." Both essays are reprinted in Meyerling, ed., *We Are All Part of One Another.*

17. For this and the following paragraph: Deming statement in *Woman Time* (a Key West feminist newsletter), Winter 1981-82; *Key West Citizen,* Aug. 18, 1985, plus her two letters to the editor, n.d. and June 4, 1978.

18. Cynthia Costello and Amy Dru Stanley, "Report from Seneca," *Frontiers: A Journal of Women Studies* 8, no. 2 (1985); and "Online Archive of the Seneca Women's Encampment," Jan. 3, 2008 (http://peacecampherstory.blogspot.com).

19. Jane Gapen (Verlaine) diary and papers, Lesbian Herstory Archives, Brooklyn.

20. Jane Gapen diary [1984], Lesbian Herstory Archives.

CHAPTER V

Alfred Kinsey and C.A.Tripp

PART I
WHEN KINSEY MET TRIPP

By 1974, I'd grown increasingly absorbed in the new scholarly field of the history of sexual behavior, and had been making periodic research trips looking for buried source materials in various manuscript libraries. "I've long said that historical study isn't 'useful' (relevant)," I wrote in my diary at the end of February 1975, "because past experience is so different from ours. Now, as regards my interest in sexual behavior in the past, I've realized its study is useful precisely *because* that experience was so different."

I also began to teach a course on the subject and to review some of the books that were beginning to appear. One that I found particularly original—despite its exasperatingly misogynistic overtones—was C. A. Tripp's 1975 book *The Homosexual Matrix.* I'd never heard his name before, but a few inquiries turned up the fact that although Tripp was 56, *The Homosexual Matrix* was his first book. Intrigued, I dug a little deeper and discovered that he'd been born in Denton, Texas, in 1919, had studied photography at the Rochester Institute of Technology, had become a staff member in the Eastman Kodak Company's research department, and had served in the Navy during World War II.

In the postwar period, Tripp and a longtime friend, Bill Dellenback, started a small photography firm. One early customer was the well-known psychoanalyst Theodor Reik, who'd studied with Freud at the University of Vienna but had fled the Nazis (he was Jewish) in 1938. Lacking a medical degree, Reik had found himself at odds with the school of *medically* trained psychoanalysts then dominant in the U.S. and decided to found the National Psychological Association for Psychoanalysis (which is still active) to train so-called "lay" analysts. Reik also wrote a number of influential books, including the 1948 bestseller *Listening with the Third Ear.*

Tripp's marginal success as a photographer coincided with his growing interest in psychology, and Reik became something of a mentor, even writing a placating letter to Tripp's parents expressing enthusiasm for their son's gifts and characterizing him as "having an unusual facility for this kind of work"—being "just such young men we need [*sic*]." But it had been Tripp himself who, in 1948, immediately after reading Kinsey's just-published *Sexual Behavior in the Human Male* (co-authored with Wardell B. Pomeroy and Clyde E. Martin), simply picked up the phone one day and called Kinsey directly. We have no detailed record of what was said, but Kinsey *did* take the call, and something about the young man's authoritative boldness caught the older man's attention.

Tripp made a point of letting Kinsey know that he was himself homosexual and was writing a book on the subject. (He *had* actually begun, though *The Homosexual Matrix* was still three decades off.) Tripp also stressed that he was a skilled photographer, perhaps having heard through the grapevine that Kinsey had decided to augment direct observation of sexual activity to filming it. In any case, he invited Tripp to visit his research institute in Bloomington, Indiana.

Tripp wasted no time. Within weeks, he showed up at Kinsey's door—and stayed for the better part of three days. After returning to New York, he sent Kinsey an extraordinary letter of thanks (and Tripp was no one's idea of a sycophant): "It is almost impossible for me to tell you how much I learned from you during my visit last week. ... Little wonder you win co-operation from everyone. ... I think it is your drive that makes every-thing such a success, then the honesty and personality stand out. For me, the greatest thing seemed to be the way you meet objections and the unspoken generosity you give at those moments when you meet some-thing in another person which is contrary to what you know to be the case, or the kind way you have of rejecting what you consider worthless." (Tripp had probably told Kinsey that he was leaning towards psychology as a career, and in response, the good doctor possibly gave mild vent to his well-known hostility, even contempt, for psychoanalysis.) "Anyway," Tripp concluded his letter, "I'm with you for life and everything I can do is not enough."

Kinsey's response was encouraging: "I very much enjoyed your visit here at Bloomington and look forward to contact with you when we come east to New York. You have been very good to offer such extended help and we shall be delighted to utilize it." From that point on, Tripp, a masterful strategist, made himself entirely available to Kinsey, eager to do him favors and proving again and again in the coming years that nothing was too much for him. Tripp never became (or wished to become) a member of the staff, but, reliable and energetic, he served as a kind of courier, a listening post in faraway lands (the East Coast). Kinsey, in turn, became Tripp's mentor, collaborator, and friend. In gratitude, Tripp would make Kinsey an occasional present of something he thought he'd enjoy, such as a recording of Gertrude Stein reading her *The Making of Americans*, or "paper-shelled" pecans. (Kinsey reported back that the pecans "bring back memories of bug hunting days in Texas, and I like them very much.")

One of Kinsey's more important early requests was for Tripp to arrange for, produce, and occasionally star in filmed sessions of sexual activity. Tripp himself had made a number of masturbation films, as well as several with an assortment of male partners—though his lover, the dancer Oliver ("Ollie") Kostock, was initially reluctant to become involved. Ollie, during the 1940s and '50s, had been building a reputation with a variety of companies that included the Alwin Nikolais Dance Theater, the Murray Louis Dance Company, and, most prominently, the Hanya Holm

C. A. Tripp and Alfreed Kinsey. Kinsey photo courtesy of Proyecto Historiador 2, Wikimedia Commons

troupe. When Tripp finally succeeded in getting Ollie to make a film, Tripp confided in a letter to Kinsey that "the psychology involved is formidable."

Tripp found it relatively easy to hire "models" for most of the films. He paid $3 per orgasm or $6 for each pair of performers. Within a few months, he'd produced, along with a considerable number of "stills," 250 feet of "motion pictures on a masturbation composite," which amounted to seven rolls. Fifty feet of it included "16mm rolls of homosexual petting and intercourse between two nineteen-year-old boys." He also succeeded in enlisting Bill Dellenback, his earlier partner in a short-lived photography firm. (By spring 1950, Dellenback had taken up permanent residence in Bloomington.) The many other diverse—and unpaid—recruits included a graduate student and his wife, the latter insisting that her face not be shown. Kinsey was particularly pleased with the still photographs, declaring them "the best that any photographer has yet made," and he suggested that henceforth he refer all magazine and newspaper requests directly to Tripp. "Thanks tremendously for this work," Kinsey added. "It is splendid, and definitely what we need." He would eventually elevate Tripp to the exalted rank—there were only 45 members—of "visiting specialist," and the only two people Kinsey saw with any regularity on his trips to New York were Tripp and the gay novelist Glenway Wescott.

Perhaps the most notable contribution Tripp made during the first two years of his acquaintance with Kinsey was securing the bulk of Robert Latou Dickinson's archives following the pioneering gynecologist's death in 1950. Dickinson was among the first obstetricians to obtain detailed sexual histories—5,200 in all—and from 1935 to 1941, he also carried out a path-breaking study of human homosexuality that strongly influenced Kinsey's own interview techniques. On learning of Dickinson's death, Kinsey immediately notified the Institute's lawyers—Morris Ernst, cofounder of the ACLU, and Harriet Pilpel, the prominent women's rights activist—for help in securing Dickinson's library, notebooks, and case histories. He also urged Tripp to put himself at Ernst and Pilpel's disposal in securing and transporting the material to Bloomington. Tripp went to work immediately, and within two weeks he was able to write Kinsey that the job had been successfully completed and that 41 packages containing the contents of Dickinson's archive were on their way via Railway Express.

Despite Kinsey's scorn for psychology, he took note of Tripp's growing interest in becoming a therapist and encouraged him to enter a doctoral program. Tripp followed his advice and enrolled in NYU's program in clinical psychology. "Frankly," he wrote, "it almost did me in." In 1957, the year after Kinsey's death, Tripp completed his degree at NYU and soon opened a private practice; as well, he taught for nearly a decade at New York's Downstate Medical Center. By the mid-1960s, his practice as a psychoanalyst thriving, Tripp and Ollie bought a house some twenty miles from New York City with a spectacular view overlooking the Hudson River at the Tappan Zee bridge. He even went back to his abandoned project of writing a book on homosexuality; within a few years he thought he finally had enough material. Doubleday agreed and gave him a contract.

After Kinsey's death in 1956, it seemed likely for a time that a fraught controversy over succession at the Institute would end with Paul Gebhard and Wardell Pomeroy jointly sharing leadership. Certain prominent insiders, however—not including Tripp—insisted that Pomeroy's "frivolous" side (which seems to have meant, in part, his "excessive" enjoyment of sex) was not to be trusted. In the upshot, to avoid a protracted battle, the mantle was passed to Gebhard, about whom Tripp had decidedly mixed feelings. In a confidential letter, he predicted "the fast erosion of the Institute's prestige within the scientific community" and declared that the outline it was circulating for a pending study of homosexuality asked "the wrong set of questions," the result of "aggressive ignorance."

Kinsey had been Tripp's hero, and Kinsey was gone. "Looking back," Tripp wrote Gebhard early in 1967, "I've decided I may never understand how a man with his [Kinsey's] 'square' background ever managed to walk thru the minefield of homosexual research without making any real errors. Of course, he didn't cover much of the ground that now lies before you. Nevertheless, he just should have made more errors; it's like some curious piece of magic to me."

MY OWN ACQUAINTANCE with Tripp began some eight years later, when the *New York Times Sunday Book Review* weighed in with a blistering review of Tripp's long-incubating book *The Homosexual Matrix*. The *Times* had assigned the review to Dr. Herbert Hendin, director of "psychosocial studies" at the Center for Policy Research—the same Hendin who two months earlier had published an op-ed in the Times warning that "the increasing acceptance of homosexuality parallels increasing attacks on the family." Harvey Shapiro, head of the *Book Review* and known to be homophobic, had his man: he promptly asked Hendin to review Tripp's book.

The review appeared on October 26, 1975. It met all the requirements— of the homophobes, that is. Hendin labeled the book "pseudoscience" and summarily dismissed its author as "an erudite con man." He mocked Tripp's suggestion that homosexual males may come from a "sexually precocious segment of the population" and accused him of attempting to "hawk" homosexuality. Hendin rejected Tripp's denunciation of psychotherapists "who try to change homosexuals who do not want to change," deploring instead those therapists who pressured or encouraged young men to accept their homosexuality.

Publishers get an advance copy of the *Sunday Times Book Review*, and Tripp's editor—at this point Tripp and I had still not met—sent me a copy of the review. I immediately wrote to Harvey Shapiro (who I knew only as a voice over the phone to discuss various review assignments) protesting the Hendin review as a "disastrously simple-minded (and misstated) summary of what is probably the most complex statement on homosexuality—on all sexuality—made in several decades at least."

I made it clear to Shapiro that I was writing to him privately, not as a "letter to the editor," in the hope that it wasn't too late to do justice to the book, perhaps in the form of a "Last Word" column, a sort of second opinion that the *Times* periodically featured. I expressed a willingness to take on the assignment, but having already come out as gay, I acknowledged that "I'm not thought to be a disinterested party," and suggested a few "neutral" names, including the psychiatrists Robert Coles, Robert Gould, and Robert Liebert. The important thing, I wrote, was not that I do a counter-review but that "this remarkable book should not be jeopardized by the small-mindedness of a single reviewer." "Nor should the *Times*," I brazenly added, "be irrevocably linked with that single point of view."

Within 48 hours, Shapiro bluntly responded: no second review would be possible. Period. Tripp dropped me a note of thanks for at least having tried and—in a letter to his friend Clark Polak (the Philadelphia gay activist, co-founder of the Janus Society and *Drum* magazine)—expressed concern that my intervention might cost me: "Duberman has gone so far out of his way in support of *Matrix*, and is cited so much in all sorts of correspondence [that] I'm sad ... the wound being opened again may bury him altogether with the *Times* in future. ... tho maybe he's already buried there." (It was hard to know. After I came out publicly in late 1971, ever fewer invitations had been arriving to write for mainstream publications like *The Nation*, *The New Republic*, and the *Times*.)

Still, the "Shapiro incident" may not have been causal, but merely coincidental. In fact, a month after my attempted intervention, Shapiro printed only brief excerpts from half a dozen letters responding to the Hendin review, omitting the one from Tripp entirely, but gave my letter a full, unedited two columns. I acknowledged in my letter that "like all highly innovative work, Tripp's study is open to challenge. I was myself bothered that some of his generalizations seemed based on limited evidence. And I think his view of female sexuality is, in part, outmoded and patronizing." Nonetheless, I went on, *"The Homosexual Matrix* is literally astonishing—it opens the eyes. Time and again Tripp takes our culture's set formulas—that homosexuality is far more characteristic of city than of town life; that promiscuity is a function of 'neurotic insecurity,' etc.—and examines them with such devastating logic and imaginative force that we can never again settle for the familiar clichés."

Tripp even dares to argue, I went on, that "sexual interest is whetted by stress and by barriers that have to be surmounted, [and that] sexual attraction hinges to a significant degree on distance and tension—'resistance' in Tripp's preferred phrase." As for Hendin, I wrote that "it was his prerogative to disagree with Tripp's analyses, but he has the responsibility to portray them accurately rather than to parody them. He also has the responsibility to uncover his own attitudinal bias, to try to understand how his distaste for a line of argument might lead him to distort its premises (thus conveniently avoiding its consequences)." "It's dismaying," I concluded, "that Tripp's book ... has been so caricatured and trivialized. I can only hope that potential readers, unlike the *Times*' reviewer, will prove willing to confront its bold, discomforting propositions."

As is well known, controversy often quickens book sales. In the upshot, *The Homosexual Matrix* would in the years ahead sell some half a million copies. But back in the mid-'70s, it looked for a time that instead the book might sink under the weight of the *Times*' displeasure. Convinced that *The Homosexual Matrix* warranted *serious* appraisal, and out of concern that its uncommon insights would be ignored and its provocations buried, I decided to put together two informal gatherings of LGBTQ+ scholars. To that end, I invited some fifteen or so lesbian and gay academics to gather with Tripp at a friend's spacious apartment to discuss the book—including what some of us took to be its shortcomings. The first session met on February 2, 1976.

Shortly before that, I got a somewhat frantic call from Arno Karlen (who I knew only slightly and who in 1972 had published *Sexuality and Homosexuality*), saying he *had* to see me, and promising that it would be "for fifteen minutes, not more." We—or rather Arno—went on for almost three hours, ablaze with outrage, denouncing Tripp's book as "junk, disreputable, dishonest." Arno had chosen to vent in *my* living room, it turned out, on the theory that—because I'd blurbed the book—I was somehow tied into what he called "the conspiracy to elevate it to respectability." I pointed out that a number of prominent figures had also praised the book, including the Johns Hopkins sexologist John Money, Kinsey's co-author Wardell Pomeroy, the anthropologist Frank Beach, and the psychiatrist Judd Marmor, president of the American Psychiatric Association. The praise, Arno fumed, "was part of a larger disintegration of standards, a *conscious* willingness to applaud the politically chic at the expense of scientific truth."

During Arno's self-indulgent rampage, I tried to suggest several times that some of his fury *might* relate to the fact that Tripp's book challenged several of his own assumptions in *Sexuality and Homosexuality*, primarily the assertion that psychiatric treatment could cure the "maladjustment" of homosexuality. When, on the third go-round, he continued to ignore the suggestion, I became explicit: "I've reread *Sexuality and Homosexuality* several times," I bluntly said, "and each time I've become more aware of its homophobic subtext." I told him that, in a limited way, I did agree with his criticism of Tripp, and in particular with his failure to cite evidence in support of some of his more suspect assertions (for example, the larger penis size of gay men). Comparable criticism regarding evidence and bias, I added, could be made of any book in the social sciences. "No!" Arno spat out, "*not* to the same degree!" With his anger verging on hysteria, and after having rehearsed the same arguments over and over, I simply called a halt, telling him that I was already late for an appointment.

PART II

Tripp's *Homosexual Matrix* Deconstructed

THE FIRST GATHERING to discuss *The Homosexual Matrix*, held on February 2, 1976, was hardly a love fest. Over a five-hour period, most of the hot-button topics relating to sexuality came up for discussion, sometimes in heated exchanges. Not having previously met Tripp, I found that I liked Tripp the man better than I had expected to, since most of the advance reports had described him as arrogant, closed-minded, and "difficult." The peremptory note did unmistakably sound now and then, but so did his warmth and charm—though I didn't entirely trust the charm, which seemed to be in the service of evasion, at which Tripp proved exceedingly skillful.

The group of some two dozen invitees was bright, well-informed, and tenacious in their criticism (a match for Tripp's own tenacity in ignoring it). None of the objections raised to his views seemed to make a dent, though I thought much of the criticism telling. I myself pressed him on the lack of supporting evidence for some of his claims, even while acknowledging that the imaginative insights I most admired about the book were in pleasant contrast to the academy's notion of what constituted "true" scholarship. "For God's sakes, Duberman," Tripp later told me privately, "Kinsey didn't base his conclusions on those umpteen thousand interviews, but on his direct observations watching sex—including watching me and a long line of lovers!" Maybe so, I rather stumblingly replied—Tripp, after all, had worked directly with Kinsey—but the book's paucity of citations, I told him, made it difficult to defend his work to literal-minded scholars.

To my mind, the most serious objection raised that first afternoon concerned Tripp's claim that sex is "focal" for males, but innately "peripheral" for females. He offered as confirmation the many consultations he'd had with female researchers about his conclusions. Annoyed at his presumptive tone, I was among those who pointed out that "we all choose our consultants, and consciously or not go to experts who we know or sense hold views comparable to our own." The anthropologist Edgar Gregersen (who would later write *Sexual Practices*) added that the anthropological literature did not confirm Tripp's sweeping statements on female sexuality: Edgar gave Mangaia as an example. It was a culture where all women have orgasms because they demand them, not because of male desire, attentiveness, or proficiency.

Tripp was a good deal more persuasive—this was 1976, before the advent of the trans movement—in his insistence that a majority of "transvestites" were not homosexuals (and vice versa). When he further trashed aversion therapy as "a joke"—and a harmful one—he found no disagreement. He also made a strong (if perhaps too encompassing) case that sadomasochistic sex was not intrinsically destructive, but instead a carefully calibrated case of "resistance." And resistance, he claimed—that is, some kind of barrier, some sort of impediment to easy access, a degree of tension, distance, alienation—was an essential element in forming and maintaining erotic attraction. In long-term relationships, he argued, the ongoing presence of "resistance" was essential to the continuation of sexual arousal. Individuals who equate arousal with roses and romance were merely acting out the nonsense of our adolescent culture. Therapists who seek "harmony"—an absence of stress and combat—were in the foolish business of leading their clients down a path that ends either in celibacy or outside affairs.

Intriguingly, Tripp also told us that at the last minute that he had pulled his chapter on aging from the book as "too far out." What he'd concluded, he said, was that homosexuals age better than heterosexuals—despite the stereotype that, devoid of family ties, they fall into despair after youth fades. The excessive focus in heterosexual American families on the children, he went on, is accompanied by the illusion—almost always disappointed—that the parents' "sacrifices for the kids" will produce grateful offspring attentive as adults to the needs of their aging parents. In contrast, Tripp argued, the emphasis on youthfulness in gay culture forces homosexuals at a much earlier point to deal with their fading attractiveness and to form strong bonds of friendship.

In direct contradiction to the long-dominant theories of Irving Bieber and Charles Socarides, the psychiatrists responsible for establishing the binding mother/absent father theory that was still the consensus view long dominant in the profession's understanding of the origins of homosexuality, Tripp insisted that anthropology proves that societies in which homosexuality flourishes are those with strong father-son bonds—thus maximizing the opportunity to eroticize male attributes. Yet Tripp also claimed that in cultures where physical bonding between males was commonplace—for example, sleeping intertwined—this practice "short-circuits" genital contact. Put another way, emotional closeness (according to Tripp) leads to genital homosexuality; physical closeness forecloses it. Several of us found the formula too pat, and its claims too sweeping, though Tripp's speculations were nonetheless intriguing and worth pondering further.

I was less suspicious of Tripp's own view of causality. He made a persuasive analogy, I thought, with how we forecast the weather. With the help of computers and memory banks, he argued, meteorologists have been able to isolate more than 100 variables that influence the weather. Even so, they have great trouble weighing, let alone controlling, the importance of any single variable in explaining a particular outcome—thus, the unreliability of weather forecasts *and* of formulaic explanations for the origins of sexual orientation. What was certain, he went on, was that human sexual behavior was primarily the result of social learning, not biology.

On several other significant issues, I found Tripp's discussion enigmatic or unpersuasive. What he seemed to be saying in regard to male "effeminacy" was that once a homosexual orientation is established, "you go out of production"—that is, you cease to "import" masculine traits. Did that mean, I and others asked, that "effeminate" men become conscious of their orientation at an earlier age than "masculine" homosexuals? Do non-effeminate homosexual men not seek masculine traits in their partners? How does one even define "effeminacy" (or for that matter, "masculinity")? What specific traits are considered essential to those definitions?

And what of the claim that all gay men are effeminate, even those disguised under layers of leather. Tripp's theory reminded me of 19th-century physics and its belief in "closed energy systems," though in truth I didn't understand that either. Similarly, while Tripp explicitly denied Freud's concept of "innate" bisexuality—the view that one is born psychosexually neutral—he implicitly assumed that some unspecified bio-logical mechanism (hormones? genes?) could interfere with the infant's sexual readiness for any and all stimuli. But hadn't he just claimed that social learning and not biology played the primary role in determining sexual orientation?

After the discussion ended and a few of us lingered, Tripp let a bit more of his hair down and entertained us with some salacious tidbits, including Wardell Pomeroy (Kinsey's co-author) telling him that the "anti-gay" psychiatrist Charles Socarides had "a large homosexual history." At the end of the afternoon, alone with Tripp, I told him about Arno Karlen's verbal rampage in my apartment. Tripp replied with a twinkle that Karlen (who in 1976 was a heterosexually married man with children) was himself one of the "106" gay men that Irving Bieber claimed in his "infamous" study to have "cured" through psychotherapy. "Though as is well known," Tripp added, Bieber "made up much of his data." He claimed further that in a radio debate with Karlen about his book, Tripp had offered to go over every citation that Karlen found suspect, but Karlen never took him up on the offer.

We held the second of the two Tripp seminars about a month later. In reaction to the position he'd taken at the first meeting that sexuality was "focal" for males but "peripheral" for females, decidedly fewer women showed up. Still, several of Tripp's pronouncements—he obviously delighted in provocation—met with considerable opposition, though it barely ruffled his composure. Probably the liveliest exchange came over his frequent use of the word "resistance"—not only in regard to sadomasochism ("an extreme form of resistance") but as a general explanatory tool. "How are you defining 'resistance'?" someone asked.

"It has many components, including individual isolation, mutual incompatibility, and anger." With respect to an S/M lifestyle, he insisted that "a tight, prudish religious belief system" was a prerequisite. "Take rimming," he suggested: "it's symbolic S/M and doesn't escalate." But the "next step"—for example, whipping—does escalate, though we don't know why. "Wife-beating," he added, "is not S/M—it's hostility." As for the relationship between social oppression and sadomasochism, Tripp added, "there is a direct correlation between a decrease in social resistance to homosexuality and a rise in aggression (biting, etc.) during gay sexual encounters, the aggression being one way of maintaining the necessary tension for erotic excitement no longer provided by social disapproval." That mouthful went unchallenged; it was simply too "packed" to allow for rapid digestion. The closest Tripp came to striking a tentative note regarding S/M was when he declared that "no one knows why some people need an especially high level of resistance in order to function sexually."

Some of us wanted a great deal more clarification and tried to get Tripp to further disentangle the various terms he seemed to use inter-changeably: anger, "resistance," and S/M. Instead, we got enticing tidbits: "Pathology is a foolish concept. A normal base line can be demonstrated in physiology—for example, the eye should be clear, not cloudy—but not in psychology." "Not even statistically?" someone asked. Tripp ignored the question, moving straight on to his next provocation: "A person late to puberty has less chance of being conditioned to homosexuality, a fact [Frank] Beach has validated in his work on rats and beagles." "'Rats and beagles!' an astonished voice rang out. Can analogies to human beings be drawn from non-primates?" Again ignoring the question, Tripp announced that "the Institute for Sex Research is today characterized more by 'conflict avoidance' than by homophobia." "Are you including Wardell Pomeroy?" someone asked. This time Tripp responded: "Wardell, sensibly, no longer works there."

A pattern of exchange had become established: when Tripp felt chal-lenged, however friendly the tone of the challenge, he tended to look through you in dumb amazement at your stupidity, or shift immediately to an anecdote which, ten charming minutes later, you realized had little or no bearing on the question. He also tended to shift terminology abruptly: in mid sentence "anger" could become a synonym for "hostility," which in turn could get equated with "aggression"—without any of the three ever being closely defined. Where one minute he seemed to equate "resistance" with "eroticism" (omitting tenderness, etc.), the next he'd be saying that resistance is a necessary but not sufficient condition for erotic arousal, and then two beats later he'd be discussing "compatibility" as no less necessary an ingredient, even though he'd earlier argued that erotic zest necessarily declines in direct proportion to harmonious domesticity. He was a maddening conversationalist, all at once bracing, elusive, seductive, amusing—and profoundly self-satisfied.

When I recounted all of this to my close friend, the literary critic Dick Poirier, it turned out he'd recently had dinner with Tripp at Gore Vidal's place. (Gore was one of many celebrities who cooperated with Kinsey in recording their sexual history.) Immensely shrewd about people, Dick's conclusion was that Tripp was a "medicine man"—meaning "an impenetrable bundle of inside information, magical insights and pure hokum. I could have listened to him all night."

AS QUIXOTIC, if provocative, as I found Tripp's claims, he proved entirely on target in his prediction of my likely reception at the Kinsey Institute. During my research travels in the past few years in search of manuscript sources relating to the history of sexuality, I found the archivists at most of the libraries I visited—and especially the Lilly Library in Indiana, the Massachusetts Historical Society, and the Countway Library of Medicine in Boston—willing to go out of their way to be helpful. Without hesitation (and with occasional glee), they dug out an assortment of "forbidden," and uncatalogued, material for my examination.

At the Kinsey Institute, however—the very citadel of sexology—the reception was quite different, just as Tripp had predicted. The night before I left for Indiana, he had me to dinner to "prepare" me for the current politics in play there. Kinsey, he told me, had been especially interested in historical material and collected a large amount of it—but it was all now under lock and key. Paul Gebhard, then the head of the Institute, was by nature a cautious man and unlikely to be forthcoming.

That proved an understatement. On my first day at the Institute, I did as Tripp advised: I told Gebhard that Tripp had made me aware of the Institute's uncatalogued storehouse of historical material and had in particular recommended that I look at Kinsey's lengthy correspondence, beginning in 1951, with an international businessmen named Sixt Kapff, who, in his letters to Kinsey, described in rich detail his homosexual adventures while traveling the world. Tripp told me that Kapff had also served as Kinsey's guide when he visited Europe in 1955, which had put to rest any doubts Kinsey may have had about Kapff's reliability as a witness. Accompanying Kapff on his varied rounds, Kinsey became fully convinced that his reports, scrupulous and unique, were a kind of "World Guide to Gay Male Sex."

Soon after, Kapff also served as Tripp's guide when on a trip to Europe. He returned home with a full set of photocopies of Kapff's lengthy correspondence with Kinsey. "[C]ertainly," he wrote Kapff, "it's a treasure trove of cross-cultural sex information, containing as it does many delicate differentiations you made on the responses, mores, and sexual variation between people." Like Kinsey before him, accompanying Kapff on his sexual rounds erased all doubt about his veracity: "no matter how extreme your sexual numbers and actions might seem at a distance," Tripp wrote him, "you were, in fact, very conservative in your estimates and number-counting, as opposed to being in any sense an 'exaggerator.'"

The two men, as Tripp put it, "became the closest of friends," visiting each other back and forth and exchanging numerous letters. After Kinsey's death in 1956, Tripp continued the correspondence with Kapff via cassette tape and—with Kapff's permission—shared much of the material with me. When Gebhard found out, he strenuously objected, but Tripp pointed out to him that he felt "entirely free to call to Duberman's attention such things as the Kapff material—material which, let me remind you again, I know about independently [from Kapff himself], not from Institute sources." In 1981, after Kapff and I began writing directly to each other, he enthusiastically gave me permission to publish whatever selections I chose from the four-way correspondence involving Kinsey, Kapff, Tripp, and myself. ("Having full confidence in your good intentions," Kapff wrote to me, "just go ahead as you think best.")

And for a time during 1981-82, I did do a fair amount of sifting and editing, making just enough grammatical corrections to Kapff s eccentric English to ensure it was intelligible without forfeiting his perspicacity and wit. But my efforts stopped when, out of the blue, Paul Robeson Jr. invited me to write his father's biography, an undertaking that would prove all-consuming. I did manage to publish some excerpts from Kapff's letters in a column I'd been writing for *The New York Native*, which I subsequently republished in my book *About Time: Exploring the Gay Past,* but by then my focus had shifted to the Robeson biography.

To return to that first day of my visit to the Institute back in 1976: when I repeated my request to see the Kapff material, as Tripp had urged, Gebhard told me sternly that Tripp was not only misinformed but that in using Kapff's real name, he'd unforgivably broken confidentiality and jeopardized Kapff's employment with a conservative foreign firm. In response, I repeated what Tripp had told me: Kapff "has never had the slightest reservations"—indeed was "delighted"—to have his letters published and had been disappointed when Wardell Pomeroy referred to him in his 1972 book (*Doctor Kinsey and the Institute for Sex Research*) as "R.J." rather than by his real name.

Changing the subject, Gebhard assured me that the Institute's historical holdings were minimal and unlikely to prove of much interest to me. Thanks to Tripp, I knew better and told Gebhard, my tone humble, that "I'd be immensely grateful" if he would have another look. He gruffly agreed: "I'll have a look." While Gebhard was purportedly "searching," I was confined for three days to the Institute's Vertical File of already catalogued and entirely "safe" material. In the end, he did let me see one, and only one, collection from the uncatalogued material, even as he reiterated his claim that the Institute possessed little else of historical interest.

I subsequently learned that furious, behind-the-scenes phone calls and letters were being exchanged, with Tripp strenuously berating Gebhard for denying "a reputable scholar" access to material that deserved wide circulation, calling Gebhard an "insufferable prig." Tripp was, in fact, rather fond of Gebhard, even though he found him hopelessly limited, and the two would stay in touch long after Gebhard left the Institute in 1982. But Tripp did deplore what he called Gebhard's "weakness and lack of leadership." He insisted yet again that Kapff had "not the slightest fear of his materials (or his identity) being revealed when in scholarly hands." Nor, Tripp added, could he "possibly have been so coy as to refer to a 'foreign traveler' [Gebhard's suggested pseudonym for Kapff] in an informal conversation with scholar/friend Duberman. To have done so would have constituted a major break in rapport with him, and an unforgivable imperiousness on my part." Besides, he added, "why in the world would the Institute be so cagey as not to mention a word of such material to Duberman, a scholar working in the field?"

Then came the coup de grace: "After all, you could close up shop and simply paint 'No' on the door; it seems to me that a main purpose of keeping the doors open is to find ways to say 'Yes' to people." To that provocation, Gebhard made no response.

Instead, he took out his displeasure on me, telling me sharply that I would be allowed to make no more than three photocopies from the catalogued Vertical File collection. If I wanted additional material, he announced, I would have to take notes by hand. I protested the policy as arbitrary and unreasonable: since he was willing for me to take notes on the material, I argued, why not let me do so in an expeditious way, through photocopying? Gebhard remained adamant. I later wrote angrily in my diary: "Kinsey's unorthodox, unquenchable search for understanding is gone."

When I got back to New York, Tripp, with pixyish delight, presented me with a complete set of photocopies that he'd made earlier of the Kinsey-Kapff correspondence, as well as a set of the cassettes exchanged between Kapff and Tripp after Kinsey's death in 1956. I, in turn, had one last story to tell Tripp: On my first day at the Institute, one of the staff had handed me a manuscript letter. "Look what we just found," she laughed. I was holding the original of Freud's famous letter to "the mother of a homosexual son"! "Someone," the staff member said, had just come upon it in the Vertical File, where it had apparently been sitting for years.

Tripp was horrified that the Institute didn't even know the provenance of the Freud letter, though Tripp himself remembered it clearly: when Kinsey published his first volume in 1948, he received a letter from a woman who congratulated him on his handling of the homosexual issue and enclosed the letter Freud had written to her on the subject years earlier. She wanted Kinsey to have it, she wrote, because he seemed the "natural inheritor" of Freud's questing spirit. Kinsey had subsequently seen to it that the Freud letter was published.

TRIPP AND I gradually lost touch. Aside from both of us being Kinseyites, we had little in common. I admired him a good deal, and mostly believed him, yet I also found him formidable and unyielding, and rarely felt at ease in his company (my problem, probably). I also sensed that discipleship was a central ingredient of lasting friendship for him, something from which I've always steered clear. I suspect Tripp found me too scattered in my commitments, and especially misguided in bothering at all with politics. He didn't seem to have any, and in regard to the gay movement, he once told a correspondent that he had "little sympathy for that brand of pleading."

We joined forces one last time when James H. Jones published his scurrilous biography of Kinsey some twenty-five years ago. I myself roasted the book in a November 1997 review in *The Nation* [which is reprinted below], while Tripp vented his contempt on his computer but seems never to have published his rebuttal. Yet it deserves to be known, since it amounts to more than a defense of Kinsey: it succinctly reveals the qualities that Tripp admired in another human being—thereby telling us much about himself.

For one, he dismissed Jones' diatribe as the priggish misreading of a man (Kinsey) who proved a capacious defender of "the sexually despised"—a man "often light and lovely, with a boyish playfulness." Kinsey had, Tripp wrote, "the most 'cleaned up' mind I ever saw." Widely liked and respected, he projected "an image of happiness, self-confidence and inner peace"—a far cry from Jones' portrait of an obsessively negative, small-minded, and mean-spirited man. Unlike the narrowly moralistic Jones, Kinsey, in Tripp's view, was neither fearful nor ashamed about sex and "felt not a fragment of guilt or conflict" about exploring it as both a scientist and a human being. He had nothing but scorn for those religious pieties that over time had resulted in sexual constriction and dysfunction.

"What was really revolutionary about Kinsey," Tripp wrote, "was his joy over sex, a readiness to celebrate it in any harmless form, and to lament it when absent." Fortunately, Kinsey's two path-breaking books on male and female sexuality appeared just before the onset of the Cold War and McCarthyism, which killed off "a certain spirit of freedom throughout the land." That spirit would return in the '60s, and then again in our own day, though Kinsey is rarely recognized as its progenitor.

PART III
In Defense of Kinsey

Duberman review of James H. Jones' Alfred C. Kinsey *in* The Nation, *1997*

BEWARE THE FACTS; they can lead you away from the truth. James H. Jones has unearthed an enormous amount of new information in his biography, *Alfred C. Kinsey.* Let no one underestimate the achievement. But let no one confuse it with an understanding of Kinsey's life and work. Diligence is the beginning of scholarship, not the end point. Through research, scholars discover what material exists. Then they must decide what it means. Jones gets high marks for industry, low ones for insight.

The most myopic moment comes near the beginning of his book and is repeated throughout: Alfred C. Kinsey was "a homosexual." Oh, really? By what definition? Jones presents evidence—full, incontrovertible, and previously known only to a small circle of insiders—that Kinsey often had sex and occasionally fell in love with other men. Yet Jones also tells us that Kinsey was lovingly married for some 45 years to Clara McMillan, and that their relationship was in no sense perfunctory, certainly not sexually. A decade into their marriage, Alfred and Clara were "eagerly" exploring various coital positions newly recommended by a friend, and they maintained a sexual relationship until Kinsey became ill near the end of his life. With Clara's knowledge, Kinsey also slept with other women during their marriage—as did Clara with other men.

Isn't it obvious that if Kinsey must be labeled, then "bisexual" is more appropriate than "homosexual"? For some unfathomable reason, Jones has chosen to ignore Kinsey's own famous 0-6 scale (0 = exclusive heterosexuality; 6 = exclusive homosexuality). By using that scale, the simplistic category "a homosexual" would be reserved for individuals whose sexual behavior was confined exclusively to their own gender. Or if not their behavior, then their fantasy life. Perhaps Jones meant to argue that Kinsey self-identified as a homosexual on the basis of his erotic fantasies, discarding as irrelevant his ability (and desire) to perform bisexually. If that's what Jones means, he's forgotten to provide the evidence or make the argument.

Insiders at the Kinsey Institute place Kinsey between a "1" and a "2"—more "straight" than "gay"—when younger, then shifting increasingly to the "gay" side of the scale as he aged, but never becoming an exclusive "6." In other words, whether the yardstick be behavior, fantasy, or self-definition, Kinsey considered his sexuality malleable (and long before Queer Theory reified "fluidity" as the signifier of sexual, indeed personal, authenticity).

Astonishingly, Jones doesn't get it. He not only persists throughout in referring to Kinsey as "a homosexual" but he tries to force Alfred and Clara's relationship into the canned mold of "homosexual man seeks cover in a heterosexual marriage." Along with vitiating all that was special and brave about the couple, Jones can't even manage a complicated version of the gay man/straight woman arrangement, presenting instead a tired stereotype of lost souls (which he bases on a few outdated articles from 20 to 25 years ago that he nervily refers to as "recent studies").

The other slot Jones drops Kinsey into is "masochist." It is one of many terms—"voyeurism," "exhibitionism," "prurience," "pathology," "perversion"—Jones slings around, never pausing for close definition. Judging from his footnotes, Jones's guiding experts on "masochism" have been

Havelock Ellis, Richard von Krafft-Ebing, and Theodore Reik, now partly or wholly superseded by recent scholarship. None of the vast literature on sadomasochism that has accumulated over the past two decades is cited, let alone argued with or theorized.

Still, *Alfred C. Kinsey* does contain a considerable amount of new information. Thanks to Jones' prodigious labors, we are now privy to aspects of Kinsey's sexual life previously known only to his family and a close circle of associates and co-experimenters. Kinsey, it seems, found that tugging on his testicles provided pleasurable/painful sensations; later in life, the stimulus had to be increased to maintain the desired effect and he took to tugging on them with a length of rope. Kinsey also discovered that the urethra was, for him, an erogenous zone, and over time he teased and plied it with various instruments, culminating in the use of a toothbrush. Later in life, he was also drawn to watching various S/M performances, but he preferred looking to participating.

These were occasional practices, not exclusive, narrowly focused fetishes. Kinsey utilized many other, more conventional outlets for sexual pleasure. How we evaluate his more "extreme" (unconventional) practices will very much depend on our own sexual histories and our willingness to explore our own fantasies. In the process, we would do well to remain modest about our inevitable subjectivity and our limited imaginations.

James Jones is limited, but not modest. He is very sure what Kinsey's behavior means, and is very quick to characterize and denigrate it—usually with heavy-handed psychologizing. Kinsey's "inner demons" are given vast explanatory powers; catch-all references to his "confusion," "anger" and "guilt" are made to substitute for any sustained, persuasive analysis of the inner man. A few samples: "By late adolescence, if not before, Kinsey's behavior was clearly pathological, satisfying every criterion of sexual perversion" (the "criterion" are not provided); he was "an exhibitionist extraordinaire"; an "aloof loner"; headstrong, stubborn, highly opinionated, gruff and arrogant; a man of "iron will" whom few liked; an unpopular teacher (who somehow attracted droves of students), a thin-skinned, manipulative elitist; a self styled martyr and would-be messiah.

This kind of crude psychologizing (which is really moralizing) is far too formulaic to inspire confidence. Indeed, several of Kinsey's surviving colleagues guffaw at such a reductive view of the complicated man Kinsey was. "It's nonsense," says C. A. Tripp (author of *The Homosexual Matrix*, and, in my view, the most rigorous and fearless disciple of Kinsey's sexual iconoclasm). "All that guilt and anger Jones keeps talking about—well, you could say that about anybody. Kinsey can't even get interested in gardening without Jones ascribing it to 'deep tensions' or explaining his scanty clothing while working the soil as a need to 'shock' people. And how naughty of Kinsey to stand nude in his own bathroom as he shaved!"

Where another biographer might, with justice, have emphasized Kinsey's remarkable capacity for open-minded exploration, Jones persists in negatively labeling nonconventional sexual behavior as "skating on the edge," or "compulsive" and "addictive" risk-taking. He can manage to credit the homophobic sexologist Richard von Krafft-Ebing as having been prompted "by deeply moral concerns," but bisexual Kinsey is merely "sex-obsessed." This is like calling Albert Einstein "physics-obsessed." And it leaves us wondering what to think about James Jones, who has devoted 27 years to researching Alfred Kinsey's "perverted" life.

Where all this becomes serious is when Jones uses his defamatory portrait of Kinsey, the man, to discredit his work as a sexologist. He does so through a morally slippery ploy: he generously quotes from Kinsey's antagonists (often mistaken), letting them do Jones's talking for him. Now and then, however, Jones's own indignant voice breaks through: "Despite his claim of coolly being disinterested," Jones hisses, "Kinsey was nothing of the sort ... enthusiasm for sex was a fundamental tenet of Kinsey's thought, and it rang out loud and clear in his writing." Enthusiasm for sex? For shame!

Elsewhere, Jones refers to Kinsey's "facade of objectivity"—as if value-free social science has ever existed, or been more than approximated as an ideal. Of *course* Kinsey's "personal needs and motivations" influenced his findings; this is primer stuff in social science. Besides, subjectivity cuts both ways: what it often means is that the sensitized investigator is able to see and reveal much that had previously been closed off to less personally engaged scholars.

The bottom-line question is whether Kinsey's personality, and personal engagement with his material, led to serious distortions in his findings. The two most common accusations against his *Sexual Behavior in the Human Male* (1948) and *Sexual Behavior in the Human Female* (1953) relate to the statistical methodology he employed in arriving at his conclusions, and especially at the finding that 37% of the adult male population has had at least one homosexual experience to orgasm, and that 4% of the male population is exclusively homosexual (or 6 on his scale *for three years* between ages sixteen and 55).

Jones repeats most of the longstanding critiques of Kinsey: "for all his posturing and bluster, Kinsey was chronically unsure of himself as a statistician ... his sample was far from random," etc. But we are not told that Paul Gebhard (one of Kinsey's co-authors and his successor as director of the Institute for Sex Research), himself reacting to criticism leveled against the two volumes, spent years "cleaning" the Kinsey data of their purported contaminants—removing, for example, all material derived from prison populations.

In 1979, Gebhard, along with Alan Johnson, published *The Kinsey Data*, and—to his own surprise—found that Kinsey's original estimates held: instead of Kinsey's 37%, Gebhard and Johnson came up with 36.3%; the 10% figure (with prison inmates excluded) came to 9.9% for white college-educated males and 12.7% for those with less education. And as for the call for a "random sample," a team of statisticians studying Kinsey's procedures concluded as far back as 1953 that the unique problems inherent in sex research precluded the possibility of obtaining a true random sample, and that Kinsey's interviewing technique had been "extraordinarily skillful." They characterized Kinsey's work overall as "a monumental endeavor."

In his shrewd way, Jones sprinkles his text with periodic praise for Kinsey the master researcher, the brilliant interviewer, the daring pioneer, the debunker of conventional morality. No heavy-handed conservative frontal assault for Jones. We learn that Kinsey was an active, loving parent (perhaps that's why we hear so little about his four children), a concerned mentor who stayed in touch with many of his students for years, a man of childlike wonder and one capable of great warmth, gentleness, and generosity. How does this Kinsey fit together with the near-monstrous one Jones more frequently portrays? It doesn't. Jones never manages a coherent portrait (and personality contradictions *can* intelligibly cohere); the pejorative assertions that dominate the book simply overwhelm occasional references to Kinsey's positive qualities.

Why this insistent pathologizing of Kinsey the man and, by implication, the devaluing of his work? The moral values that have guided Jones's choice of emphasis come into sharpest focus in the contrasting way he treats two of Kinsey's closest associates, Paul Gebhard and Wardell Pomeroy. Gebhard, who gave Jones four interviews and whose testimony is crucially enlisted against Kinsey at various points, appears to have been the only male staff member unwilling or unable to sleep with men; he is pronounced "a free spirit," "a very likable man" with "a terrific sense of humor." Wardell Pomeroy, who distrusted Jones and refused to see him (now, with Alzheimer's, he is unable to defend himself), loved all kinds of sex with all kinds of people; he is dismissed as a "sexual athlete or superstud ... a randy boy in a man's body," with "a character of little substance."

Get it? The exclusively heterosexual Gebhard wins the kudos (Jones even dares to claim that among his associates "Kinsey probably respected Gebhard the most professionally"). Pomeroy, a man *by other accounts* of great charm, intelligence, and warmth, is dismissed as a vain creature "whose taste in partners could be described only as broad, if not indiscriminate." "He fucks just everybody and it's really disgusting," says one of Jones's informants—who clearly speaks for Jones.

James Jones has not understood, or does not approve, Kinsey's foundational message: erotic desire is anarchic and will necessarily break free of and engulf all simplistic efforts (like Jones's) to categorize, and thus confine it. Kinsey's work will survive this book. ∎

CHAPTER VI

Lincoln Kirstein

PART I
FRIENDS AND LOVERS

I THOUGHT *I was done with Lincoln Kirstein. In 2007, when Knopf published my biography,* The Worlds of Lincoln Kirstein, *I felt confident that I'd tracked down just about every extant bit of evidence on the man. That included not only his own massive archive in the New York Public Library, but those of his friends and colleagues; I'd also interviewed dozens of those who knew him best. But then I got my comeuppance. A large collection of family correspondence came on the market that had previously been held in private hands.*

I first learned about the new material when its owner, who I didn't know, called me out of the blue to ask if I'd do him the "great favor of having a look" at the material, and advising him whether or not it was "significant." I ran not walked to his apartment. After several hours looking through the material, I told him that in my view the letters were of considerable historical value—and he expressed delight and gratitude. The gratitude, alas, proved fleeting. I hadn't asked for any fee for my expert services but did say, as a sort of quid pro quo, *that I'd very much appreciate the chance to study the collection further—and even, conceivably, to buy it myself, if my limited means would allow. He said he would "think it over" and would call me. During the many months that followed he did exactly the opposite: he used every ruse imaginable to prevent me from even seeing the collection again—out of fear, apparently, that my further familiarity with the material might diminish its value. It became clear that he aimed for a sale to an archival library with deep pockets. I didn't qualify.*

Not one to give up, I finally traced him to his lair; he turned out to be the owner of a small photography gallery. Horrified at the sight of me, he was curt and tightlipped—though through other sources I learned that the prestigious and wealthy Houghton Library at Harvard (where over the years I'd often done research) had bought the collection. Short of owning the Kirstein correspondence myself, that was for me the best possible outcome: Houghton generously allowed me to cart off many hundreds of pages of photocopies.

At roughly the same time, I was astonished to learn that yet another privately held Kirstein hoard had surfaced—and been immediately commandeered by the wealthy Ransom Center at the University of Texas. This second storehouse proved just as rich and rewarding as the collection the Houghton Library had acquired—and its keepers no less generous in allowing me unrestricted access. The Ransom collection consisted of the extended and revealing correspondence between Kirstein and his close friend, the painter Pavel Tchelitchev. Both Kirstein and Tchelitchev were difficult, complicated men, and their friendship was periodically strained. Yet their bond held, and Kirstein's letters to "Pavlik" turned out to be more revealingly personal than any others I'd seen—full of acerbic wit and shrewd insight into the doings of the international set of gay artists that included, among others, W. H. Auden, Christopher Isherwood, Stephen Spender, Philip Johnson, Glenway Wescott, E. M. Forster, Osbert Sitwell, George Platt Lynes, Romaine Brooks, Virgil Thomson, and the painters George Tooker, Jared French, and Paul Cadmus. The Kirstein-Tchelitchev correspondence was also unusually candid, and sometimes astonishingly acid about George Balanchine and the struggles of the New York City Ballet, which Balanchine and Kirstein had cofounded.

What to do with this second treasure trove of material? My initial impulse was to publish a revised version of my Kirstein biography, but I quickly realized that expanding a book already 723 pages long would be prohibitively expensive, given the likelihood of limited sales—especially since the new material, lavish though it was, didn't fundamentally change the portrait of Kirstein that I offered in my 2007 biography.

As the next best option to a second edition of the biography, I decided to condense the new material into several extended articles. The Gay & Lesbian Review *seemed the best possible venue, since (I'm guessing) it has an educated readership already familiar with many of the figures who appear in the correspondence and would likely prove appreciative of Kirstein's candid-camera takes on their personalities and accomplishments. The material falls rather naturally into three parts, which are presented here under the headings "Friends and Lovers," "Balanchine Comes to the U.S.," and "Rivals and Idols."*

Lincoln Kirstein was born in 1907 to a newly prosperous Jewish couple—his father Louis had risen to a top executive post in Filene's, the famed department store. As a young man, Kirstein was precocity personified. At age seventeen—as one of the new letters reveals—he wrote a friend that he was "very low—particularly because I get no time to go to the museum and when I do I get interested in brilliant conversation and never work; I haven't done a decent drawing in years. ... I've just about come to the conclusion that you must have the whole cake or none." Soon thereafter, as an undergraduate at Harvard, he founded not only an avant-garde gallery, the Harvard Society for Contemporary Art—a precursor and model for New York City's Museum of Modem Art—but also the *Hound and Horn* literary journal, which became an outstanding outlet for contemporary writing.

By the time he turned twenty, Kirstein had also become (in his words) "deeply addicted" to the ballet. As a child, he'd watched Anna Pavlova dance, and on family trips to Europe while still a teenager, he'd continued to see a number of prominent ballet companies perform. (Some time later, he even took classes in New York with Michel Fokine, one of ballet's most celebrated pioneers; Fokine did not encourage Lincoln's dancing: "too big, too awkward, too old" was the gist of his message.)

Arriving in London on his first solo trip to Europe in 1927, Kirstein's ex-boyfriend, Howard Doughty (later the author of a distinguished biography of the historian Francis Parkman) met his ship dockside in Southampton. Together, they hit the ground running, all but bursting with excitement and energy. They made "intoxicating" visits to the National Gallery and the Tate, where, in between his adoration of Veronese and El Greco, Kirstein pointed out to Howard which lads wandering around the gallery he "would or would not like to go to bed with." He wrote home to Mina, his older sister and confidant, that "the people are perfectly charming and there is a great deal of male pulchritude, especially in young pups."

By this point, Kirstein had seen most of the repertoire of the Serge Diaghilev company—then the reigning sensation—including George Balanchine dancing the role of the wizard Kastchei in *Firebird* (as well as two pas de deux the young choreographer had done for another company). Nothing else moved him, Kirstein firmly decided, as much as ballet. However, through his whole life he would retain a passionate interest and involvement in the fine arts, and would be highly regarded as a critic and connoisseur, an adviser to MoMA, and a champion (and financial supporter) of artists as diverse as Elie Nadelman and George Tooker.

But his passion for the ballet took precedence early on. Over the next few years, he kept returning to Europe, seeing every company, every leading dancer and choreographer, multiple times. (He became so knowledgeable that in 1935, while still in his twenties, he published *Dance: A Short History of Classic Theatrical Dancing.*) Though Lincoln saw much to admire, no one in his view compared to George Balanchine—to his "energy and invention prodigious." With the death of Diaghilev in 1929 and the collapse of the Ballets Russes, Kirstein began to harbor the dream—against all odds—of himself creating a company, one that would be devoted above all else to Balanchine's choreography.

Yet it wasn't until 1933 that Kirstein and Balanchine actually met.

The path had been tangled: as a result of helping Romola Nijinsky finish her biography of her husband Vaslav, Kirstein gradually met a number of people close to Balanchine, including the designer "Bébe" Bérard, Bébe's companion, the director Boris Kochno, and the captious painter Pavel ("Pavlik") Tchelitchev, who'd done decor and costumes for Balanchine's current company Les Ballets 1933. Gradually, Kirstein was invited to sit in on rehearsals—during which Bébe plied him with "coarse" remarks, Kochno was "disdainful," and Tchelitchev took credit for the libretto to Errante, Balanchine's most recent work.

Les Ballets 1933 had been made possible by the generosity of the wealthy English socialite Edward James. The bisexual, deeply eccentric James, an extraordinary character unto himself, deserves at least a brief sidebar (he also deserves a biography). Kirstein initially patronized James as a mere dilettante who happened to have inherited great wealth from his father's huge railroad holdings, but—as the two new collections of letters make clear—he soon changed his mind. James invited Kirstein to his legendary Sussex estate, West Dean Park, where he found the walls covered with fine early Dalís and Magrittes, as well as other avant-garde art. James, a pioneering and consistent supporter of surrealism, was himself a poet—Tchelitchev illustrated one volume of his verse—and the author as well of the novel *The Gardener Who Saw God* (1937). Kirstein was so impressed with the mansion and its beautifully kept grounds—a titanic 6300 acres—that he talked at length with James about the importance of turning his home into a national trust—which James eventually did in 1964, in the process creating a notable refuge for artists and craftsmen.

Kirstein's relationship with James remained peripheral, unlike his immediate and lasting friendship with Tchelitchev. Thanks to the two new manuscript collections, that friendship, in all its ups and downs, emerges in rich detail. In their intensity, hyperactivity, and theatrical ardor, Kirstein and Pavlik had comparable temperaments, and Kirstein was especially drawn to Pavlik's mesmerizing conversation—he described one journalist as "a marinated white louse," a fashionable lady's mouth as "the entrance to the Holland Tunnel," a rival's eyes as reminding him of "two poached eggs in a urinal." Counterbalancing Pavlik's entrenched malice was his brilliance, his originality, and his willingness to pronounce himself a "monster"—"impossible" and "obsessed." Kirstein would become convinced of Tchelitchev's extraordinary gifts as a painter, and in the years ahead, as Pavlik's once-bright reputation continued to fade, he would remain a staunch advocate. Like all intense relationships, the two men would have some bruising quarrels; the longest ones had to do with Pavlik's profound narcissism—nobody was ever sufficiently appreciative of his genius—but also involved Kirstein's extreme distaste for Charles Henri Ford, Tchelitchev's devoted partner (and co-author of *The Young and the Evil,* one of the earliest gay-themed novels); yet the Kirstein/ Tchelitchev bond nonetheless held firm.

Though Kirstein had been gradually meeting many of the artists centrally connected to Balanchine, he had still not met Balanchine himself. The first occasion was quite accidental. After watching a performance of Balanchine's 1932 ballet *La Concurrence,* Kirstein and some friends went back for drinks to Kirk and Constance Askew's place (he ran the New York branch of the Durlacher Gallery, and the couple's home in Manhattan would become a fashionable salon). One evening, the young choreographer Frederick Ashton, with Balanchine in tow, arrived at the Askews, when Kirstein was also a guest. It was a small gathering and Kirstein was able to talk alone with him for some time. Though Balanchine was a man of deep reserve and few words, Kirstein found him "wholly charming," though he worried that Balanchine "aspired through his teeth as if he really had T. B." (In fact, he did, and a round of illness and alarums would soon follow.) Balanchine even confided to Kirstein—perhaps testing the extent of his rapt devotion—that he hoped someday to come to the United States, that "with 20 girls & 5 men he could do wonders. Americans have great potential."

That was interest enough for Kirstein. He went instantly into overdrive—which could be a fearsome sight—determined somehow to bring Balanchine to America and to start a new company for him. A mere three days later, the two men had lunch alone. This time, they talked in considerably more detail about the prospects of Balanchine coming to America, and (as Kirstein wrote in his diary): "We got frightfully excited about it all. I visualized it so clearly. He wants so much to come ... says it has always been his dream. He would give up everything to come."

Determined as Lincoln was to bring Balanchine to the States, the path was full of obstacles. To appreciate them, we need to begin with the story of Lincoln's sister Mina, ten years his senior. In the early 1920s, when Lincoln was a teenager, Mina was on leave from her teaching post at Smith College and sharing a small, 18th-century house in London with an ex-student, Henrietta Bingham, daughter of Robert Worth Bingham, owner of *The Louisville Courier-Journal* and future ambassador to the Court of St. James. Henrietta had been in one of Mina's first classes at Smith, and the two women, only a few years apart in age, had fallen in love and decided to travel together in Europe.

Mina didn't think of herself as "lesbian," but she was not apologetic about her relationship with Henrietta, describing it as "an extremely beautiful and honest one." However, unlike Henrietta, Mina's primary attachments for most of her life would be with men. That said, her affair with the tall, strikingly attractive, and charismatic Henrietta was more than a brief fling. For years after their relationship ended, their lives remained intertwined, and the protective Mina would for decades faithfully answer the call to extricate the fragile, unstable Henrietta from assorted plights.

One day in 1922, when still living with Henrietta in London, Mina stopped to browse in a bookshop near the British Museum. The owner, a tall, blond, blue-eyed 29-year-old named David Garnett, started to chat her up—yes, that David Garnett, a prominent member of the unorthodox Bloomsbury set, which also included Virginia Woolf, Vanessa Bell, the iconoclastic homosexual historian Lytton Strachey, and a host of other now legendary people. Before long, Garnett invited Mina—and Henrietta—to tea, and in the weeks that followed, all three became friends. The two young, attractive women were soon introduced to other members of the Bloomsbury circle, including Strachey, Dora Carrington—who was immediately smitten with Henrietta—and Dora's somewhat reserved (for Bloomsbury) husband Ralph Partridge.

Garnett later claimed that he'd fallen for Mina that very first day in the bookstore. Yet their relationship never became sexual, due entirely to Mina's misgivings (she blamed her own "strong if often inactive sense of Puritan morality"). She and Garnett would remain deeply companionable friends for decades, while Garnett would never be at a loss for sexual partners (including Henrietta Bingham—to Mina's annoyance). In 1922, he was already a husband and a father, and throughout his adult life took male as well as female lovers. One of his more extended affairs was with the painter Duncan Grant, the two sharing a house with Virginia Woolf's sister, Vanessa Bell, who gave birth to Grant's child, Angelica. Bloomsbury was, as we now say, "sexually fluid." (Years later, in a triple somersault, Garnett would marry Angelica.)

Mina and Lincoln (at this point still a teenage schoolboy) shared details of at least some of their sexual adventures. In one of the recently acquired letters at Houghton Library, Lincoln reports that his father had gotten a massage from "the most handsome Swede I ever saw. I would have loved to but feared the results." He also conveyed the news that he and his close friend Howard Dougherty were having sex, and that Howard had expressed astonishment at how easily Lincoln got an erection. "How one's ex-boyfriends do pile up," the fifteen-year-old Lincoln nonchalantly added.

In 1924, Lincoln again spent his summer in Europe, and Mina introduced him to some of the Bloomsbury crowd. The contacts, though, were mostly superficial—he barely glimpsed E. M. Forster at some gathering (though a decade later, the two would become friends). The only Bloomsburyite Lincoln got to know reasonably well that summer was the economist John Maynard Keynes who, despite his many sexual encounters with men, would soon marry the Diaghilev ballerina Lydia Lopokova. Keynes took Lincoln to Gauguin and Cézanne exhibitions, and when Lincoln expressed reservations about Cézanne, Keynes urged him to "keep your eyes open, clean of received opinion and prejudice." It was advice that Lincoln took to heart. He would later write that Keynes had "launched a radical reformation in my naïve judgment."

TWO YEARS LATER, Lincoln became a freshman at Harvard, where he proceeded to ignore most of his classes and to spend his time founding, remarkably, both an avant-garde art gallery (the precursor and model for the Museum of Modern Art) and a pioneering literary journal, *Hound and Horn*. Even as a young man, Lincoln's finely tuned antennae were quick to filter out artistic mediocrity and to encourage promising new voices. Like nearly everyone else, however, he now and then proved surprisingly tone deaf. While a modernist in sensibility, Kirstein was and would remain a moderate modernist: he published Ezra Pound in *Hound and Horn* but not James Joyce. In the realm of painting, he would always favor representational art over cubism and abstract expressionism, sometimes promoting the work of lesser figures—William Rimmer, Alex Colville, Honoré Sharrer—while dismissing someone like Fernand Léger as "stiff as static machinery, the stenciled formula of a genial mechanic."

Years later, in the 1950s, when abstract expressionism ruled the art world and Kirstein's close friend, the painter "Pavlik" Tchelitchev, accused him of a blanket distaste for it, Lincoln fired back a firm denial (the newly recovered letter is in the Ransom Center): "I no not hate abstract art, as you insist; I recognize the abstract purity of Mondrian, and of certain classic Cubist Picassos. ... But [Jackson] Pollack and [Theodoros] Stamos and [William] Baziotes and all the rest of them who think they are abstract are actually only accidental. ... They think by twirling the handle they can unlock the safe; they think the sounds of any struck chord have their own significance; and it may be true there is an order in accident, but it is an inferior order."

In the 1930s, Lincoln began to make occasional trips to New York City, where before long he met the then famous free spirit Muriel Draper, twenty years his senior, whose coach house on East 40th Street was a mecca for "high bohemia." In one of the letters to Mina, Kirstein, barely out of his teens, described his initial impression of Draper, opting for a blasé, debonair pose: "She had [with her] one of the nastiest little homosexual boys I ever saw. … I acted pretty well the innocent Harvard freshman all health and tanned. … The talk was clever, depressing, and crazy—honey, she is so cuckoo. … She was dressed all in white—with a mauve lipstick. … I could quite see she has a good heart and beneath the galvanization of her nerves … she is quite sweet, kind, and fine."

During subsequent trips to New York, Kirstein got to know Muriel better—much better—and to appreciate her a great deal more. Before long, they began what would be a decade-long intermittently sexual affair, which, by the time Kirstein moved to New York in 1930, greatly intensified. By then, Kirstein had come to appreciate—to marvel at—just how special Muriel actually was: she "has all barriers down all the time" and is "quite without conventional restraints." Throughout the '30s, Kirstein would see more of Muriel than anyone else; he called her his "dominant companion and influence," and through her gained entrée into much of New York's smart set.

Later, their relationship would become attenuated, as Muriel became increasingly absorbed in pro-Soviet activities and as Kirstein's devotion to the dance and art worlds absorbed most of his energy. Like so many others on the Left—though not Muriel—Kirstein's once pronounced leftwing views morphed into a kind of vague liberalism, and politics itself no longer held much interest for him. Still, he and Muriel never lost track of each other entirely. In 1947, on one of her many trips back and forth to Moscow, she seemed to him "old and tired"; he thought it possible that "she will one day drop dead of exhaustion, but I guess that is the way she wants it." Still, in 1949, again on her way back from Moscow, Kirstein found here "as enthusiastic as ever … still marvelous, like the best of the old days. She goes to China and Mexico; how she manages, I'll never know; except that no one seems to care." By that time the Cold War had set in, and the House Un-American Activities Committee soon proved that *it* cared, denouncing Muriel for "Communist-front" activities. When she died of a paralytic stroke in 1952, Kirstein wrote that "part of my life [is] gone. ... She stays with me much of the time; she educated me and focused me and I am forever grateful."

DURING MOST of the 1930s, Lincoln had shared Muriel's political views, and, when in London in 1933, he became so agitated about the rise of the Nazis that he attended a Fascist meeting, the better to gauge their sentiments and influence. He came away railing at what he called "the Fascist face—mean, self-assured ... and intensely mediocre: it is something to spit at." He deplored the fact that Viscount Rothermere, proprietor of the popular *Daily Mail*, was engaged in a "frenzy of rapprochement with Hitler." (In 1939, Rothermere sent congratulations to Hitler on the annexation of Czechoslovakia and his "great and superhuman" work.) There were too many Rothermeres in England for Kirstein's taste—or peace of mind (he was, after all, Jewish)—though he counted on the country's essential soundness.

On that same 1939 trip to England, Lincoln looked up Henrietta Bingham, currently busy at the American Embassy, where her father had recently become Ambassador to England. "Her charm," Lincoln reported to Mina, "now fits all around like a glove—but what is inside I'd rather not think of." He further reported that Henrietta's new girlfriend was the actress Hope Williams (she starred opposite Jimmy Durante in the 1930 Cole Porter revue *The New Yorkers*), though he'd been told that Tallulah Bankhead was courting Henrietta as well. Lincoln also spent time with Mina's old friend (and would-be lover) David Garnett, who took him to several gatherings of the Bloomsbury clan, including a party at Roger Fry's, the esteemed art critic. The sibling Sitwells, Osbert and Edith, were there, as was Virginia Woolf (whom Kirstein initially managed to mistake for her sister Vanessa Bell), looking—he wrote to Mina—"very gaunt in a lace cap, and frightening." At another Bloomsbury gathering, a picnic with Duncan Grant and the Woolfs, Virginia's husband Leonard told Kirstein that "he is completely mystified as to F.D.R.'s policy; he feels he has no interest whatever in Europe—which is what everyone here thinks."

It was on this same trip that Lincoln met the non-Bloomsburyite writers Stephen Spender and E. M. Forster, the former through *Hound and Horn* connections, the latter through William Plomer, a young novelist whose 1926 *Turbott Wolfe*, a denunciation of South Africa's brutal racial policies, had caused a sensation. Spender brought along Tony Hyndman, his lover at the time, and Kirstein (as he wrote in his diary) fell "acutely in love" with their relationship, with "their life together." He took immediately to Hyndman ("simple, frank, yet cunning ... and entirely male"), somewhat less to Spender. He thought the latter "slightly wet behind the ears," and with a "spiteful" side—as when he characterized his friend Christopher Isherwood as "a small man whose jealousy and intrigues rise from his height." When Kirstein later met Isherwood—whom he subsequently referred to as "Issyvoo"—it was in Los Angeles, where Isherwood was working for Goldwyn and (according to one of Kirstein's newly released letters to Mina) "wildly unhappy," drinking too much, and worrying aloud about whether he should return to England (where he and Auden had been widely denounced for abandoning the Motherland in her time of need). Kirstein accurately predicted that Isherwood would not return.

PART II
Balanchine Comes to the U.S.

BY 1933, Lincoln Kirstein's long-simmering search for a way to establish a classical ballet company in the United States picked up steam and intensity. His interest in the ballet had initially quickened on his various trips as a teenager to Europe, where in 1929 he'd seen Diaghilev's Ballets Russes. That same year, with Diaghilev's death, the ballet world had become rent by factions. A number of émigré artists had been trying to lay claim to his mantle, and to find venues, patrons, and, they hoped, companies that might make their existence less precarious.

George Balanchine, who'd been Diaghilev's last important choreographer, succeeded in putting together a group called Les Ballets 1933, a young company of some fifteen dancers, including Toumanova, Derain, and Roman Jasinski. None of this would have come to pass had it not been for the events of a decade earlier, when Vladimir Dimitriev, a former baritone in the Marinsky opera company, successfully engineered exit visas from the Soviet Union for a small group of artists, the so-called Soviet State Dancers. Among them were Balanchine, Tamara Geva, his first wife, and the ballerina Alexandra Danilova, who would become his "unofficial" second wife.

Lincoln went up to Hartford to confer with his friend Chick Austin, the youthful head of the prestigious Wadsworth Athenaeum, who showed him the half-completed new International Style addition to the museum; Lincoln noted in his diary that "his little auditorium is perfect for small ballets." Chick, like Lincoln, was a serious advocate of the arts and an audacious innovator. As director of the Wadsworth Athenaeum, he'd transformed Hartford's reputation as the stodgy headquarters of the insurance business into an important center of cultural ferment. Lincoln knew that, although Chick was married, his erotic preference was homosexual, and he hinted to Lincoln, who also preferred men, about having recently indulged in "some highly irregular pleasures," saying that he'd tell him more some other time.

Most people saw Chick Austin as a charming, engaging, outgoing man, but Lincoln had a far different take on him. He intuited "glimpses of acute hysteria, like lightning in his conversation; a person of many splits whose energy could collapse at almost any moment, I think, if he was either confined or pressed. Really vicious: that is, unimaginative, morally repetitious & lazy." Lincoln's chief interest in Chick Austin was to get him involved in some way, somehow, with his ballet plans. Lincoln suggested that the Athenaeum host a "Ballet Demonstration," which he thought he could arrange for the following year. It was an idea Chick apparently "warmed up to." Lincoln said he'd provide more details soon.

WHEN IN EUROPE during the summer of 1933, Lincoln—26 years old at the time—met with Balanchine, and the two had "a long and satisfactory talk" in French. Lincoln found him "wholly charming." A few days later, they had lunch, Balanchine arriving nattily dressed in a gray flannel suit, "his strong, delicate Caucasian face very animated" (as Lincoln wrote in his diary). They talked in some detail about the possibility of an American ballet, with Lincoln briefly mentioning Chick Austin's Museum at Hartford as a possible site.

Lincoln then got "frightfully worked up" and, able to "think of nothing else," sat down and wrote his now-famous sixteen-page letter to Chick. It began with a grand theatrical flourish: "This will be the most important letter I will ever write you ... my pen burns my hand as I write: words will not flow into the ink fast enough. We have a real chance to have an American ballet within 3 years time. When I say ballet, I mean a trained company of young dancers—not Russians—but Americans with Russian stars to start with." Years later, Lincoln claimed that he'd deliberately chosen "an optimistic style" in writing to Chick. But "calculated optimism" doesn't capture a tone that sings with ardent intensity; his words leap off the page with an almost libidinous passion. "You will adore Balanchine," he tells Chick. "He is, personally, enchanting—dark, very slight, a superb dancer and the most ingenious technician in ballet I have ever seen." Then, knowing his audience, Lincoln appealed to Chick's homoerotic side by describing Roman Jasinski, likely to be the new company's male star, as "extremely beautiful—a superb body."

There had been earlier attempts to find a home for ballet in the United States, but although Anna Pavlova (from 1910 to 1925) and a few other internationally famous stars, as well as Diaghilev's Ballets Russes on its 1916-17 tours, had successfully drawn audiences, there'd been few opportunities to study classical technique and a scant tradition of indigenous choreography. Lincoln insisted to Chick that the planned-for school "can be the basis of a national culture as intense as the great Russian Renaissance of Diaghilev. We must start small. But imagine it—we are exactly as if we were in 1910. ... Please, please, Chick, if you have any love for anything we do both adore, rack your brains and try to make this all come true. It will mean a life work to all of us [and] incredible power in a few years." He assured Chick that he was not being "either over-enthusiastic or visionary."

But of course he was being both. Drunk on possibilities, perhaps feeling it might be now or never, Lincoln couldn't help throwing caution—along with absolute truthfulness—to the wind. Even if he'd been capable of a more modulated tone, it might not have appealed to Chick's own audacious nature. Bravado and amplitude were mother's milk to both men. If Chick was going to bite, the nervier the vision, the better.

No sooner had Lincoln returned to London than he received word from Chick that he'd already raised three thousand dollars from some dozen people, with the architect Philip Johnson (five hundred dollars), Jim Soby of MoMA (five hundred dollars), and Eddie Warburg, scion of the wealthy Warburg clan (one thousand dollars) giving the largest sums. The extraordinary Muriel Draper, already close to Lincoln, was also trying to raise money for the enterprise, though she confessed in a letter to him that she was having trouble envisioning the "poor Russians" in Hartford, "stopping for a Western at a lunch wagon." Her letter upset Lincoln because he knew she was at least "half true" about the cultural disjunction between the cosmopolitan Russians and the conservative business elite of Hartford.

Finally, on July 26, the long-awaited cable from Chick Austin arrived: "Go ahead ironclad contract necessary starting October 15 settle as much as you can bring publicity photographs museum is willing can't wait." Lincoln was elated and immediately wired Balanchine in Paris. He in turn notified Lincoln that his friend Vladimir Dimitriev would be a necessary part of any plans. When Lincoln met Dimitriev, he was impressed with the older man's solidity and shrewdness. At age forty, and with considerable experience in the dance world, Dimitriev could be a formidable ally—or antagonist—depending on whether he felt Balanchine's interests (and his own) were being sufficiently protected.

Lincoln could tell, he wrote in his diary, "how afraid they are to be left high and dry." The commercial failure of Les Ballets 1933 in London meant that Balanchine was feeling particularly tender at the moment. He continued to insist that he did want, above all, to come to the United States, but as everyone agreed, it would be "a big risk and ... very difficult to actualize." Besides, though he claimed a lack of interest in them, Balanchine had recently received several offers to stay in Europe, including an invitation to go to Copenhagen as *maître de ballet*, and to stage for Ida Rubinstein, the well-known and wealthy actress-mime, a Stravinsky-André Gide work for the Paris Opera.

Dimitriev, Lincoln wrote Chick, felt that the project fell into two distinct parts: a school to train dancers and a ballet company to perform, with everything "at first" centered on "the foundation of a school … nothing at all should be mentioned about a company or ballets." Lincoln urged Chick to set up a private corporation, arguing that it, and not the Athenaeum trustees, must hold "the whip hand." He reiterated that "such a chance as now presents itself comes but once in a lifetime," and lamented that it should be at a time of such general economic distress. "When I think," he wrote Chick, "of the cash spent on the bushes and shrubbery of the Philadelphia Museum, of the people who collect stamps and matchboxes, I go mad. This will be no collection, but living art—and the chance for perfect creation."

Ready or not, the day of Balanchine's arrival was suddenly upon them. In the early evening of October 17, 1933, Lincoln, Chick, and Eddie Warburg gathered dockside to greet Balanchine and Dimitriev as they debarked from the *Olympic.* The group then went immediately to the duplex apartment Lincoln had rented for Balanchine on the thirty-fourth floor of the Barbizon Plaza at 58th and Sixth. He had decided to splurge on the steep twelve-dollars-a-night rental to help create a favorable first impression.

After dinner, Lincoln had the first of what would be many "heavy" talks with Dimitriev about plans for the school, Dimitriev telling him firmly that the importation of Pierre Vladimiroff, the prominent ballet teacher, was an absolute "necessity." Dimitriev also made clear that the European offers Balanchine had had "would have paid him a lot had he accepted them." Lincoln boldly replied that he "knew Balanchine's services were not to be named in mere figures, but if it was money he wanted he wouldn't be here." The next morning, it was off, by car to Hartford. On the way they talked politics, with Balanchine and Dimitriev expressing their grave fear about "the coming of communism" to the United States, and how no Russian "has any civil rights anywhere."

After inspecting the museum's new theater, the Russians declared that it was "a big disappointment; there is no height; they couldn't use any scenery in it ... the floor is too hard for dancing, the whole thing too small," that no more than 24 people at most could be put on that stage. Dimitriev said it might do well enough for rehearsals, "small ballets," or school performances, but no more than that. Dimitriev came quickly to the point: Hartford was impossible. It was too far away from New York, the facilities were unsuitable, the cost of living too high, and Chick's dilettantism (he'd made the mistake of remarking at one point that he himself would paint whatever scenery was needed) boded ill for a serious venture.

When Chick wasn't present, Dimitriev stated flat-out that Hartford was *not* really a needed preliminary. Why waste time in a provincial backwater, and tied to a dilettante like Chick? They could open the school straight off in New York under the auspices of MoMA—especially since Eddie Warburg had just given it a $100,000 check. Dimitriev felt that "Chick was wholly unimportant," and that they "never could work with him." Lincoln expressed his feeling that they had to have some sort of a sponsor in order to convince the public that this was not just another dancing school. The more everyone talked, the more Hartford faded into the background.

Heading back to New York in the car, Balanchine abruptly told Lincoln that he didn't seem "as interested" as he "should be" in girls. As they passed through Harlem, Balanchine asked him (in words Lincoln recorded in his diary—and perhaps in exaggerated form) if he'd "ever screwed a negress." No, Lincoln said, "but he'd always wanted to"—which would have come as surprising news to any number of Lincoln's closest friends. "Alors," Balanchine responded, "we will go together." Obviously, Lincoln hadn't yet brought up the subject of his sexual preference, nor had Balanchine apparently surmised it for himself or heard about it from the many others who knew. Either that or Balanchine was playing cat and mouse. Dimitriev later confided to Lincoln that he "really didn't understand" Balanchine, that he "had no sentiment, liked casual fucking ... no heart"; he was of "another generation."

As for MoMA, the director Alfred Barr read the prospectus Lincoln drew up "with great sympathy," and made several useful suggestions for improving it still further. But he told Lincoln frankly that he thought the whole idea was "utopian," that "no Americans could submit to the necessary discipline" for creating an American ballet; in addition, Barr emphasized his belief that "European sources" were responsible for all American art—that there was "no possibility of calling anything primarily American."

Nonetheless, Lincoln notified Chick that the Russians had turned down Hartford as "unsuitable." Chick, in turn, "exploded" with resentment, and Eddie Warburg felt that "a definitive meeting" with him, without the Russians present, was necessary. Lincoln agreed and the two headed up to Hartford. The meeting *was* definitive—and unpleasant. Chick had already decided to save face by telling the local press that the venture had unexpectedly turned commercial and that the Athenaeum could not possibly lend its good name to that sort of enterprise. He intended to announce publicly that he was voiding the contract with Balanchine and Dimitriev, apparently not realizing (or caring) that the contract was already void, since neither man had as yet signed it.

When face-to-face with Chick in Hartford, Lincoln could feel his "just resentment." He told Chick how sorry he was that things had turned out the way they had, and made "several polite attempts to engage" him in conversation. They failed. Chick told him "bitterly" that he'd "hypnotized Eddie and betrayed him." Within twenty minutes the meeting was over. Lincoln felt that Eddie Warburg himself lacked any profound interest in ballet and it was questionable how long he would stick. Then there were all those people, from Archie MacLeish to Alfred Barr, who believed the project was misguided from its inception. And perhaps worst of all, despite a printed notice soliciting applications, no students were banging down the doors seeking instruction. That is, with one exception. A "boy" named Erick Hawkins, whom Lincoln remembered seeing in Harvard Yard, came by to say he'd already studied with the modern dancer Harald Kreutzberg and now wished to learn ballet from Balanchine. This was the same Erick Hawkins, of course, who would subsequently shift his allegiance to Martha Graham, become her lover, and play an aggressive role in her company before going on to found his own.

Then, just as Lincoln's gloom began to thicken, he and Dimitriev finally found "a dream place" for the school at 637 Madison Avenue, a space "better than anything [that] could be imagined." That same day they signed the papers for incorporation that they'd long been working on, with parity for all four participants: Lincoln, Eddie, Balanchine, and Dimitriev.

These encouraging steps were suddenly jeopardized when Balanchine fell seriously ill. Once back in New York, Balanchine—by now running a high fever—was taken to a Dr. Geyelin for X-rays. Soon after, Geyelin came to the hotel and said—in front of Balanchine—that the films had revealed "an active tuberculosis spot" and he would have to go to the Presbyterian Hospital for at least two weeks. Then, out of Balanchine's hearing, he told Lincoln and Dimitriev that there was "another darker spot on his lung which might be a really serious thing. If so, he would have to go away for six months perhaps." In any case, "he could not live much longer than ten years, if that long." In response to Lincoln's direct question, Geyelin advised them not to sign any lease for the school—which they'd already done.

The number of students who had showed up to enroll did begin slowly to climb, yet at the end of 1933, only some seventeen of them (by Lincoln's estimate) were paying fees, which in total were projected to bring in about $10,000 during 1934. In the sketchy budget the four partners had drawn up, expenses came to roughly $22,000, with rent ($94 dollars a week) and salaries the major items; Vladimiroff topped the list at $150 a week, and Balanchine and Dimitriev each got $100. (All these figures, in today's terms, would be approximately nine times higher.) That left a considerable projected deficit, even without factoring in any of the much-desired and discussed plans for performance and expansion.

To cover the deficit Eddie Warburg pledged $12,000 a year and Lincoln (from his father) eight; those sums did theoretically cover the deficit, but Eddie soon proved his unreliability. One day, he'd declare himself "satisfied with the way everything was going," and the next, privately tell Lincoln that he was "consumed with apprehensiveness about the future finances of the ballet school," that he was wary of committing himself to what seemed like a bottomless pit, and that he doubted if Balanchine "understands American taste sufficiently to give them what they want."

Lincoln constantly had to play nursemaid to Eddie, reassuring him about everything from the school to his hemorrhoids to the endless crises attendant on his endless psychoanalysis with the brilliant but unscrupulous Russian émigré Gregory Zilboorg. (George Gershwin was another of his patients.) Lincoln thought Eddie to be essentially "soul-less" and without any real commitment to anything. But out of both self-interest and friendship (at his best, Eddie could be a charming companion), Lincoln played out his role of concerned confidant—half the time wanting to strangle him. One night, when Eddie had a bad cold, Lincoln stayed overnight in order to administer steady doses of tea and lemon. On another, Eddie asked Lincoln to talk him to sleep, and as he did (so Lincoln recorded in his diary), Eddie "became amorous and over a long sleepy period gradually worked himself down and me up"—but Lincoln, "moist," stopped him. That seems to have been the only time Eddie attempted sexual contact, though Lincoln occasionally recorded other instances of Eddie's homosexual escapades.

Though his father Louis, a prominent partner in Filene's department store was wealthy, Lincoln had no significant financial resources of his own, or none he could touch anyway, in order to meet his pledge to the school of eight thousand a year; in truth, as he wrote his father, "I have no idea how much money I own myself, that is, in my own name." Louis had grown accustomed to paying his son's bills and providing him with a monthly allowance to cover incidental expenses, but constantly hectored him about his financial irresponsibility—even though it was Louis who'd set up the framework that perpetuated it: he'd kept Lincoln in the dark about his own assets, even after he'd turned twenty-one, and then, from his own pocket, had indulged his son's constant overdrafts. As a result, Lincoln had become incorrigibly inept at keeping reliable financial records and had long since learned, when pressed, to turn to his parents to bail him out.

Lincoln had seen himself as something of a co-creator, with Balanchine, and for months (while Balanchine convalesced), he'd been dreaming up ideas for new ballets based on American themes—Flying Cloud (about the clipper ships), Custer's Last Stand, Pocahontas, and (one that did interest Balanchine) a ballet based on the Rover Boys books. Still, Lincoln fully understood Balanchine's "righteous fear of dilettantism," and he had no doubts about who the chief creative force was. But Dimitriev and Balanchine's combined remarks, sometimes cruelly overstated, made him increasingly feel like some sort of incompetent office boy, someone incapable of carrying out even the minor tasks assigned him. It upset Lincoln and at times made him resentful. He tried to harden himself against feeling bitter toward the Russians, though (as he put it in his diary) "their iron lack of emollient words" did nothing to help his hurt pride. Lincoln had a habit, when feeling emotionally wounded, of believing that his current mood would be permanent ("I will never meet Balanchine or Dimitriev on friendly terms again," and so on), but he vowed to break the habit this time around, to work himself through his resentment. Yet the wound went deep, and he had trouble adjusting to what their harsh words had revealed about the diminished creative esteem in which they held him and the peripheral role they saw him playing in future plans.

Yet even during the worst of his pain, Lincoln did recognize that he remained "influential" and most of the time was able to see clearly that "Balanchine can be ably and efficiently influenced, if it is sufficiently indirect, flattering, and if the suggestions are validly imaginative. What my role would have been had I not been, as now, disappointed," he wrote in his diary, "I have, now, no idea. As a matter of fact I thought hardly at all of what I'd do, imagining only consecutive and charming collaboration." Yet instead of holding to his decision to be "cold-blooded" and coolly aloof, while concealing his resentment, Lincoln in fact lurched quite quickly in the opposite direction, turning his anger inward, blaming himself for all that had gone wrong, indulging an orgy of lacerating self-recrimination and a humiliating outburst of apologetics.

It was as if he couldn't manage to sustain an emotional middle ground, couldn't simply acknowledge where he may have made some mistakes or come up short, even as he justifiably held to account those who'd evaded their own inadequacies by trying to blame them on him. Instead, he tended to lurch between fierce denunciation and savage self-blame. Always a man of extremes, he dealt all his life in hyperbole, crudely lashing out at others or holding himself infernally culpable and damned. What he called his "demons" rarely allowed, in personal relations as well, for a cool appraisal or for more than a fleeting sense of inner peace.

Good news finally came from Dr. Geyelin; after examining Balanchine over the winter, Geyelin declared, somewhat to his own surprise, that Balanchine "might be the case to refute the old idea one could not get well from T.B. while in New York and working." That verdict helped to dissipate months of gloomy apprehension and backbiting—though hardly ushering in an uninterrupted reign of harmony and sunny satisfaction. The School of American Ballet was, after all, a newborn; as with most infants, peaceful interludes were all but guaranteed to give way to some rude wailing and sudden spitting. Within weeks of the general rapprochement, Eddie Warburg was sitting Lincoln down for yet another lecture about his shortcomings, and a renewed insistence that he go to see his analyst. "You aren't exactly mean," Eddie said, "but your nervous jumpings-about and your shortness with people gave a bad impression."

Eddie was a good-natured softie compared to Dimitriev, who'd picked up on Lincoln's infatuation with Harry Dunham, one of the student dancers, and decided to have the conversation that Lincoln had long been "dreading." When the two were alone one day, Dimitriev told him—so Lincoln described the encounter in his diary—that he "couldn't understand

Lincoln Kirstein and George Balanchine

Americans. He'd been here five and a half months and he'd only met pederasts: Eddie and I never went out into the country, etc. with young girls: Were all Americans queer?"

Where Dimitriev could be openly abusive, Balanchine could be coolly dismissive. As Lincoln wrote in his diary, Balanchine could be "suggestible in small doses, in cafeteria intervals," but "a formal conversation tires him." After one talk between them about legal and financial matters, Lincoln could feel "Balanchine's slight contempt" and it left him all "loose and worried" and prone to nightmares; in one bad dream, "Balanchine a murderer; myself shipwrecked. Disaster and guilt all around."

During the winter of 1934, Lincoln and Balanchine did have at least a few discussions involving "creative" issues. What Balanchine primarily wanted from Lincoln was not creativity or collaboration, but small-task efficiency—and large sums of money. Lincoln was perfectly willing to sweat and toil in the trenches, and did so prodigiously, but efficiency at niggling detail work wasn't well suited to his off-handed nature, his baronial sense of consequence, and his stirring dreams. Being relegated to treadmill routines amounted to an insulting misreading of his temperament and talent, of his high intelligence and genuine artistic sensitivity. Lincoln had envisioned himself as sitting at the helm of an ocean liner, not working the ropes on the assisting tugboat. Feeling unappreciated and underutilized, he turned increasingly to the ego-soothing pursuits of writing ("my bitterness against Balanchine and Dimitriev conveniently keeping me in my room"), lecturing, and socializing.

Lincoln felt that he, more than Balanchine, knew what might be most special about "*American* dancing," about what he called the "unique, indigenous and creative style of American dances, choreographers, and composers." "Instead of setting a stereotype of remoteness, spectral grandeur and visionary brilliance," he wrote in an April 1938 column in *The Nation*, "Americans are volatile, intimate, frank. ... The most important thing about American dancers is the retention of their amateur status and their nearness to the audience ... the frontier spirit of spontaneous collective entertainment where everybody got up and danced as they could, still persists. But with a difference. Our dancing artists have selected and amplified all that is most useful in the amateur spirit to make of it a conscious and brilliant frame for their individual theatrical projection"—and he explicitly included not merely ballet or "modern" dancers but also the can-do "hoofers" Fred Astaire, Paul Draper, Ginger Rogers, Eleanor Powell, Buddy Ebsen, and Ray Bolger.

"Volatile, intimate, frank" were shrewd if contestable definitions of the American essence (certainly in dance, "energy" and "athleticism" might just as easily serve), yet at the very least, Lincoln had put his finger on some recognizable, canny half-truths, and throughout his life, he would continue to hone his definition of "American."

IN THE FIRST FEW YEARS following Balanchine's arrival in the States late in 1933, Kirstein wholly immersed himself in the back-to-back crises, artistic and personal, that seemed to descend without letup, and which threw into serious doubt the entire notion of forming an American ballet. For much of the first year, Balanchine's precarious health alone threatened to sink the ship; he himself tended to minimize the seriousness of his condition, but Kirstein knew better and had to constantly play nursemaid, ensuring Balanchine's comfort, watching over his diet, shuttling him from one doctor's office to the next—even as he puzzled over the specialists' contradictory diagnoses. At one point, a specialist found "two active but diminishing spots" on Balanchine's lungs and prescribed injections of insulin that the previous specialist had advised against. To avoid alarming the patient, Kirstein—even while fretting over the contradictory diagnoses and elusive prescriptions—had to control his own, not inconsiderable, mood swings. (Later in life, he'd be diagnosed with bipolar disorder. When W. H. Auden was at one point asked about Lincoln's "erratic" behavior, Auden replied: "everyone has moods and Lincoln's should be respected. Lincoln always means well ... he's a very good man.")

When his health finally stabilized, Balanchine had a burst of creative energy, and no one was more thrilled than Kirstein. For three years in the early '30s, Balanchine and the fledgling company (which called itself the American Ballet) provided the dance interludes at the Metropolitan Opera, which led to a full-scale production of Balanchine's Orpheus (with Tchelitchev's set and costume designs). As a result, Balanchine started to get commercial offers and he signed on to do a Broadway show, "On Your Toes"—which proved an enormous success. That, in turn, led to still other assignments to choreograph musicals, including Rodgers and Hart's "Babes in Arms."

Despite this success, Balanchine's prime interest remained what it always had been: creating an American ballet school and company. His detour to Broadway, though, alarmed Kirstein, even as it gave him more of a chance to exercise his own talents. Picking from among some dozen dancers already attached to the American Ballet, he formed a touring company, the "Ballet Caravan," which for a few months of each year for four years, toured the country. Kirstein's conviction that Balanchine stood head-and-shoulders above all other choreographers hadn't weakened: the Caravan primarily performed and spread awareness of the master's genius. That genius, in Kirstein's view, uniquely centered on the virtuosic body in stark, swift, clean motion, unconnected to sentimental narration, with movement an end in itself, devoid of anything superfluous.

At the same time, Kirstein initially hoped to include ballets that had at least the outlines of a traditional story line, and in particular with identifiably American content that referenced everyday life. With the Ballet Caravan under his exclusive control, it became possible for Kirstein to commission works with a strong narrative line. Many of those ballets have become standards in the repertoire: Lew Christenson and Elliott Carter's "Pocahontas"; Eugene Loring and Paul Bowles' "Yankee Clipper"; Christenson and Virgil Thomson's "Filling Station"; and Loring and Aaron Copland's "Billy the Kid."

Kirstein continued to value Balanchine's masterful genius, but thanks to the new letters that have turned up we now know that his experience in running the Caravan gave Lincoln a new confidence in his own judgment. In a letter to Tchelitchev, Lincoln vowed that henceforth he would "criticize and be harsh with him [Balanchine] when I feel like it ... instead of being scared by his uniqueness and genius." Yet ironically, by the time Balanchine had had his fill of Broadway and returned full-time to the American Ballet, Kirstein's interest in exploring the American past through dance had sharply diminished. It wasn't a matter of Balanchine *compelling* adherence to his neoclassical vision, but rather the result of Kirstein's lessening involvement after the 1930s in left-wing politics and, as an offspring of that, a diminished interest in American-themed narrative dance. Unlike Kirstein, Balanchine had always been politically conservative and deeply religious, and when *he* turned, briefly, to American subjects in the ballets "Western Symphony" (1954) and "Stars and Stripes" (1958), it would be in a spirit of joie de vivre rather than moral earnestness.

Kirstein had also come to realize that he was temperamentally ill-suited to the many demands of managing a touring company. The

Houghton Library's new collection of family letters tells us a good deal more than we've previously known about the multiple responsibilities of running a ballet company and the multiple demands it made on Kirstein's limited patience—and mounting exasperation—for the mundane details of daily life. Brilliant, deeply serious, and widely read, Lincoln never lost his "affection" for the Caravan and its accomplishments but, especially during the last year of touring, he developed, to his own surprise, "certain sudden murderous instincts" toward his "little troupe." "I can't stand easily," he wrote home, "the unremitting gaiety and good clean fun of one and all." He sometimes felt "like I was on a small tramp steamer with a co-educational high school during a calm that lasted for days." When the Caravan reached North Dakota and Montana, he drolly wrote his sister Mina that they were "scenic states with beauteous fjords and waving savannas"—i.e. "the most desolate, bone-dry dreary landscape I ever saw." His only comfort was that the train food was inexpensive: Swiss steak and whipped potatoes cost 65 cents.

When Lincoln decided to give up the Caravan in 1938, he confessed in a letter to his mother that it was "much, much harder than giving up the *Hound and Horn* [his earlier literary journal for which" it had turned out, there was "no public."] He felt the Caravan, on the other hand, *did* have an audience: "night after night we see our public—only there's not enough of them … it's too bad to quit just on the brink of something [but] there's no use of wailing." Ballet could only make money, he concluded, if done on a large scale, which meant finding the resources to further build up the American Ballet company. He didn't relish the prospect of returning to his role of second (or third) fiddle: "Everything connected with the stage," he wrote to his parents, "fascinates me, but I hardly ever see it now. Someone else, anyone else, could manage the mechanical side better than me, but there isn't anyone else in my position. The thing has to have a head and I'm it."

After the touring finally came to an end in 1938, Kirstein suddenly came up with a new idea, one that might, on the side, serve as a more creative outlet than "laying out the master's clothes." Still interested, if to a lesser degree, in left-wing politics—much later, he would join the Selma March—he came up with a "divine" idea for a new ballet he called "Memorial Day." Its theme would be "democracy in crisis" as represented in Civil War iconography. He planned to write the libretto himself and asked his friend, the composer Aaron Copland (with whom he would always have a good relationship) to write the score—a commission Copeland accepted enthusiastically. For a time, the project consumed Lincoln; he sent his sister Mina letter after letter (all in the new Houghton collection) detailing his progress and using her as a sounding board for his ideas.

He was especially keen to get Mina's take on the possibility of getting the prestigious Mercury Theater involved. John Houseman (who'd been Mina's lover) had, in 1937, co-founded the Mercury with 21-year-old Orson Welles, and Lincoln hoped Mina's influence would lead Houseman to put on "Memorial Day" first as a concert, and then open it for a theatrical run. Though Mina had earlier come through at the last minute with a crucial donation that allowed the legendary Houseman/Marc Blitzstein production of "The Cradle Will Rock" to open, she wasn't able to interest Houseman in "Memorial Day."

Kirstein, in fact, had all along had a low opinion of Houseman; at one point, when describing him to Mina, Kirstein made a telling and uniquely revealing comparison: Houseman, he wrote, is "as negligible and as corrupt as Balanchine, except George is a cynic, disinterested, sick and has genius." It's a comparison that takes the breath away. There's no way of knowing how Kirstein, in his own mind, was defining "negligible" and "corrupt," but clearly not in a way that was complimentary, thereby revealing that his occasional bitterness toward Balanchine—it was never a steady state—could reach a depth which hasn't previously been known.

In the upshot, Kirstein revised and redrafted his libretto for "Memorial Day," accepting many of Mina's suggestions for revision, though he came to see the whole project as "very pretentious." No one, in any case, proved willing to showcase it. Disappointed, he went back to working in the traces, once again focusing his attention full-time on developing the American Ballet School and company.

After World War II—in which Kirstein served as a private and ended up being one of the Monuments Men who discovered the huge Nazi horde of stolen art buried in the Altaussee mine—the ballet company reconstituted as a unit connected to the City Center, the large mosque-like building on West 55th Street devoted to cultural events and offering low ticket prices. In its director, Morton Baum, Kirstein found a sympathetic soul, but City Center lacked the resources needed to guarantee the ballet an extended season, much less a permanent home. Still, by 1950 the American Ballet had achieved enough prominence and recognition for London's prestigious Covent Garden to offer a five-week engagement.

It proved enormously successful, and Kirstein, in a published article, brilliantly pinpointed why the company's unique style—Balanchine's style—had finally gained the recognition it deserved. His distinction lay, in Kirstein's words, in "a leanness, a visual asceticism, a candour ... and sometimes a galvanizing, acetylene brilliance, a deep potential of incalculable human strength." What fascinated Balanchine, Kirstein wrote, "was the human body's instinctive, yet scarcely unconscious, expression of its era—our corsetless, all but skirtless ... era, where good social and theatrical manners are more a problem of individual obligation and affection than the reflection of the devotion for, or authority felt resident in, sovereign or system."

Steadfast and unwavering in his public praise of Balanchine—and Lincoln meant every word of it—privately, we now know, Kirstein would occasionally let loose to an intimate friend like Pavlik Tchelitchev his accumulated hurt over the master's dismissive treatment. In the correspondence now available at the University of Texas, Kirstein let Pavlik know that during the negotiations with City Center, he'd "counted so much on his [Balanchine's] aid, and in a way, I felt somewhat deserted by him." Kirstein freely acknowledged to Pavlik that he himself could tell "what is wrong after I see it; but he [Balanchine] knows before, and he has the authority to work with the musicians which I will never have." Yet from Lincoln's perspective Balanchine seemed oblivious to the company's everyday logistics, its need for constant tending, and unappreciative of the grueling toll it took on Lincoln's time and energy. "Perhaps I wrong him," he wrote Pavlik, "But he is like ice; and his genius for composition is unsupported by taste or intellectual curiosity."

THOUGH HOMOSEXUALITY was omnipresent in the ballet world, it seems never to have been, in any explicit way, a point of contention between Kirstein and Balanchine, perhaps in part because Lincoln, in 1941, married Paul Cadmus' sister Fidelma—though neither before nor after the marriage did he stop having sex with, and sometimes becoming deeply attached to, other men. The dancer Pete Martinez, one of the great loves of Kirstein's life in the late '30s and early '40s, not only lived with the Kirsteins for a time but became a close and trusted friend to Fidelma. Later, the painter and curator Jensen Yow would fill a similar role.

Whether and to what extent these relationships (and others) were ever discussed between Kirstein and Fidelma remains unknown. Paul Cadmus was already dead when I began work on *The Worlds of Lincoln Kirstein*, but I talked at length with his long-term partner, Jon Anderson, who told me that Cadmus' sense was that Fidelma understood early on that "Lincoln simply needed his close relationships with men—and that was that."

One could argue, if intent on categorization, that Kirstein might best be viewed as "bisexual." He'd had affairs with women early in his twenties, including one of profound importance to him with the cultural doyenne, Muriel Draper. That he cared deeply as well for Fidelma seemed "certain" to Jon Anderson, who felt that their relationship, at least during the early years of the marriage, definitely had a sexual component. As I wrote in my biography, "the cynical conclusion would be that Lincoln married in order to foster his career. Yet that seems far too cynical, given how little he would bother to cover up his homosexual activities—and how much he genuinely cared for Fidelma."

What seems nearly as certain is that, to Balanchine, homosexuality was simply incomprehensible—of no interest, and vaguely suspect. Distant and reserved by nature, Balanchine rarely discussed his or anybody else's private life, yet he of course knew that male (not female) homosexuality was commonplace in the ballet world. We get an indirect clue to Balanchine's attitude towards it in the figure of Vladimir Dimitriev, his most trusted adviser in the early years after his arrival in the States. Dimitriev proved a relentless advocate for Balanchine's business interests; and he was no less outspoken about Kirstein's homosexual affairs.

Early on, Kirstein became deeply infatuated with one of the school's first students, Harry "Bosco" Dunham, a "small blonde from Ohio" in his early twenties who'd already had an affair with Paul Bowles (who warned Kirstein that Bosco was "nuts—that sitting down in a chair was drama to him"). Until Bosco came along, Kirstein had been so preoccupied with the multiple issues connected to putting the ballet on its feet, that for a considerable period, he had been celibate. (As he wrote in his diary: "Streets full of sailors and marines. I keep my eyes neatly averted.") But Kirstein found Bosco "wholly charming" and noted in his diary "the unmistakable solar plexus pains of strong attraction and longing which I have not felt since I can't remember and which I thought up to now were forever dulled by jacking off and concentration." Bosco responded in kind, but he proved wildly unpredictable and soon left the school and the city. (He would die in World War II.)

But before then, while Bosco was still in attendance at the school, Dimitriev became aware that he and Kirstein were having an affair. Kirstein somehow discovered that Dimitriev was regularly opening his mail—including his lovesick letters to Bosco. Shocked, he confronted Dimitriev, who—instead of expressing apologies and regret—"made fun" of Kirstein's predilections. "I can't understand Americans," Dimitriev boldly told him. "Were all Americans queer?" Yes, Kirstein angrily replied, "We are the nation of the great intermediates" (he'd been reading Havelock Ellis). Henceforth, he wrote in his diary, "no intimacy would be possible" with Dimitriev, and he would confine their interaction to "an efficient working school and business basis."

Soon thereafter, Kirstein noticed a tone of "slight contempt" from Balanchine when the two of them talked. Unlike Dimitriev, who was something of a bull in a china shop, Balanchine's style was indirect, coolly dismissive. Yet the contempt was unmistakable, and it left Lincoln, as he confided to his diary, feeling "loose and worried" and prone to nightmares. What's more, Balanchine's deprecatory attitude toward him carried over into their work together. Lincoln had expected a collaboration; what he got was an off-handed assignment to raise money and attend to the multiple small tasks of an administrative assistant. In one of the newly acquired letters, Kirstein poignantly reveals how deeply wounded he felt all of his adult life at Balanchine's patronizing view of him—and Kirstein wasn't a whiner and never indulged in self-pity. "Balanchine returned," Lincoln poignantly wrote, "he is as cold as ice. ... I can't expect that his nature would change. ... With me, it is no use; I neither interest or amuse him, and he has no basis upon which we can speak ... it makes me feel sad that I can talk with all the other people with whom I work, and George seems to have no interest ... the only thing he really loves is music ... for this he has a passion, and it is wonderful and disinterested, but on the other things, he leaves me alone—with no trace of caring." Kirstein's suffering, familiar to several generations of gay people, rises in remonstrance against those "superior" others who have for so long, and casually, inflicted it.

In all the long years that followed, the basic contours of the Kirstein-Balanchine relationship remained constant. An occasional business lunch or dinner aside, the two men never became friends, nor even socialized other than incidentally. Kirstein always retained his profound conviction of Balanchine's genius, and he devoted himself to creating the most ideal circumstances possible for its expression. His zeal did occasionally falter—the result of emotional exhaustion or the demands of his own multiple projects—but his central conviction of Balanchine's unmatchable brilliance held steady. When Balanchine died in April 1983, Kirstein stepped in front of the curtain the following night and told a hushed audience, in a voice that slightly trembled, that Balanchine "is with Mozart, Tchaikovsky, and Stravinsky. I do want to tell you how much he valued this audience, this marvelous audience ... you kept us going fifty years, and will another fifty. One thing he didn't want was that this be interrupted. We will proceed."

IN THE POSTWAR period, Kirstein and his wife Fidelma often saw Isherwood and his current lover, the photographer Bill Caskey. In 1947, the couple visited the Kirsteins in their beloved summer hideaway on Fire Island. Caskey had a reputation in some quarters as an aggressive, disruptive "truth-teller," but Kirstein liked him enormously, describing him as a "no nonsense … tough little customer … cold as ice underneath." Isherwood had already published two of his most famous works, *Prater Violet* and *The Berlin Stories*, and during the Fire Island visit he shared parts of his private diary with Kirstein, who found it (as he wrote Mina) "a very remarkable precise English commentary, in a rather rigid evangelical tone of the intimate horrors of our time; realistic, very detailed, astonishingly honest and cold. … Like a more intelligent Pepys or Evelyn, but combined with amazing portraits and narratives."

Years later, in the mid-1960s, Don Bachardy—who had long since displaced Caskey as Isherwood's life partner—paid a visit to New York to promote his drawings and portraits, and he stayed with Kirstein and Fidelma in their house on 19th Street. The visit was not a success. Bachardy reported to Isherwood that "Lincoln is still manic and oh! so difficult"—an understandable reaction given Kirstein's sometimes severe mood swings during these years. Less understandable was Bachardy finding him "boring to be with"—an estimation that no one else ever shared.

When Kirstein gave Bachardy the handsome commission of $2,000 to do some drawings of the New York City Ballet Company, Bachardy himself called the payment "extravagant," unattractively adding in a letter to Isherwood that "if Lincoln is going to throw his money around, I see No reason why Kitty [Bachardy's pet name] should be criticized for taking off his little hat (very respectfully) and catching a coin or two." Bachardy also mocked Kirstein's critical tastes, writing that he "doesn't have the faintest idea of what's any good, and if he did, wouldn't have the courage of his conviction"—an estimate that can only be called astonishing, given Kirstein's fearless public opposition to abstract expressionism when it was at its height of popularity. He was no less fearless in defending various representational artists (including Andrew and Jamie Wyeth) whom the smart set disparaged.

Bachardy concluded, rather hair-raisingly, that Lincoln "is the most awful coward, and will back down at the slightest bark from any ass, including Madam Balanchine, who may be a genius as a choreographer but is just a vain, silly know-nothing about other things, most particularly 'the visual arts'"—descriptions of both men of breathtaking obtuseness. Not surprisingly, soon after Bachardy's visit, Kirstein's friendship with Isherwood became distant to the point of disappearance.

Far from fading into the woodwork rather than offend, Kirstein would sometimes speak his mind with such ferocity as to produce considerable offense and, in some cases, a rupture in relations. One case in point is his reaction to his brother-in-law (and close friend) Paul Cadmus' 1945 painting Lust, the first in what became a famous series titled *The Seven Deadly Sins*. Pulling no punches, Kirstein told Cadmus that the painting was "horrible": "it is so full of hate and disgust, in an active way, that it is quite paralyzing." Kirstein went on to admonish Cadmus for his "aching agony about the flesh. I suppose it partly comes from hating being queer, and partly from [the] curdled Catholicism of your nasty youth ... maybe the nicest thing about all of us is our poor half-stiff peters and stretched, hungry cunts."

Cadmus was a gentle soul who avoided conflict, took Kirstein's intemperance in stride (however hurt by it), and stayed close to him throughout their long lives. And Kirstein did his part to make that possible. As I wrote in *The Worlds of Lincoln Kirstein*: "Lincoln could be recklessly impatient with people, bluntly and hurtfully saying what he felt at the moment, but he was at bottom a bad hater; he would secretly do an important favor for someone he wasn't speaking to, would loan money to an acquaintance whose talent he'd lost confidence in, or would 'forget' two weeks after a shouting match that it had ever taken place, casually embracing the person who'd recently been his fierce antagonist."

The writer Donald Ritchie put his finger on another essential ingredient in Kirstein's personality: "You are a very moral person," he wrote to

Kirstein, "in this world of slipping and slithering and sliding standards there are some which remain inviolate … you stand for these and observe them." An example of such standards is Kirstein's reaction to Gertrude Stein's behavior during World War II. One of the newly released letters in the Ransom Center collection from Kirstein to Tchelitchev begins by praising "lots of young rich Parisiens who behaved magnificently [during the war], tricked the Germans time and again under the disguise of being silly and mondain." He could not say the same, he went on, for Gertrude Stein "writing non-stop" under the protection of Professor Bernard Faÿ, a specialist in American literature and a close adviser to Marshal Pétain, head of the pro-Nazi Vichy government. Later, when Faÿ was tried as a collaborator, Stein wrote a letter in his defense.

Kirstein was angered, too, at a number of other artists—he named Charles Despiau, André Segonzac, Roland Oudot, and André Derain—all of whom had accepted an invitation to Berlin in 1941 to attend an exhibit of the Nazi-endorsed painter Arne Brecker. They did so, in Lincoln's view, "not by necessity but to curry favor." Kirstein wrote from Europe to Tchelitchev: "I learn a lot about evil and I have developed a hate of people that frightens me." He was pleased after the war when the ballet luminary Serge Lifar was tried and imprisoned for having seen to it that the lights of the Paris Opera be turned on—after all the workmen on the premises had refused to do so—in order to give Hitler a personal tour.

Kirstein downplayed his own dramatic experiences during the war, the result of a lucky break (though he was only an army private) in being assigned to the now famous Arts and Monuments Commission. He and his commanding officer, Captain Robert Posey, through a series of accidental tips, found themselves hot on the trail of the famed polyptych, *The Adoration of the Lamb*—the so-called Ghent Altarpiece painted by the brothers Hubert and Jan van Eyck between 1426 and 1432, stolen by the Nazis and hidden, as the war turned against them, at some unknown location known to be a salt mine.

Thanks to the Ransom Center's newly acquired Kirstein-Tchelitchev correspondence, we now know more about the location of that salt mine in Austria's Alt Aussee region, which had become, by 1945, the central assembly point for looted treasures ultimately destined for Hitler's "super-museum" at Linz. The Alt Aussee mine had ideal climate-controlled conditions for storing art, and the Nazis had converted it into a state-of-the-art storage facility. In March 1945, with the war going badly, Hitler had issued what became known as the Nero Decree ordering the destruction at supply sites of anything that might be of use to the Allies. Martin Bormann, Hitler's secretary, sent a letter to August Eigruber, the Nazi officer in charge of the Alt Aussee region, that seemed to make it clear—or so Eigruber insisted—that works of art were to be understood as included under the Nero Decree.

The advancing Allied armies regarded Alt Aussee as unimportant strategically and even somewhat dangerous, given the remnants of SS troops known to be hiding out in the mountainous terrain. But when Posey and Kirstein informed General Patton that a vast amount of stolen art was probably buried in the Alt Aussee mine, he redirected the Third Army to the site. Scattered SS troops still guarded the mine, which was known to be wired for detonation with 500-kilogram aircraft bombs. Were the bombs to go off, they would certainly have collapsed the mine and buried the art. August Eigruber, a devoted follower of Hitler, was determined to carry out the Führer's Nero Decree and completely destroy the mine.

He was foiled by a group of anti-Nazi Austrian officers, in cooperation with a number of brave local miners who'd been active in the Resistance. Working secretly at night, the miners somehow managed to elude the SS guards, remove the bombs from their crates, and set off enough explosives to seal the opening to the mine without damaging the art within. The Third Army arrived at Alt Aussee on May 8, one day after Germany surrendered unconditionally at Reims. The debris blocking the entrance to the mine was soon cleared away, and, with one of the miners as their guide, Posey and Kirstein, holding up acetylene lamps, were the first to enter. They opened two padlocks on an iron door, and there at their feet, unwrapped, lay the eight panels of *The Adoration of the Lamb*. Over the next few days, a cornucopia of other treasures emerged, including a Vermeer self-portrait and Michelangelo's marble Madonna from Bruges.

PART III
Rivals and Idols

KIRSTEIN'S relationships—unlike the course of friendship with Paul Cadmus--did not always follow a pattern of reconciliation following a blow-up, occasionally because the other party refused, but more often because Kirstein would neither seek nor accept a renewal of friendship. Sometimes, too, there would be no dramatic explosion; Kirstein would simply lose interest in a person and allow a friendship to gradually lapse. One case in point was the composer and critic Virgil Thomson ("He is the coldest-blooded of all," Kirstein wrote Tchelitchev.) Stephen Spender was another. Early on in their friendship, Kirstein had admired Spender's poetry, but before long his opinion of him took a nosedive. By the end of the 1950s, Lincoln would write to Donald Ritchie: "I have no respect for Spender as poet or person"—and their contact soon after diminished to nothing.

Lincoln's rejections of British poet Edith Sitwell, composer Marc Blitzstein, and writer Glenway Wescott were more caustic and severe. Of the three, he knew Sitwell the least well (though he was close to her brother Osbert and admired him as "daring and honest"). Kirstein and Edith Sitwell had met initially in the 1930s, through Tchelitchev, who was then very close to Edith. The two shared, in Kirstein's view, operatic temperaments, "a venomous hatred of everyone, except a very few close leeches," and a penchant for vitriolic gossip. Among much else, Edith came to the disastrous conclusion that she was in love with Tchelitchev—though like everyone else in their circle, she'd often been exposed to his lyrical descriptions of the beauty of boys and was never in doubt about his intimate relationship with Charles Henri Ford. Sitwell's persistence led to coloratura quarrels between the two that further excited her ardor; the two would remain in contact for some thirty years, but were most in harmony in their letters.

In the early 1950s, Kirstein—possibly for Osbert Sitwell's sake—encouraged Edith to do a series of dramatic readings in the U.S. She chose to read from Macbeth, with Glenway Wescott opposite her. Attending a rehearsal, Kirstein found the combination breathtakingly awful: "Edith thinks Lady Macbeth [is] a sort of old maid aunt; Glenway thinks Macbeth is … Rabbi Stephen Wise [then a well-known figure]. She uses a microphone; he uses his, er, natural voice. The combination is not to be described. One's averted eyes will never re-avert."

Unlike Spender, who Kirstein had initially held in high esteem and thought less and less of over time, Glenway Wescott never attained any altitude from which to fall. Kirstein first met Wescott and his partner Monroe Wheeler (for many years, the head of publications at MoMA) in the early '30s in Europe. He'd liked Wheeler from the start, found him "charming and delightful," knowledgeable about ballet and shrewd in his judgments of people. His reaction to Wescott was another matter entirely. At their very first meeting, he and Lincoln "quarreled steadily for 2 hours" (so Lincoln reported to Mina), "saying how important it was to live in France—for anybody and everybody—and I saying how necessary it was for a writer (like himself) to get back to his own country."

Kirstein's initial impression of both men held. Through the years that followed, he came increasingly to admire Wheeler. He had, in Lincoln's view, a "selfless" and "sunny" nature, and was "always sympathetic [to other people's] crises, whether of money matters or personal gaffes." When Tchelitchev at one point was desperate to find studio space, Wheeler created one for him in his own office. Another time, when the painter was, in Lincoln's view, "certifiably mad, determined on devouring fame, with unappeasable hunger," it was Wheeler who supplied the "surplus of patience and affection" (Kirstein's words) that succeeded in calming him down.

As for Wescott, from the start Kirstein thought him "chi-chi," a frivolous mediocrity—and he never changed his mind, despite the fact that Westcott's second novel, *The Grandmothers* (1926), had won the Harper Prize and been a bestseller. (His 1940 novel *The Pilgrim Hawk* still has its fans.) During the life of Kirstein's touring Ballet Caravan, Wescott came to him at one point with an idea for a ballet he called "The Dream of Audubon," but Kirstein wouldn't touch it, finding it "very old hat and full of nonsense." Wescott had many well-placed friends and admirers, including Jean Cocteau, Marc Chagall, Somerset Maugham, Thornton Wilder, and Katherine Anne Porter, but Kirstein (and Hemingway, too) remained a stubborn detractor.

If anything, as the years went by, Wescott seems to have annoyed Kirstein more and more. He concluded, through the years, that Wescott was a lazy, whiney conniver, and for five years during the late '40s and early '50s, Lincoln flat-out refused to see him socially, even in a group gathering. The animus was apparently mutual. At one point, Wescott wrote Kirstein a testy letter telling him to "stop fooling around as a dilettante in the arts" and stick to raising money for the ballet—advice that amounted to the implicit verdict that money-grubbing, not art, was all that Kirstein was suited for (a view that for Lincoln painfully echoed Balanchine's initial attitude to him).

The only other gay artist of the day about whom Kirstein felt as consistently negative was the composer Marc Blitzstein—a judgment that stands out as one of the few exceptions to his generally shrewd assessment of people. In my biography of Kirstein, I make reference to his mixed feelings about Blitzstein, but it's only with the new Ransom Center letters that the depth of Kirstein's dislike becomes apparent—though the reasons for it remain obscure. Some of the antagonism, probably, was politically based, relating to what Kirstein referred to as Blitzstein's "Stalinist shenanigans." Spender did belong to the Communist Party, and, in the late '30s, the Moscow purge trials were fresh in everyone's memory.

In 1938, ten days before the play *Danton's Death*—with music by Blitzstein—was due to open at the Mercury Theater, Blitzstein, "in a state of extreme agitation" (according to John Houseman, who headed up the Mercury), wanted to cancel the production, fearing that the critics would equate the play's ruthless Robespierre with Stalin. According to Houseman's 1972 autobiography *Run-Through*—and its accuracy has been persuasively questioned—Blitzstein insisted that a meeting be arranged with V. J. Jerome, a CP spokesman and editor of *The Communist*. Several meetings proved necessary before a compromise could be reached. Some of the more obvious Robespierre-Stalin parallels were removed from the play and, in return, the CP agreed not to boycott it.

Kirstein furiously denounced the decision to allow the CP to act as censor, and, for good measure, he dismissed Blitzstein's music as "lousy" and his influence on the production as "fatal." When the mostly unfavorable reviews appeared, Kirstein put the blame squarely on Blitzstein—on (as he wrote Mina) his "rigid Stalinist tactics plus self-indulgent hysteria. Marc is a Jewish fascist and robbed the play of any point or idea." He bracketed Blitzstein with Jerome Robbins and Leonard Bernstein as "self-pitying" men of "the Jewish resentment school. ... [E]ven success" did not cure them.

Mina—no blushing violet—refused to sit still for her brother's attack on Blitzstein, who she regarded as an "irreplaceable friend." Nor was she alone in defending him. Orson Welles—a man not easily pleased—had warm feelings toward Blitzstein throughout his life. "He brightens a room when he enters it," Welles wrote at one point; "he is mannerly, widely educated, unaffectedly civilized, a man of natural authority and unstudied charm. If he sounds a little too good to be true, he is, almost, just that." Some fifteen years later, after the Cold War had set in and the House Un-American Activities Committee began to hunt down left-wing artists, Blitzstein would be among those called to testify. Unlike the director Elia Kazan, who did name names, Blitzstein bravely challenged HUAC's right to interrogate him and refused to implicate anyone else, which led to his indictment in 1951 under the Smith Act—and to four years (1954-1957) in prison. A few years later, in 1964, the 59-year-old Blitzstein was murdered by three sailors he'd picked up in a bar on the island of Martinique.

THANKS TO the extraordinary letters from Kirstein to Tchelitchev, we're able for the first time to see in detail how extraordinarily generous and forgiving Kirstein could be to the people he cared deeply about. He first met Tchelitchev in the early 1930s and, in Kirstein's words, they "raced into intimacy at a hundred miles an hour." Kirstein saw from the first that Tchelitchev had a "mild, but clinging paranoia," leading him to turn the merest slight into an unforgivable act of treachery. Tchelitchev's reliance on astrology and numerology reflected, in Kirstein's view, his need to remain on permanent guard against "malevolent forces" that lay everywhere in wait. Volatile, headstrong, overbearing, Tchelitchev saw himself (as Kirstein once put it) as "a modern magus," a cosmological messenger privy to nothing less than the mathematics of time and space, a cabbalistic master of the universe.

Yet Kirstein stuck around, drawn by Tchelitchev's high energy and intelligence, and his entrancing talk—along with a truckload of talent that Kirstein believed augured well for a major artistic career. In the coming years—indeed, until Tchelitchev's death in 1957—Kirstein (who always took on too much) knocked himself out acting unofficially as both Tchelitchev's agent and publisher, praising and promoting his work, publishing his drawings, writing articles extolling his "mastery," setting up gallery shows, even publishing a full-length book on his work.

Yet all that was not enough, in Tchelitchev's view—not enough to satisfy his gigantic ego. He complained to Kirstein that the latter's commentary on his major paintings, *Hide-and-Seek* and *Phenomena*, showed an insufficient understanding of their profound metaphysical importance. For years, Kirstein swallowed these complaints without bothering to contradict them. While he himself has sometimes been wrongly portrayed as a person of volatile self-absorption, Lincoln was in fact that rare friend who went about quietly doing a multiplicity of favors and kindnesses, often for people who lacked his own considerable gifts—and neither sought nor expected gratitude.

Tchelitchev's churlishness did finally produce at least a muffled protest from Kirstein: "I am not pretentious enough to say that I understand Boehme or Paracelsus. I said I had read them, and I had no comparative reading material upon which to base a cosmology for a study of *Phenomena*." That mini-storm passed, but a few years later, a mutual friend repeated to Kirstein comments that Tchelitchev had publicly made about how "bored" he'd become with Kirstein's repetitive—and "impossible"—fears about the precarious financial situation of the New York City Ballet, even after it had a triumphant engagement at Covent Garden. The unjust complaint hurt Kirstein deeply. At the time Pavel made his remark, the company couldn't even afford new costumes for the upcoming season, and the repertory had to be dictated by what already existed in wardrobe. Tchelitchev lacked the grace even to add a compliment about Kirstein's remarkable contribution to making ballet a viable and reputable enterprise in the U.S.

Only once before had Kirstein let Tchelitchev know that his "megalomania every so often is a hard cross for even your most devoted friends to bear ... you forget that other people besides yourself ... need reassurance and encouragement, too; oh well, it's of no importance." But it was, and this time, with Tchelitchev badmouthing him to mutual friends, Kirstein expressed his resentment in a letter—though, remarkably, in rather gentle terms. He reminded Tchelitchev that he "never falters" in his admiration for Pavel's art, nor in doing "what I can to further" it. Perhaps, he poignantly added, "you will even admit that I have feelings just like you, and they can be hurt, just like yours." Moreover, he went on: "You are an expert in USE. ... USE is a very ugly word, and while we all need each other, it seems to me a pity that it's reduced to that level." He then retreated to the philosophical: "We all pay for our preoccupations in one way or another; yours is paid by your monastic isolation and your separation from people, and I know this [is] necessary, but in your remoteness and clarity, think of those who are condemned to be in the middle of a howling mob [a ballet company] and who continue their work in getting ephemeral things done not exactly out of delight."

The two managed to avoid an explicit break. Kirstein even wrote the catalogue for Tchelitchev's 1951 show, and Tchelitchev made Kirstein (not his longtime companion Charles Henri Ford) the executor of his estate. Yet by then, as Kirstein told Tchelitchev: "the time has long past when you and I could talk to one another," and within a year or so even their correspondence petered out. On occasion, when Tchelitchev was low on funds, he would still appeal to Kirstein for help; a check was always sent. At least once, when Kirstein was "very close to a complete breakdown," a mutual friend appealed to Tchelitchev to invite his former friend to come and stay with him in Italy; he refused.

Only two people come to mind who invariably met Kirstein's high standards, who entirely escaped his pungent wit, and captured his admiration without qualification: E. M. Forster and W. H. Auden. He had briefly met Forster via Mina's Bloomsbury connections in the 1920s, followed by a more substantive meeting a few years later, after which he pronounced both Forster and his longtime companion, the married policeman Bob Buckingham, "charming." (As Kirstein campily wrote to Mina: "I'm not tired of policemen and he was adorable.") Although Kirstein and Forster saw each other infrequently thereafter, when they did, Kirstein was always smitten with Forster's shy sweetness and unassuming wisdom. He was, Kirstein pronounced, an "angel."

One of Forster's visits to the U.S. coincided with one of Kirstein's bouts of acute depression, from which he was just emerging. Forster had had his own experience with depression, and, in a letter to Kirstein after seeing him, he cautioned against "frenzied activity," adding "you are not well enough ... for my taste and hopes. ... You were so overtired and accused yourself of things that did not exist." Kirstein had also told Forster that in his despair he'd found himself drawn to Catholicism, a temptation Forster discouraged. Catholicism, Forster told him, isn't "for those who do not grow up in it ... its assertion that it has worked, that it is a success, ought to be rejected in the realm of the spirit."

But if Kirstein thought of anyone as a "hero" (as opposed to an "angel"), it was W. H. Auden. Of all his many friendships, none would prove more satisfying and durable than his connection to Auden. Before he'd ever met him, Kirstein had read "The Orators" and considered it the greatest poem in English since Eliot's "The Wasteland." He later became certain that Auden was "the greatest English poet of our time"—and also something of a secular saint. (He referred to Auden's longtime companion, the volatile Chester Kallman, as "a sort of hair-shirt that Auden put up with as penance for his 'sins.'")*

One episode in particular epitomized for Kirstein Auden's remarkable human qualities. In 1949, Kirstein became smitten with one of the company's principal dancers, "Herbie" Bliss, and while Kirstein (unlike Balanchine) rarely became personally involved with members of the ballet company, he felt that he genuinely loved Herbie, and the two men began an affair. Temperamentally, though, Bliss was unstable to the point where Kirstein feared he might turn to suicide. Once, when Herbie disappeared, not even showing up for rehearsals, Kirstein became frantic and called in the police. Herbie did finally turn up, but with "no explanation" for his behavior. At another, particularly frightening point, Herbie became so distraught that Kirstein called on Auden for his help. Auden spent three hours with Herbie, telling him (so Kirstein reported) "many useful things." "Auden is wonderful," he added, "so kind, sweet and gentle." Within less than two years, the affair with Herbie was over. "I never see Herbie," he wrote Tchelitchev in June 1951; "he is muted, decent, accurate, and not very interesting." Kirstein could have been referring either to Herbie's dancing—the London critics had generally found him lacking in "personality"—or to his manner when with Kirstein. Or both.

When Auden died in 1973 at age 66, Kirstein told a friend that ever since their meeting in 1937, Auden had been "the strongest influence in my life." He felt certain that "the glory of [Auden's] ... verse and the wisdom of his presence" would survive. "He was a magician who continually rehabilitated the commonplace. He undercut pomposity by his common-sense and no-nonsense candor."

Kirstein himself would live on until 1996, leaving behind a different sort of legacy, a compound of turbulent suffering, profound integrity, and immense achievement. No saint was he, secular or otherwise, but a human being, tormented, gifted, and unaccountably brave. ▪

---

* See the following essay "W.H. Auden and Chester Kallman: Separately Together" for an attempt to view Kallman in a somewhat more positive light.

CHAPTER VII

W.H.Auden and Chester Kallman

SEPARATELY TOGETHER

Chester Kallman is the bad boy of the standard W. H. Auden story. In its extreme version, the tale goes something like this: In 1937, Kallman, a sixteen-year-old freshman at Brooklyn College, slyly maneuvered an introduction to the esteemed thirty-year-old poet, bedded him down that very night—re-awakening Auden's long-disappointed, long-simmering hope for a lifetime companion, a "true marriage"—and hung on ever after, fitfully available, a slattern of promiscuous lust, an abuser of trust, a financial leech, a glib, destructive, talentless dilettante, the saintly Auden's "hair shirt" (the latter, Lincoln's view).*

But is there any degree of truth to this woeful assessment of Kallman? Let us start at the beginning, when Auden and Kallman first met. In several manuscript collections, material is now available that allows for a

---

* Three manuscript collections have been of central importance in writing this piece: the Auden-Kallman correspondence at New York Public Library; the James Merrill papers at the Ransom Center at the University of Texas at Austin; and the Harold Norse Papers at the Lilly Library at the University of Indiana. Three secondary sources have also been exceptionally helpful: Richard Davenport-Hines, *Auden,* Heineman: 1995; Dorothy J. Farnan, *Auden in Love,* Faber & Faber, 1984; and Edward Mendelsohn, *Early Auden, Later Auden,* Princeton University Press: 2017.

far more nuanced description of Kallman himself and of his relationship with Auden. More is involved here than attempting to revise our understanding of one relationship. The rescue mission has broader resonance: the need to "queer" history, to interpret it from the vantage point of our own cultural perspective (keeping in mind that all historical writing is interpretive). For too long, the commentary on past LGBTQ+ lives has been in the hands of mostly conservative, mostly straight academic historians and critics who tend to define "healthy" or "authentic" relationships as ones that center on lifetime, monogamous pair-bonding—the ultimate signpost of something called "maturity."

Auden (and his many biographers) share that definition of what constitutes a successful relationship, but Kallman (who's had no biography) did not. A good-looking young blond of full-lipped sensuality and—as he was pleased to advertise—"well-hung," Kallman was from an early age cocksure (pardon the pun), confident of his seductive prowess and buoyantly shameless when satisfying his abundant sexual appetite. Even before meeting Auden, Kallman had already told his father (his mother had died young) that he was "queer," that he saw nothing wrong with it, and had no wish to "outgrow it." Bright, clever, and keen-witted, by age sixteen Kallman was already enrolled as a freshman at Brooklyn College. He'd been sexually active since the age of twelve, having his first serious affair with an older Brooklyn College student and fellow poet named Harold Albaum. (He later changed it to Harold Norse, became part of Allen Ginsberg's circle, won considerable recognition, and lived into his nineties.)

In the Norse Papers at the Lilly Library, Norse describes Chester Kallman in 1939 as a young man whose "charm and powers have become a legend." Many others who knew Kallman in his youth tended to regard him as a singularly "glamorous" creature. Starting at age twelve, he had (in Norse's words) habitually "molested adults in subway toilets" and fearlessly approached attractive men on the street. In his 1989 autobiography, *Memoirs of a Bastard Angel*, Norse emphasizes other aspects of Kallman's character: his nature was "essentially benign" and kind-hearted, though his campy, merciless wit, "an acid rain of mockery," sometimes concealed his affectionate nature. Chester also had from an early age a profound passion for music and for opera in particular, identifying, diva-like, with its exaggerated emotions.

After his first sexual experience with Auden in 1939, Kallman delightedly

Chester Kallman and W. H. Auden

reported to Harold Norse that the poet had exclaimed, "Thank God it's big!" "Talk about groveling!" added Kallman naughtily, "He'd stay down all night if I didn't remind him that even I am not inexhaustible." From the start, in fact, Kallman viewed the two as sexually incompatible: Auden deplored anal sex, while Kallman's primary pleasure lay in getting fucked. As Auden once wrote in his journal: "To me the act of fucking, whether heterosexual or homosexual, seems an act of sadistic aggression, to submit to it, masochistic, and neither actively nor passively have I ever enjoyed it." To Kallman, such a view was unthinkable heresy.

When on an out-of-town trip with Auden about a year after they met, Kallman wrote Norse that he was sexually bored: "When I do get back to the city I expect to spend 3/4 of my time flat on my stomach biting into pillows, listening to the music ... of the bed-springs." It didn't help that Auden was an inept, awkward lover. Although he'd had his share of sexual adventures in Berlin in the 1920s, his dormant Christianity (by 1940 he was about to recommit to his idiosyncratic version of the faith) fed his uneasiness about sensual indulgence. Kallman, born Jewish, was adamantly secular and regarded sex as a source of unequivocal pleasure.

Their views on homosexuality itself were no less at odds. Auden felt that it was a misfortune, a "crooked" disorder. He kept changing his mind about the infirmity's origins, but his negativity remained a constant. During his Freudian phase, he saw it as "an unconscious criticism of the mother as a love-object"; at other times, he thought it a form of adolescent rebellion or a flight from intimacy. Consistently and ruefully, he viewed homosexuality as a "backward" or "regressive" form of attachment—not a variation of authentic love but an impediment to it. Before meeting Kallman, Auden had considered his erotic life a failure—a narcissistic derangement, as he saw it, limited and barren.

His attitude reflected, of course, standard psychiatric assumptions of the day. However brilliantly original in his deployment of language and comfortable with his own personal eccentricities, Auden was utterly conventional in his views on sexuality and gender roles.

Kallman, a gifted poet—though he'd never find a comparably unique poetic voice—rejected conventional views about romantic love and monogamy, and freely indulged his guiltfree enjoyment of "immoral" sexual pleasure. His attitude looks ahead to the 21st century, while Auden's seem anchored in the late 19th.

What made Kallman a better candidate for Auden's affections than previous attachments was their shared class origins, Kallman's precocious intelligence, and his passion for language. Soon after meeting him, Auden wrote the poem "Heavy Date":

> *I believed for years that*
> *Love was the conjunction*
> *Of two oppositions;*
> *That was all untrue;*
> *Every young man fears that*
> *He is not worth loving:*
> *Bless you, darling, I have*
> *Found myself in you.*

Auden was now able, with lapses, at least to consider the notion that homosexuality was something other than a curse—that is, if experienced within the context of a committed relationship and performed (in his words) with "a person with whom I shall be one flesh." From their first meeting, Auden was obsessed and adoring. Kallman, for his part, seems to have realized early on that he'd found in Auden a soulmate, yet he never confused that with having found a sexual partner who could magically and enduringly meet his erotic needs. Not even in the short term.

Kallman wanted sex often and with a variety of partners—and he was open about it. He never pretended to Auden (or to anyone, for that matter) that he was equally smitten, and he never agreed to sexual fidelity. Auden knew the terms of the relationship from the beginning. He sometimes suffered greatly, especially in the early years, from Kallman's amorous wanderings, yet he refused to relinquish the relationship. He saw in Kallman the life partner he'd given up all hope of finding and was wise enough to realize that love was, after all, far harder to find than sex. His description of himself (to Christopher Isherwood) as "a real Victorian wife," though perhaps written with tongue in check, wasn't far off the mark.

For a time, Kallman continued to see Norse almost daily, and he continued to cruise relentlessly—and unrepentantly. Auden may have fallen madly in love (if defined as obsession), but Kallman had not. He liked and admired Auden, was powerfully drawn to his genius, his awesome phrase-making, his magnetic story-telling and outlandish erudition, his gallant generosity of spirit. But he was not drawn to Auden's sometimes domineering ways, cantankerous moods, stubborn, sometimes gruff, certitude—and most assuredly *not* to his fleshy, unathletic body and limited, clumsy sexual repertoire.

Not least, Kallman enjoyed having an entree into Auden's glamorous world. When the two went cross-country in the summer of 1939 on what Wystan insisted on calling their "honeymoon" ("Such a romantic girl!" Kallman wrote Norse), and bought "wedding rings" to mark the occasion (Kallman refused to wear his), their first stop was a two-day visit to Thomas Mann and his family in Princeton, followed by a layover in Baton Rouge to see Katherine Anne Porter and her husband, a meeting in Taos with D. H. Lawrence's widow Frieda ("a marvelous woman," Kallman wrote Norse), and, finally, a leisurely stay in California with Christopher Isherwood. (Judging from his published diaries, Isherwood over the years would continue to have mixed feelings about Kallman. He liked him "much more" as he grew older, writing in a 1948 diary entry, after an Auden-Kallman visit, that Kallman "is very funny, and so anxious to be friendly that it is quite touching. ... [He] said to me: 'I feel at last that you really don't disapprove of me.'")

Kallman kept a zealous eye out at bus and train stops for attractive young men, reporting in a letter to Norse that he'd "almost precipitated a domestic crisis by groping a boy sitting next to me between Jacksonville and Tallahassee. Boy, I think, was straight avec un basquet, ma chere, that he kept adjusting. Wystan was quite rightly exasperated, the boy merely removed my hand with a slight smile." When forced to become aware of Kallman's "antics," Auden more typically kept discreetly silent. Thrilled that "the marriage of true minds" he'd long sought was actually at hand, Auden seems to have hoped that once Kallman's teen years were behind him and his hormones less rampant, he would turn more domestic—and monogamous. But that, as he would unhappily learn, was not to be.

IN THE VERY EARLY days of the relationship, Kallman may have been briefly caught up in Auden's ecstatic fantasy of enduring "oneness" and may even have shared and encouraged it. Soon after their initial meeting in April 1939, Auden had to leave New York for a few weeks to fulfill a teaching engagement at St. Marks School, and during May and June, Kallman sent him several letters underscoring his devotion. In one, dated May 13th and in apparent response to Auden's parched need for validation, Kallman provocatively replied, "Why this self-abasement? Can you be assured?" He did try: "I love you, I love you, I love you." In a subsequent letter, Kallman even suggested (without saying as much outright) that he'd been giving his cruising a temporary rest: "You worry about the sailors and I wile [*sic*] away my time imagining you teaching some student French in bed... We're both wiling [*sic*] away time groundlessly I think."

Ten days later, in another letter, Kallman reiterated his devotion: "Dear, I do love you!" and soon after followed up with "this love business is beginning to tell on me. I miss you disturbingly much—damn you darling." He even reassured Auden regarding their different preferences in bed: "I am quite convinced, we are not different, darling, not at all—just a bunch of healthy youngsters who come in different positions and look at different people, but we're quite all right, eh?" As if brought back to reality, Kallman signed the letter "Your little whore."

The honeymoon was brief. Within a year of their first meeting, a crisis arose when Auden discovered that Kallman had fallen for a handsome, well-built young Englishman known only by the pseudonym "Jack Lansing," and had started seeing him with some regularity. Auden was shocked at the depth of rage this "betrayal" aroused in him. He felt that he knew for the first time "what it is like to feel oneself the prey of demonic powers, in both the Greek and the Christian sense, stripped of self-control and self-respect, behaving like a ham actor in a Strindberg play." But as Humphrey Carpenter—the Auden biographer who has shown more sympathy toward Kallman than any other—has written: "Chester's behaviour was only to be expected. He had never loved Auden with the same intensity as he was loved by him ... and Auden ... had in his eyes the role of patron and protector rather than lover. Even this had its difficulties, for Chester sometimes resented Auden's patronage."

Following Auden's stormy reaction over "Jack," Kallman played his trump card: he announced that he and Auden would no longer have sex. And he meant it—though the two would stay together as a couple, and each would find in the other not only his best friend but a mutually reliant "co-conspirator." As Auden put it in a mid-1940s letter: "I need your interest and your help more than you know (or allow yourself to know)." For his part, Kallman stressed "that, in whatever context it may be, or whatever interpretation it may be subjected to, I love you."

It was Kallman who opened Auden's eyes to the wonders of opera. The two came to share a lifelong passion for the form and starting in the late '40s co-wrote a series of opera librettos, the most successful of which was Stravinsky's *The Rake's Progress*. The original deal for "The Rake" was made between Auden and Stravinsky—until Auden, with typical generosity, simply told Stravinsky that he'd be taking on "his friend" Chester Kallman as co-librettist. When a surprised Stravinsky reacted negatively to the news and was clearly upset, Auden assured him that "Mr. Kallman is a better librettist than I am"—and in fact Kallman did prove to be an extremely gifted one. After working together for a time, Stravinsky (whom Kallman referred to as "the mighty anal") wrote him directly to say that he had "found your poetry most expressive and flexible for my music." Not only was Stravinsky delighted with Kallman's contribution but (according to Stravinsk's associate, Robert Craft) "was quickly won by [his] ... intelligence and sense of humor." Kallman (according to Craft) was "easier to understand than Auden, and could bring out ... [Auden's] dormant affability, as well as subdue his tempers ... Bluntly stated, the Stravinskys were happier with Auden when Chester Kallman was present."

Yet Kallman never found, either as a librettist or a poet, anything like Auden's dedicated vocation; perhaps his talent simply wasn't deep enough—besides, Kallman never shared Auden's highly disciplined work ethic; his concentration was much too sporadic. And then there was alcohol. At least one friend—the distinguished poet James Merrill ("Jimmy")—came to view Kallman as a prime and sad example of a significant talent destroyed by alcohol—and "gay self-hatred." As early as 1951, when Merrill attended the premiere of *The Rake's Progress* in Venice's glittering La Fenice theater, Merrill noted that at the curtain call—a roaring ovation, with the librettists joining Stravinsky onstage—Kallman looked like "a vision of Sin, puffy and purpled and scarred."

When Harold Norse ran into Kallman during roughly the same period, he lamented (or pretended to) that the brilliant, demonic boy he'd once known had disappeared. Perhaps, Norse wrote in his notebook (now in the Lilly Library), "Having been too close to him at an early age, I saw him when all was promise, intimations of grandeur. Now, that's over... Also, his social manner [is]... close to the Jewish ham actor. Lots of mugging, always one eye on the effect, never quite true, sure of itself, given." Norse, though, was being harsh, as we know from other, more appreciative observers, like Isherwood or Merrill.

Still, there was no gainsaying the decline over the years in Kallman's promise (and as well his good looks). When he and Auden were apart, they exchanged letters (Kallman sometimes belatedly) about everything from literature to publishing to money—which Kallman often needed and which Auden usually sent. Auden would periodically urge Kallman—believing that "no friendship... can endure without cool, clear 'minds-to-hearts'"—to yield less automatically to his impulses, particularly in regard to sex, and to activate a more rigorous routine when it came to writing. But to no avail, perhaps partly because Auden himself relied heavily on alcohol and Benzedrine.

They were also explicit in their letters about their separate sex lives, with Kallman always having far more to report. "Divine soldier and his friend," he wrote Auden at one point, "both hotter than the nuts of hell—just want to fuck all night long." At another point he mockingly chastised Auden for going to the Turkish baths when in Michigan: "Shame on you, Wystan. ... By the way, has anything been thrust at you through the Ann Arbor 'glory holes'?"

For the remainder of their lives, Wystan and Chester continued to live together for part of each year; their affective, though not sexual, ties remaining closely entwined. The "marriage" that Auden had as a younger man desperately longed for, held. They spent winters in New York City and summers first on the island of Ischia and later in the cozy Austrian town of Kirchstetten. In their later years, much to Auden's regret, Kallman began to spend increasing amounts of time in Greece, where casual sex was much more available. By 1963, he'd substituted Athens for New York and he and Auden from then on lived together only during the summer. The separation greatly deepened Auden's gloom and loneliness; nor did it help Kallman to rally his resources: more of his energy went into cooking than poetry. He became a master (and hugely messy) chef, once turning out a dinner of Chicken Marengo and chocolate soufflé for twelve on the same evening he moved into a new apartment.

He also fell in love—with a young soldier named Yannis Boras, who was admiringly described by Jimmy Merrill's partner, David Jackson, as having "the patience and affection to put up with terribly strange lives... [he had] that great talent which understands what is human and what is simply a nervous surface." Tragically, Yannis, age 26, died in 1968 after being hit by a drunken driver. A bereft Kallman turned more and more to drink. As for Auden, in his later years he'd have an occasional, brief affair, but sex had never been at the center of his life and its absence seems not to have bothered him much; he described himself in his 1966 poem "Fairground" as one of those who'd put "their wander-years behind them," who "play chess or cribbage,/ games that call for patience, foresight, manoeuvre,/ like war, like marriage."

If he didn't miss sex, he most certainly missed Kallman; the habit of a shared life had become central to his sense of well-being. In the hope of regaining some form of community, Auden accepted Oxford's offer of a permanent residency and returned to England early in 1972.

Kallman approved the move—not least because, as he wrote a friend, Wystan had of late been imposing "rather hair-raising tension... on every-one near him in New York, me especially." For a brief time, Auden seemed happy and relaxed at Oxford. But too much had changed; too many old friends were gone, too many donnish rituals discarded. There were few amenities, and even less conviviality. His friends feared that he would drink himself to death. Miserable and ill, Auden suffered a fatal heart attack in 1973, age 66. It was Kallman, devastatingly, who found his body. Hearing the news, James Merrill wrote to him: "It may not always have been plain to you... how greatly he loved you & relied on you; but it was to the rest of us. I mean, always was." Shocked and heart-broken, Kallman never recovered. A year and a half later, he too was dead, at age 54.

NEARLY EVERYONE who has written about Chester Kallman has essentially described him in words that might suggest a "borderline" personality: as a spoiled and selfish sociopath, a sexual predator, an irre-sponsible parasite interested in little more than indulging his insatiable sexual appetite. Sometimes explicitly, but usually by implication, Kall-man's critics profess bewilderment over Auden's profound and lifelong attachment to him.

Kallman could cause Auden pain and public embarrassment, but that stream ran in both directions. Auden's uninterruptable monologues and outbursts of rude, grumpy arrogance inflicted their own share of discomfort on Kallman.† Besides, being the spouse of an acclaimed genius, and considerably younger as well, could be an onerous role that encouraged superficial dismissal as a mere appendage, a sponge. Kallman was in fact too gifted simply to bask in reflected glory; he was more its victim.

The point isn't to parcel out "blame" more evenly but instead to recognize that from their very first meeting, an "electric spark" passed between Auden and Kallman that in the coming decades would often dim but never go out. Though their relationship, like most—like all?—could be contentious and troubled, they saw in each other the likeliest candidate either would ever know of a "true marriage"—and not primarily (as often suggested) because of dovetailing neuroses. Kallman was far more of a genuine partner than is usually credited. "I rely absolutely upon your critical judgment," Auden once wrote him, and in another letter he stated flat-out that "you are the one comrade my non-sexual life cannot do without." Kallman often influenced Auden's taste, held his own with him intellectually (surpassing him in aphoristic wit, though never matching his erudition), and proved genuinely and generously supportive during difficult moments.

Auden could now and then sound a note of homosexual "chauvinism," but far more often he saw his "condition" as a curse, and possibly even a crime. "It's wrong to be queer," he told a friend in 1947, "all homosexual acts are acts of envy." When *The Kinsey Report* was published the following year, Auden wrote a review that he himself characterized as "so anti-homintem" that he tore it up. In 1950, he titled his review of a new biography of Oscar Wilde "A Playboy of the Western World: St. Oscar the Homintem Martyr."

Chester Kallman shared none of those views. He was comfortable with his homosexuality and delighted in sex. That has almost certainly been a contributing factor—arguably the most important—to his undeservedly negative press. ▪

---

† See, in this volume, "Kirstein: Part III: Rivals and Idols" for an adoring view of Auden that never mentions (let alone credits) the importance in his life of Kallman.

CHAPTER VIII

Andrea Dworkin

THE WOMAN I KNEW

MOST PEOPLE *know Andrea Dworkin simply as a radical feminist prominent in the anti-pornography campaigns of the 1980s and '90s. Yet this is only one aspect of a complex, intriguing woman who authored a dozen books, and was a passionate, tenacious activist for social justice. My biography* Andrea Dworkin: The Feminist as Revolutionary *(The New Press: 2020) was based on her rich (and previously closed) archive at Harvard's Schlesinger Library. Having unimpeded access to the archive allowed me to write a comprehensive account of her life. Still, as I was putting this book together, I realized that I had something more I wanted to say—this time, about our personal relationship.*

*Andrea and I became friendly in the early 1970s as a result of working together in the anti-Vietnam War organization REDRESS. Since our friendship was centrally linked as well to the early years of the Gay Academic Union, it also throws some light on gay male-lesbian attempts to work together politically.**

Early in 1973, a group of mostly young academics began to meet informally to discuss what we might do to make the university world a

---

* For more on the Gay Academic Union, see Duberman, *Midlife Queer,* University of Wisconsin Press (1996), pp. 49-59.

more accepting environment for gay people, and also to foster the study of gay and lesbian lives. After months of discussion and debate, we decided to focus on several goals: to pressure the American Association of University Professors and other academic organizations to protect the rights of openly gay faculty; to serve as a support network for the many isolated gay people on campus; to pinpoint needed areas of scholarly research; and to originate pilot programs for course work in lesbian and gay studies.

We decided to call ourselves the Gay Academic Union (GAU), and, as a way of announcing ourselves and beginning the work of reducing homophobia on the nation's campuses, we set about planning for a conference that fall on "The Universities and the Gay Experience." From the beginning of the planning sessions, one problem loomed large: in the early 1970s, women were still scarce on academic faculties, and "out" lesbians were scarcer still. We were also aware that the early post-Stonewall organizations—the Gay Liberation Front and the Gay Activists Alliance—had been rent with bitter struggles over what the women justifiably protested as "male chauvinism." Determined from the start to deal openly with these real and difficult issues, some of the gay men connected with planning the GAU conference formed a consciousness-raising group to discuss our own acknowledged sexism. As a result, most of the attendees took a firm stance about the need to ensure that women would have equal representation on GAU's steering committee. But the vote wasn't unanimous. Some of the men took vocal exception to the introduction of what they called the "irrelevant" issue of feminism, and, in response, some of the women expressed doubt as to whether they would continue to attend meetings.

Enter Andrea Dworkin. As an eighteen-year-old undergraduate at Bennington (where she'd had affairs with both men and women, including the wife of a dean), Andrea had already become politically active around antiwar and feminist issues. As early as 1964, she'd been arrested during a street protest in Manhattan protesting the war in Vietnam and had spent four days in the Women's House of Detention, where two male medical examiners treated her so brutally that she'd bled for days afterwards.

Soon after, Andrea went to Europe to live and write. For a time, she found "true love" on the island of Crete, but then moved to Amsterdam, where she met and married a Dutch anarchist who turned sadist and badly beat her. Finally escaping, she worked briefly as a prostitute and then returned to the States.

Living at the poverty level in an East Village tenement, she was befriended by the short story writer Grace Paley and the well-known poet Muriel Rukeyser. Both women believed in Andrea's talent and took her on as a part-time assistant. She also went to work for REDRESS, the anti-Vietnam war group, and it was at one of its meetings that she and I first met and were soon drawn to each other. At the time, Andrea was putting the finishing touches on what would become her celebrated (and also widely criticized) first book, *Woman-Hating*, and she asked both me and Muriel (also involved with REDRESS) to read a final draft. Muriel found it stunningly good and called Andrea to say (as she reported to her parents) that "she thinks it's one of the most important books of our time—wow!" I was somewhat less enthusiastic, but believing as I did in Andrea's talent, sent her to Hal Scharlatt, my own editor at E. P. Dutton.

Hal did encourage her, though Andrea complained to me about his "heavy vibes" and wrote her parents—adamantly, as was her way—that she "won't agree to certain changes they want to make." I told her that she was way off the mark in regard to Hal, that not only was he a brilliant editor but an entirely reasonable one, and as well one of the gentlest, kindest of men. Andrea grumbled but took my word for it. She did have an implacable side when it came to protecting her writing, but contrary to what became a standard charge against her, that was hardly the sum of her personality. Over the years, her army of critics would denounce her as an inflexible virago, yet interviewers who met her personally would comment again and again on how surprised they were at her soft-spoken, gentle manner—and her uncommon ability to listen. Andrea on a public platform was often fierce and truculent; in person, she was usually empathic and generous. I vividly remember the time I opened the door to my apartment after she and I had had a heated political disagreement at a GAU meeting the night before—and found her standing there shyly holding a placating bouquet of flowers.

When I first suggested to Andrea that she join me at a GAU meeting, she was reluctant. First of all, she pointed out, she wasn't an academic and besides, her sympathies were focused not on the plight of gay people but on the mistreatment of women.

Andrea Dworkin. Photo: Alexander Caminada

Still, as an act of friendship, she did finally agree to give GAU a try. She'd already decided from her early experience of gay male politicos that many of them were blatant sexists, and, to make matters worse, were unwilling to acknowledge it. Almost all of the original organizers of GAU self-described as political *radicals* (i.e. *not* "mere" liberals), and were, in my view, far more aware than most men that, as creatures of the culture, they'd internalized a belittling, patronizing view of the inherent abilities of women. As it would subsequently turn out, within two years of its establishment, GAU would come under the control of a small group of decidedly *conservative* gay men—at which point I, and most of the other pro-feminist men, resigned. The organization itself collapsed a year later.

All that lay in the future. Back in 1973, by way of thanks for having put her in touch with Hal Scharlatt at Dutton, Andrea took me out to dinner at Max's Kansas City, then all the rage. We ended up talking nonstop for five hours that night—talking "with a kind of electricity" (as I wrote in my diary) that I'd rarely known before. I also discovered that—despite all of those REDRESS meetings—I knew next to nothing of Andrea's personal history, nor she of mine, and after filling in the blanks we settled into a searching political exchange that was formative in shaping my activism in the years ahead. Throughout the evening (as I somewhat feverishly put it in my journal), "rockets kept going off in my head, butterflies in my stomach. We kept completing each other's sentences, shaken at the similarity of experience and perception, overjoyed at the confirmation that we were not singular freaks but parts of an emerging community (nervously) willing at last to talk about what we had all long wanted to hear, to demystify the desperate secrets, [and] to end the separation in ourselves, and the society, between the private and public voices." We wanted to embrace the manifold, fearful sexual fantasies that peopled our dreams and to view the deviations from traditional gender norms "as enrichments to be openly encouraged, not shameful deviations to be carefully concealed." At the time of our dinner, Andrea described herself as bisexual, leaning more toward the heterosexual side, at least experientially. Within a few years, she came out as lesbian; though after what she called a "wild" youth, she thereafter settled into a more subdued sexuality. She would soon meet John Stoltenberg, who became her life partner.

Andrea helped me to clarify my own understanding of bisexuality. It was not, she insisted, the equivalent of—and could even serve as a fortification against—androgyny. That is, to have sex with both genders (as the binary then had it) in the same way—for example, to be always dominant or always passive—could keep us from the realization that each of us has a wide, if fettered, spectrum of sexual impulses and gender fantasies. As I told Andrea that night at Max's, I'd often berated myself in the past for what I labeled my "inconsistent" desires in bed, and saw my varying moods and acts as a function of an "incomplete" or "muddled" sexual identity. Andrea assured me that what (back then) was often called "role confusion" was what we should now regard as the rejection of rigid definitions of permissible needs.

She also reinforced my already strong conviction that women, gay men, and people of color were involved in a common political struggle against a shared oppressor: the dominance of the heterosexual White male and our own deep-seated wish to become like him, to play his macho role, to incorporate his macho body, to offer ourselves—even gratefully—to his macho mistreatment. I'd already come to believe (as I wrote in my diary) that "the primary obstacle that had been preventing a gay male/feminist alliance from maturing was the gay male denial of his own marginality and gender non-conformity"—which was especially true of the white, middle-class gay men who dominated the current political movement.

At the time, I'd somewhat smugly assumed that I was already more conscious of sexism as a prime enemy than were most gay men. What I now began to see more clearly was that the "enemy" wasn't solely "out there" but also within ourselves. In that regard, I was hardly exempt from scrutiny. As I put it in my diary: "my enjoyment of the company of women is sometimes based on the stereotypic qualities I invest them with—'understanding,' 'sensitivity,' 'intuition'—the same gender expectations deep-seated in the culture and whose consequences make women afraid of success, and men disdainful of emotion."

DISCUSSION of the advantages and pitfalls of a feminist-gay alliance became frequent in GAU, and in the course of the argument, one remark stayed with me. It came from "Marilyn," a warm and wise historian of science who I'd immediately been taken with when she first appeared at the meetings. She broke through one of our more heated discussions to say, with just a trace of irritation, "You need to get it through your heads that in the eyes of the straight world, you gay men are *all* considered feminine."

Andrea underlined another incisive point: she strongly urged us to distinguish between the willingness of some of the gay men to become better informed about feminist concerns and the views of a group called the "Revolutionary Effeminists," which in those years enjoyed considerable notoriety and whose ideology was exemplified in the writings of Kenneth Pitchford (married to the prominent feminist Robin Morgan). In Andrea's view, which complemented and strengthened my own, Pitchford tended to see "female" traits as inherent and fixed, and she deplored his call for homosexual men to "copy" those traits and to subordinate their own needs in the name of bringing Womanhood to power.

Andrea encouraged me to see the Pitchford model as static and tyrannical, a confinement of women to a limited set of biologically induced traits, and of homosexual males to a no less traditional "effeminacy" historically linked to some sort of genetic deficiency. At that stage in my own rapidly evolving views on sexuality and gender, Andrea's words were heady stuff. Here was a radical perspective that not only rejected traditional straight male dominance but also some of the strategies—like the essentialism of the Pitchford model—then being deployed to undermine it.

Andrea lasted only a few months in GAU. She told me that she felt worn down by the resistance of most of the gay men at the meetings to acknowledging their own entrenched sexism. It was a point that in general I didn't contest, but I did take issue with Andrea's blanket assumption— and told her so—that this particular group of gay men was no more open to a "salvage operation" than men in general. Although our consciousness about sexism may well not be at the optimal level needed, we weren't as uneducable as she insisted. If true, that meant there was some hope that gay men and women *could* manage to work together, and our combined force would increase our clout and our potential ability to produce social change.

Andrea didn't buy it. She believed that the "primary emergency" for women was feminism, not homosexuality. My counterargument was that we were capable of more than one commitment at a time; few of us—and certainly not Andrea—lived in so single-minded a cocoon, or had such a limited supply of energy that we had to confine ourselves to single-issue politics. I did agree with Andrea when she broadened her indictment to include "leftwing" gay men in general for their "abysmal ignorance of feminist writings" and for failing to incorporate "the social analysis that radical feminists have done in these last years." Which is true, I wrote in my diary: Some of the radical gay men "are reading [Stanley] Aronowitz, [Murray] Bookchin, etc. with serious regard, but [Kate] Millett, [Robin] Morgan, [Ti-Grace] Atkinson, and [Angela] Davis not at all, or with the most obvious condescension." On the whole, I was more optimistic than

Andrea in believing in the plasticity of some gay men, but the conversation between us would ebb and flow, with neither us giving much ground. Our relationship, in fact, wouldn't last beyond the mid-'70s. No personal anger was involved; our political paths simply diverged.

WHEN ANDREA resigned from GAU, she did so with a bang. Late in 1974, in a blistering open letter, she denounced the organization for its "insufferable arrogance and male supremacy." By then, at least as regarded GAU, I didn't disagree. Over time, the organization had become unexpectedly inundated (it seemed that dramatic at the time) with a growing number of openly anti-feminist gay men, most of them tenured academics, whose ranks and influence would continue to grow and who, pushing aside those of us with at least an incipient feminist consciousness, ended up controlling the organization. How they did it remains, even today, a considerable enigma.

PART OF THE LASTING legacy of my friendship with Andrea was an audacious insight of hers that has stayed with me, and deepened. What she saw in her clear-eyed way—and would greatly suffer for—was, as she put it, the need "to break down the dichotomy between how we talk to ourselves and (perhaps) our closest friends, and how we present ourselves in our formal, social roles." What was needed was an effort to present ourselves publicly with the same complexities and contradictions which we privately entertain in our fantastical heads. To bring those utopian impulses to the forefront of consciousness would surely be belittled as besotted exhibitionism, but that risk had to be run. To talk frankly and in detail about our private fantasies and "shameful" behavior represents (when not powered by mere exhibitionism) an honest impulse to understand the potential range of our desires—and to share that self-scrutiny openly.

It would mean, too, making an effort to use words as genuine instruments of communication rather than, as currently, a means of deception and disguise, or as a tool for control—that is, a device for *preventing* communications that might threaten to upend accepted definitions of humanness and relationships of power. Andrea pointed out that the attempt at full-out honesty, especially at first, would often fail; the words might come out as an indulgent grab bag of unfelt laments and arch postures—in other words, what we had long since been trained to show. But the impulse behind those attempts, if it remained authentic, would at least represent the buried wish to break away from the exchange of falsely meager messages, to bridge the gulf of separation.

It didn't matter, Andrea argued, that our initial attempts might fall lamentably short. That would only mean that the effort was deficient, the communication incomplete. How could it initially be otherwise, coming from people schooled to conceal "improper" needs—and thereby main-tain the traditional taboos. We needed to at least make a start toward what many of us were beginning urgently to feel: that people have to talk to each other in different ways about different things. A start is a start, not a completion. The need is there: to universalize—but not homogenize—freakiness, to allow people to see that what they've been taught to hide as individual shame could be converted into bonds of commonality. ▪

Addendum

Allies or Enemies? The Relationship between the Feminist and Gay Male Movements*
1975 and 2023

I WANT TO EXPLAIN my reasons for thinking that the feminist and gay movements are natural allies and why, logical though the alliance may be, the partnership is currently in disarray, due in particular to the con-troversy, both with each other and within each movement, over whether gender is biologically or socially shaped. Feminists in particular, both then (1975) and now (2023), differ profoundly over which behavioral traits are or are not biological in origin. In gay life, too, there are varied views on whether some behavioral traits are givens or are responses to socialization. My own sympathy in the debate lies predominantly with radical feminism, by which I mean that I mostly accept the conclusion of Shulamith Firestone and others that patriarchy and hierarchy (along with racial and class distinctions) are the dominant social units of repression, and that the nuclear family is a central institution for perpetuating "things as they are." I also agree with the radical feminist insistence that certain anatomical differences (themselves upended by the transsexual and transgender revolutions)—like genitalia, lactation, menstruation, plus the female's greater capacity for multiple orgasm—are grounded in biology, yet social attitudes toward those behaviors have throughout history varied wildly in regard to "respectability."

The same is true of most of our behavior: it is learned, not biologically determined. "Mothering," for example, may come as naturally to men as to women. The family unit, which conservatives view as divinely ordained, may not be the best available environment for raising children. (However, as yet we haven't managed to conceptualize, let alone put into practice, an alternate mode of child-rearing that—for the child—is clearly preferable to the ongoing pattern.) As for other so-called "innate" male-female differences, the research to date has overturned a variety of established truisms. The majority of researchers currently assign most differences between the sexes to socialization, not to biology. Many of the myths surrounding gender are no longer considered valid: girls are not more "social" than boys or more "suggestible"; boys are not more analytic, more achievement-oriented, more affected than girls by their environment. Girls are less willing to be alone, or more strenuously motivated

---

* This piece is reconstructed from typed notes taken down in 1975, and recently revised. Terminology (and much else) has changed over the past fifty years, and even terminology has shifted. "Gay" has given way since 1975 to "queer" which in turn is today used more or less interchangeably with LGBTQ+, with the "T" for "trans" in the forefront of current discussion. To accommodate the assorted shifts in terminology—without, hopefully, updating and misrepresenting my views at the time.

I made (and have now revised) these remarks as part of a panel discussion sponsored by The National Gay Task Force on December 6, 1975. The other panel members were Charlotte Bunch, then editor of the feminist quarterly *quest*; Bert Hansen, professor of history at SUNY, Binghamton; (Betty) Achebe Powell, conference chairwoman of The Gay Academic Union; Kathy Samuels of the Women's Action Alliance; and Ronni Smith of the New York State Division of Human Rights. Jean O'Leary moderated. Charlotte Curtis and Roger Wilkins of *The New York Times* presented questions to the panel.

to "please." Nor are young girls more "interactive" during play, nor less "aggressive" and more "empathic" towards others, nor less "analytic" or less motivated to achieve.

Still hotly contested is the superiority of girls in verbal skill and of boys in visual-spatial ability. Even here, the battle seems to come down primarily to semantics, and in particular to the sometimes casual acceptance of so-called male "aggression" as an innate trait without even defining it. There isn't even agreement as to whether "aggression" should be confined to a *conscious* intent to hurt. Indeed, there's a strong argument to be made that the behavior labeled "aggressive" is more accurately regarded as "competitiveness" or "assertiveness"—both of which, it's widely agreed, *are* the product of social learning and not of biology. But if scientific rigor has laid to rest many of the so-called distinctions between the genders, current findings about the lack of significant differences between boys and girls have not persuaded the general public. Most Americans continue to believe the older "truths," the values by which they themselves were raised. Traditional-minded women and men have not been eager to surrender their basic understanding of who they are, nor the familiarity, comfort, and control of their respective domains—the home or the workplace. Besides, as the traditionalists might argue, "scientific truths" also change through time and particularly in response to society's shifting need to valorize some forms of behavior and disparage others.

Perhaps the safest tack for now is to accept that some innate, limited biological differences between the genders do exist—and to immediately add that they don't much matter. That is, given the large range of skills and temperaments among women, some—and probably many— are entirely capable of filling every role that men currently monopolize (though some of the men are quite unsuited to perform the roles assigned to them). Given the rawness of the debate over gender, equivocation and puzzlement are for now probably inevitable, perhaps even desirable. In regard to the *social* roles men and women currently play, however—and reintroducing gay men into the discussion—there are a few confident generalizations that can be risked with a fair amount of certainty.

1. Gay men are usually (and I certainly include myself, or at lest my earlier self) men first and gay second in their value set and behavior, in their competitiveness and ambition, in their wish to share straight male privilege and power. For many, their bottom-line priorities are assimilationist: let us join the male club that runs the show. On a less conscious level, the mantra becomes far more primitive: we seek alliance with straight men against all women. (I firmly believe, though, that straight men, as a group, harbor greater hostility toward women than do gay men as a group.)

2. Straight women are much less threatened by homosexuality than are straight men. It logically follows that a shared vision, sympathy, and cooperation between all women and gay men does exist, a shared sense of what is wrong and what might make it better.

3. I have a strong personal sense that feminism has much to teach me—has already taught me. Feminist social analysis seems to me far ahead of anything currently being produced by gay men. It does seem to me that some few women—straight and lesbian—are doing the most to disclose the inadequacies not simply of our social institutions but the limitations placed on our definition of "humanness." In this regard, basic inquiries into male/female "differences" have often gone unexamined. It does not minimize the importance of politics to suggest that any alliance between the feminist and gay movements based on unexamined assumptions about gender is not one likely to stay glued together.

In this regard, let me bring up another (embarrassing) question that these days I've learned not to ask. What does my lack of erotic interest in women mean? Does it imply to some degree, a phobic response? Why else would I not develop sexual feelings toward women for whom I feel deep affection? To what extent do, or should, affection and lust coincide? Phrased this way, these questions sound dangerously close to traditional medical theory about male homosexuality, and reflect exactly what the larger society wants us to believe. But the fact that we don't like the people making certain statements, doesn't prove that those statements are, in part at least, wrong—though we do know that they have been exaggerated and misused.

In any case, to the degree that a phobic reaction on the part of (some? many?) gay men exists toward women (and possibly as well—I simply don't know—some lesbians toward men) talk of a "natural alliance" may be dubious. I prefer to believe that sexual disinterest does not necessarily imply any degree of repugnance (even though psychiatry has long insisted that it does). I prefer that belief but I'd be an ostrich if I insisted that what I want to believe has as yet been fully demonstrated to be true. ▪

CHAPTER IX

The Two Eds

A FIFTY-YEAR LOVE STORY

Co-authored with Michael Kammen

IN 2010, MICHAEL KAMMEN, *the Pulitzer Prize-winning (People of Paradox) historian, an acquaintance from years earlier, asked me for some advice about gay history and culture. Michael taught at Cornell throughout his academic career, and at some point he learned that the university's archival division had recently acquired a large manuscript collection—the Wormley/Crouse Papers.*

"Wormley" was Edward Wormley (1907-1995), a modernist designer of furniture and interiors, who in the mid-20th century gained prominence for combining the avant-garde modernism of the Bauhaus and the International Style with certain features that derived from classical design. When Playboy in 1961 chose the six most prominent designers of the day for a feature article on modern American furniture, it included Wormley, along with Harry Bertoia, Charles Eames, George Nelson, Jens Risom, and Eero Saarinen. Nationally prominent in mid century, Wormley also won a number of prestigious awards, including the Elsie de Wolfe Award from the American Institute of Decorators, the Distinguished Designer Award from the American Society of Furniture Designers, and an honorary Doctorate in Fine Arts from the Parsons School of Design in New York City.

The "Crouse" of the Cornell archive was Edward Crouse (1908-1975), Wormley's lover of some fifty years. Born in 1908, Crouse was orphaned at ten, and he and his two sisters had been lovingly brought up by an aunt and uncle. Even as a youngster, Crouse adored the theater, regularly built sets and staged plays at home and hoped for a time to become an actor. As an adult, he became director of theatrical productions at the University of Georgia and, during World War II, at the Army base in Greenland. Though he'd gotten a master's degree in journalism at the University of Wisconsin in 1936, that profession had never engaged him, and after the war, he joined Wormley's firm as an "associate" specializing in lighting.

Knowing that Kammen was heterosexually married and had two sons, I was delighted that a straight scholar, and one of distinction no less, had finally expressed interest in some aspects of gay life and culture. After our exchange in 2010, I didn't hear from him again, put the matter aside, and simply assumed—accurately, as it would turn out—that he was working away steadily on the Wormley-Crouse project. Then, in 2013, I received the sad news that Michael had died at age 77.

Earlier this year, I contacted his son Daniel and then, at his suggestion, his mother Carol Kammen (also a Cornell historian). She couldn't have been more cordial and promptly sent me a copy of the nearly 200-page manuscript Michael had completed, as well as a thumb drive of a substantial portion of the Wormley/Crouse archive.

Carol and I agreed that Michael's manuscript was too sketchy a work-in-progress to warrant publication, especially since his first-draft prose lacked the nuanced sophistication characteristic of his previous work. I myself had no wish to undertake a full-length study of the two Eds. Yet I thought that a condensed selection of their actual correspondence, along with commentary to help contextualize the material, would be a labor worth undertaking. Its real worth, it seems to me, lies in the detailed evidence it provides of the rather commonplace texture of two intertwined gay male lives during a fair portion of the last century, demonstrating that the period before Stonewall was not one of unbroken dread and repression for gay people.

Michael's extensive originating labors, plus the usefulness of his manuscript in providing background details, makes it obvious that his name should be listed first as the true parent of this joint project.

Born on New Year's Eve in 1907, Ed Wormley was a sixth-generation American of German descent. When he was two, his working-class family moved from one small Illinois farm town (Oswego) to another (Rochelle), where he passed through the public schools, all the while nourishing his early attraction to interior design through correspondence courses. At least as early as 1920, he met another artistically inclined teenager, Ed Crouse. The two went to the same schools, took hikes, camped out—and, by 1925, had become lovers. "What would the world think," Crouse wrote Wormley that year, "could they but glance at our letters?" He didn't much care—"if our neighbors talk about us, let them talk"—though he did think they could be "freer and happier" if they lived in a city. (The urban image conflicted somewhat with Crouse's equally intense fantasies of a "rose-covered cottage," yet they would ultimately manage both.)

Inseparable since adolescence, both men came out to their families at eighteen, and without any notable wringing of hands, perhaps in part because as announced atheists and aspiring aesthetes, they'd already come to be regarded as creatures outside community norms. Both men came from financially modest and emotionally cramped backgrounds. Wormley "adored" his mother (as she did him), and, later in life, after she and her husband divorced, she would live with her son for extended periods. In contrast, he and his father were never companionable; Wormley thought his father was "embarrassed" by him, and their relations were never good. Crouse, for his part, lost his mother at an early age and was raised by an indigent father who occasionally sold insurance and unsuccessfully became a preacher on the side. An additional trauma in Crouse's young life resulted from being raped at age thirteen—an episode about which we have no details. He and his two sisters were essentially brought up by an aunt and uncle who, fortunately, doted on them.

Sex between Wormley and Crouse would never be particularly intense—and never based on exclusivity. There was in fact an imbalance in their erotic attraction to each other from the start, with Crouse less interested in Wormley than vice versa. Nor did they ever seem to hesitate in writing each other detailed letters when apart about their assorted sexual encounters, with Crouse (a classically handsome blonde with an athletic physique) the more active of the two.

Wormley, though pleasant looking, was no Adonis—decidedly not when compared to Crouse. Short (5-foot-5) and stocky with a slight limp left over from a mild case of childhood polio, Wormley had to do much of the initiating when they did have sex, and it mostly consisted of him fellating the well-endowed Crouse.

Both agreed that the sex between them was often enjoyable but wasn't their primary bond. Crouse especially realized early on "that, truly, our friendship is *not* founded on sex [*his emphasis*]." What would keep them together for fifty years wasn't sex but love: a compound of compatible values and tastes, the comforting assurance of emotional fidelity, concern for the other's well-being, and intense pleasure in each other's company— all of which made it possible to survive some long periods of separation and major differences in personality. Wormley's temperament was less given to extremes, was well integrated, and highly functional. Crouse, ironically, though physically stronger and more attractive, was more emotionally brittle, more easily discouraged and unsettled.

Crouse graduated high school in 1925, a year ahead of Wormley, and enrolled in the University of Wisconsin. He was initially unhappy there and berated himself in a letter to Wormley (whom he soon nicknamed "Buster," or sometimes "Bus") as "a flat failure because of my lack of perseverance." Yet on campus he grew increasingly popular, was elected vice president of his fraternity and president of the glee club, and would periodically toy with the idea of marrying a woman and "settling down." It would "give me self-confidence," he explained to Buster, and would be "a stabilizing force." In contrast to Wormley, who never felt any erotic or romantic attraction toward women, Crouse, until his late twenties, would now and then decide that he'd found this or that woman at least margin- ally appealing, and he'd experience periodic turmoil and shame about being "odd." For an even longer period, he held on to the determination at least to appear "regular."

Yet it was a fantasy he couldn't sustain: "Gee, Buster, I don't know what I'll do if our plans all fail. If I have to live alone, or with a woman, I'll never be happy." By the 1930s, Crouse would often refer to Wormley as his "wife" (as did Wormley sometimes). In fact, Wormley would prove to be the stabilizing force in their relationship. An amiable, lively, and articulate companion, he was as well that rare phenomenon: a man who remained modest and sensible even as he grew prominent.

Catalog for the exhibition The Other Face of Modernism, *1997, Lin-Weinberg Gallery, New York.*

After graduating from high school in 1926, Wormley was able—thanks to a loan from his aunt—to move to Chicago (some eighty miles west of Rochelle) to study at SAIC, the School of the Art Institute. Even as a youngster, he'd felt sure that he wanted a career designing furniture and interiors, and SAIC had an international reputation. Alas, Wormley ran out of money after three terms at the school and had to leave, though his luck turned when he landed his first job. It was with the interior design studio of the prestigious Marshall Field department store, which quickly recognized his talent and, after a two-year apprenticeship, commissioned him to reproduce a collection of 18th-century English furniture. He and Crouse continued to see each other whenever possible, but it would be many more years before they could actually live together.

Crouse, too, made a firm career choice when still young: by age ten, he was building sets, making costumes, and performing weekly before a loyal audience of his two sisters and his uncle and aunt. His passion for the theater would never diminish, but he lacked Wormley's drive and focus; he seemed to imagine that opportunities for a theatrical career would somehow magically materialize. None did. On graduating from Wisconsin in 1929, he drifted into a job on the copy desk of the *Racine Times-Call.*

That summer, he took some journalism courses at his alma mater. A close college friend, Lorrie N. Douglas, tried to warn Crouse against simply drifting into a career that held no basic appeal for him: "Let journalism suffice for the breadwinner for the time being," Lorrie advised, but "find a purpose in life ... why not be more than a dilettante ... make Dramatics your career, Ed. Admit that you like it more than anything you've tried and go after it in a thorough, mature, and serious way."

The friend, while acute in analyzing Crouse's inability to concentrate and mobilize his energy, was in essence asking him, then in his twenties, to change his core temperament, to stop longing for something as abstract as "happiness" and face the fact that "you yearn for things that don't exist ... one must become reconciled to the truth that life is precarious and unstable." Ed had neither the ethical profundity nor the moral stamina to face so challenging a set of prescriptions; few of us do. Faced with a sternly worded directive, he grew uneasy and resentful: the demand was simply beyond his unsteady, shapeless temperament.

And yet, although Crouse's own efforts (as well as his credentials) remained minimal, he somehow managed to land a job as an instructor in journalism at the University of Georgia. (Academia was not a particularly desirable or competitive profession at that time.) Still, Ed's luck held: the student drama club on campus—perhaps because he looked like an actor—asked for his help in staging productions. And he made good at it. During the '30s, he staged three productions a year, received periodic promotions, and, in 1939, was appointed to head up a new department of drama (with the added bonus of no longer having to teach journalism, which he loathed).

THROUGHOUT THIS PERIOD, Wormley and Crouse continued to see each other regularly and between visits wrote frequent and candid letters. At one point, in 1934, Crouse—the more sentimental of the two—sat down and read through Wormley's letters from the preceding five years. He was impressively honest in telling Wormley flat-out that his letters were "so damned good, and so sincere. Mine, by comparison, must be a sorry lot. I know a lot of them have been pretentious—I mean pretending." He added that "despite all our ... ordeals and self-searching ... we've had pretty happy lives, and made immeasurably more so by each other's companionship. I think often how utterly empty the world be without you, if you were to die.... I've realized so definitely and strongly this year that you are essential to my existence."

He also let Wormley know, with sympathetic glee, that he'd come across one of his friend's early letters in which even he had described a half-hearted attempt at heterosexual intercourse—as if to say "you see, I wasn't the only one who thought and hoped I could settle down with a woman" (though Wormley, unlike Crouse, in fact never harbored, other than fleetingly, any such explicit thought). What Crouse quoted back to his friend from Wormley's youthful letter was closer to an example of resigned disinterest:

> She drew me down into her lap and said I was like a little boy ... then she embraced me like a bear and wouldn't let my lips go ... she almost carried me to the bed ... my mind was working overtime, and my blood vessels not at all. She tried to give me "entrance," but complained that I hadn't sufficient erection. And that was true enough. I felt ... pliable as putty, passionless as can be.... When finally I made an effort to get up and go, she clutched me tightly again and the process began anew, this time with better success. I ... realized self-consciously that "I am actually having intercourse." ... [She] prosaically disentangled herself, fetched me a towel, and unconcernedly and disgustingly raised her gown and dried herself with an awkward straddle and stoop.

When only 23, Wormley moved on from Marshall Field to the Dunbar Furniture Company in Berne, Indiana (about a three-hour drive from Chicago), where his talent soon won him an appointment as "sole designer and stylist." He would remain at Dunbar's for 37 years, living eleven of those years in Chicago (in what was locally known as Fairytown, the gay area) and then moving to New York City. Over time he would assemble a loyal staff and amass considerable wealth, reputation, and awards. As early as 1931, he was already earning enough to afford a trip to Europe, where he traveled, enthralled, with a casual friend. Still essentially a young man from the provinces, Wormley was smitten by Europe's assorted aesthetic wonders.

This first trip inaugurated a lifetime of passionate travel and self-education in the arts. He would turn into a man of cultivated, urbane taste—but without the usual snobbish veneer. (He comes across throughout his life as an unpretentious, compassionate man, impressively free of standard status anxiety.) For the rest of his life, always accompanied by Crouse, Wormley became an ever more adventuresome traveler, venturing over time far beyond the confines of Europe.

The effect of his travels on his own work was powerful: his furniture became increasingly distinguished for its superb construction, the imaginative use of unfamiliar woods and fabrics, and perfectionist detailing. Understated and sophisticated, like the man, Wormley's deceptively simple yet elegant designs rapidly gained a following. His furniture came to be known as "nostalgic modernism"—a combination of past and present—exemplified by his widely applauded "Janus Collection" in 1957. Wormley himself chose the title "Janus"—the Roman god of two opposing faces, which had been associated since at least the 15th century with homosexuality.

While Wormley's horizons were steadily expanding, Crouse's path grew more precarious. While he and Wormley continued to see each other frequently (and often wrote three or four letters a week), when alone Crouse often felt isolated and morose; there's even evidence of a breakdown at one point. When preoccupied with a student stage production, Crouse was even-keeled, and when a play went well and applause redounded, he could become downright euphoric. But between productions, he bemoaned being "stuck in the sticks," declared most Southerners to be "vapid," was tempted to take a menial job in Chicago so that he and Buster could live together, and gradually increased his intake of alcohol. He had several car accidents, each time escaping without injury or arrest, yet he would never heed Buster's advice to avoid drinking and driving. Crouse's good looks remained intact for a while longer, and he usually had little trouble picking up tricks—often married men—for casual sex.

In contrast to Crouse's comparative isolation, Wormley lived in the heart of Chicago's "Fairytown" (also known as "Towertown"), his apartment close to the central gay cruising area of North Michigan Avenue. During the '30s, a considerable gay subculture had formed in Chicago and like New York City—though unlike most of the country—was known to non-gay residents and to some extent integrated into the life of the city (Chicago "is going pansy," *Variety* reported).

As the historian David K. Johnson has persuasively argued, while the psychiatric definition of homosexuality as an "illness" was thoroughly entrenched by the 1930s, the sociological studies of gay men in Chicago that were done at the time show a "striking absence from the narratives of these young gay men ... [of] any internalization of the notion that homosexuality is a sickness. ... It belies the notion that, prior to World War II, gay men led tortured, isolated lives." At the risk of overstating the matter, it can be said that the prevailing view for at least a segment of the gay male population was the same one Ed Crouse had expressed to Wormley when they were still teenagers: "If the neighbors talk about us, let them talk." In a 1934 letter, Wormley re-affirmed that sentiment: "I feel no shame for anything we have done."

Wormley quickly made friends with his neighbors, enjoyed their parties, and occasionally accompanied them to one of the many "mixed clientele" cabarets (the gay bar scene only developed after the repeal of Prohibition in 1933). Yet as he wrote Crouse in 1934: "I make no acquaintances that I value very highly ... we came through so much together in those Crucial Formative Years that true rapport with new friends is virtually impossible." Temperamentally, Wormley was more a discrete spectator than an active participant. He also had a marked, and widely shared, disdain for the many "swishy" men who were part of the mix at the cabarets.

One evening, Wormley agreed to accompany a friend to the annual Halloween ball for queer (yes, that term was in common use in the '30s) people, but he found it "the most disgusting and pathetic spectacle I hope ever to witness. There were about a thousand present, including a sprinkling of soldiers, sailors, and policemen. Fully half that number were in 'drag' ... nobody looked happy or gay, and the painted faces were too sad to describe."

Somewhat more prudish and less given to sexual adventuring than Crouse (and certainly more prudent about mixing alcohol and pickups), Wormley—despite a time-consuming professional life—did his share of openly pursuing sex and even frequently picked up and paid taxi drivers. In the early '30s, he and his co-tenant would have numerous bachelor parties in their Chicago apartment (he called them "let us be gay" gatherings), but when they turned into orgies, Wormley remained aloof, his sense of decorum offended by what he called "tired and aimless lovemaking." He even had an occasional misadventure, robbed and beaten by a trick, though neither he nor Crouse endured many episodes of victimization—and certainly not the kind of police entrapment that during the Fifties became so familiar.

BY THE MID-1930s, the pattern of their relationship had been set. "I feel closer to you than to anyone else in the world," Crouse wrote Wormley, "and I know our relationship is not built on sex, to put it bluntly." They pretty much accepted each other as they were: Crouse gave up encouraging Buster to make an effort "to change your outward manner" and appear more "regular," though acknowledging that Buster and he were "regular-appearing" enough. Wormley, in turn, gave up what in retrospect he called his "body worship" of Crouse and decided to believe Crouse's insistent claim that "platonic affection ... is the only kind that lasts."

Only once, apparently, did a serious crisis arise in their relationship. Crouse decided he was hopelessly in love with a former student who'd starred in several theater productions at the University of Georgia. By getting him drunk, Crouse managed to seduce him and for a time persuade him that "swinging both ways" was perfectly acceptable; soon, though, he admitted defeat. Throughout the crisis, he kept Wormley informed of the liaison's ups and downs in seemingly needless detail (even sending photos of the student). Wormley was tolerant to a fault, tactful and supportive. If he felt any hurt, he concealed it impeccably when writing to Crouse. In a letter of June 18, 1938, for example, he wrote Crouse that his newfound love

> sounds like a nice boy, and his pictures are appealing. ... But poor, sweet, confused darling, why do you feel disgusted? Why does it all seem so cheap to you? I don't feel those things—ever—about my relation with you, or even for taxi-driver incidents ... our kind of physical pleasure and love is just as "natural"—because it is so widespread—as the "regular" kind. ... The one thing I fear and dread, my sweet, about the possibility of your forming a happy alliance sometime with some charming boy who loves your attention is that such a relationship may upset the schedule of visits and vacations we have come to spend together. They are my real life. I couldn't give them up without enormous loss of happiness. Would a threesome work? I hate to think of it... Now please don't pine, and remember I shall love you always and want to help you. If I only could. And don't talk about suicide!

Wormley's loyalty was unwavering. "Call it love, call it damn-foolishness," he wrote Crouse, "I think about you to the exclusion of my work. ... When I have left you I exist in a state of incompleteness. That sounds like the most utter rot to read but I mean it." Yet Wormley was no foolish romantic. Astute and sophisticated, he recognized the difference between the infatuation characteristic of an early stage in a relationship when one is still blind to the beloved's very real quirks and inadequacies, and the long-term love that's fully aware of a partner's limitations and accepts them as part of the package.

BY THE LATE '30s, Wormley had fully grasped the indelible nature of Crouse's unsteady habits, his lack of perseverance, his depressive moods, his growing reliance on alcohol, and his "bantering elusiveness"—and continued to love him anyway. "Our long association," he wrote Crouse at one point, "has become so involved, that it seems to me that any analysis you or I could give it, with the meager knowledge that we—or indeed, any psychologist whom I have run across—have, would be too facile." These were the words of a mature and sensible man.

With the outbreak of World War II, the two Eds experienced long separations. Wormley took his civic responsibilities seriously, joined the Office of Price Administration as chief of the furniture unit, and relocated to the capital. He considered his OPA work of considerable importance to the war effort and stuck to it conscientiously. He'd always been the more public spirited of the two, though both men were political liberals, decidedly sympathetic to the plight of Black Americans—and rather off-handedly anti-Semitic. Wormley's wariness of "Hebrews" became considerably diluted over time, and by the 1940s, an increasing number of his friends were Jewish.

Crouse, for his part, enlisted in the Army in 1942, though in a decidedly callow spirit: "I can't delude myself into believing I have any noble motive in it," he wrote Wormley. "I still feel more than anything else about the war that it is utterly childish and foolish." Thanks to his experience with theater, Crouse was assigned to the Division of Welfare and Entertainment, which kept him far from the battle lines. He ended up a first lieutenant stationed in Greenland as the Entertainment Director for the base command. Yet despite praise and commendation for his work, his unhappiness steadily deepened during the war and he self-medicated with increasing amounts of alcohol. When Wormley made the decision in 1944 to move to New York City and to start his own design firm, Crouse volunteered to become an associate specializing in lighting effects. Discharged in August 1945 with the rank of captain, he spent a year teaching at Syracuse University—just enough time to remind him how unhappy he was in academia and how much he wanted to live with Wormley.

When they finally moved in together for the first time in February 1947, they'd seen little of each other over the previous three years, and both had changed—in opposite directions. Wormley's career and income had increased rapidly, and Crouse acknowledged his awe of his friend's heightened achievement: "you are the luckiest and I guess the happiest person I know," Crouse wrote. "You've always been sure of what you wanted and you've always got it." As for himself, he acknowledged that he "no longer had any confidence"—"I've just started being pedestrian I guess. ... I've got to bestir myself. The old charm has worn thin." Given his low self-esteem, Crouse turned not to building a career of his own but to heightened cruising and carousing, racking up a growing list of car accidents and arrests for drunk driving. It got to the point where Wormley deviated from placid acceptance to open confrontation: "You, my boy, just fuck, fuck, fuck, like a rabbit. I wish you [would] think about yourself a little more, or ... give some indication of it." He then hastened to add that "I am not lecturing or even disapproving in any except a concerned sense: concerned first because of what you mean to me, and then for yourself, your eventual health."

Crouse offered up a half-hearted defense, claiming on the one hand that Wormley had "an exaggerated idea of my activities" and admitting on the other that "I don't like to stay in my room alone at night. The more I think about my present work, the less confident I am that I'm not just marking time waiting for something I don't know what. I have no desire to make a real career of my work or anything else I can think of. I just want to have plenty of money and not work except putter about the house and go away when I want to in a nice car with you." And go away they did, traveling regularly—and expensively. Over time, they covered a fair portion of the globe, ranging from Mexico and the Caribbean to multiple five-week trips to Europe and eventually to Southeast Asia.

By the mid-'50s, Wormley's talent and hard work had established him as one of the country's leading designers. He not only continued to serve Dunbar as an affiliated independent but also designed the large "Precedent Group" for the well-established Drexel Furniture Company. He was featured in *House Beautiful*, photographed by Karsh of Ottawa, and able to purchase outright a large duplex apartment in Manhattan's expensive East '50s. He also became an ardent and outspoken Democrat, supporting Adlai Stevenson in the 1952 presidential race and later George McGovern in his losing campaign against Nixon. By

1958, Wormley was giving buffet supper parties for the likes of Edward Durrell Stone, the distinguished architect, and John Bauer, director of the Whitney Museum.

It's a testament to Wormley's continuing love and concern for Crouse that he regularly made sure that despite his own busy, glamorous life, he'd willingly leave all that behind—temporarily, that is—in order to go off with Crouse on extended vacations. Their shared time alone probably had a lot to do with keeping their relationship afloat. In fact, though, we don't know much about their relationship for the period following World War II—for the simple reason that they were seeing each other frequently and no longer exchanging a steady barrage of letters describing their intimate lives. We do know that at some point Wormley took over the management of Crouse's finances, that he bought a separate co-op apartment for Crouse nearby (and moved his divorced mother into his own apartment). We also know that Crouse continued to work for Wormley's firm, though his job description remained vague and unfulfilling (though he did install the display for Wormley's masterful "Janus" collection in 1957).

WHEN WORMLEY, in 1967, turned sixty, he surprised the design world by announcing his retirement. His explanation to the editors of *Home Furnishings Daily* (which they printed in a two-page tribute to him) was that "there's more to life than work—even if you like it. We know so little of the world. I want to read the books I've bought but never read, and go to new places and revisit old ones." (In his reading taste, Wormley was something of a "highbrow," appreciating Faulkner, for example, long before he was widely hailed, and greatly admiring Richard Wright's *Native Son*. Crouse, for his part, was fascinated with jazz and blues as early as the 1920s.) Over the previous few years, Wormley had bought up extensive property, including a small cottage on a pond in Weston, Connecticut to which he gradually built additions, including a heated swimming pool. Crouse moved back in with him, and together they set about raising American Kennel Club-registered Pembroke Corgis, socializing with nearby friends, and, of course, traveling.

There were other, less salubrious continuities. Crouse continued to drink and to get into car accidents, once having his license suspended for a year. By 1974, his health began to fail. Although he had emergency surgery for a bladder stoppage, he continued to pass blood and stones in his urine. His condition—there never was a firm diagnosis—rapidly declined and, with Wormley holding his hand, he died on November 25, 1975. Wormley avoided having to watch the funeral director take Crouse's body away and wrote in his pocket calendar: "I'll never get used to his not being here with me. 60 years, but not long enough ... dear sweet man."

Six months later, he still missed Crouse "dreadfully," though over time, his grief gradually eased. He began to see old friends, renewed contact with relatives, and eventually agreed to give lectures and to attend various gala occasions in Manhattan. In 1977, he resumed his lifelong love of travel, and, as late as his mid-'70s, took trips to India, Japan, and South Korea. In the early 1990s he suffered two strokes, and died in November 1995 at age 87.

Today, the two Eds will probably be seen as a perfectly ordinary couple. And that, I think, is why the reclamation of their story is important. It's rare, first of all to find the record of a long-lasting same-sex relationship documented in such intimate detail. More significantly still, their correspondence adds further and needed testimony to counter the standard view that gay male life in all the long decades preceding Stonewall is the unaccented, unvarying story of secrecy and despair.

Wormley did not regard himself as some sort of freak, a cursed aberration. And even Crouse, despite his inability to mobilize his gifts and his reliance on alcohol, was able to form a long-lasting and mutually supportive union that survived sexual incompatibility and never demanded, or even considered, monogamy and a secure, shared domicile, as central to their mutual commitment; both acknowledged from the start that they were entitled to independent liberty. The story of the two Eds is, finally, a love story. Love does not flourish in every climate. And a quiet life can be a gift from the gods. ▪

CHAPTER X

The Artist as (Reluctant) Activist

MARY MEIGS AND ROBERT RAUSCHENBERG

PART I
Mary Meigs

This is a sales pitch. It's also a rescue mission—of a book and a person. The book is *Lily Briscoe: A Self-Portrait*; the person is its author, Mary Meigs (1917-2002). Never heard of her? Join the crowd. Though Meigs was a gifted painter and a remarkable writer with an intriguing personal history, today she's all but unknown—even among those immersed in lesbian history. I myself stumbled upon her accidentally ten years ago in the course of researching *A Saving Remnant*, my dual biography of two social justice activists, David McReynolds and Barbara Deming.

Through mutual friends, Deming and Meigs first met in 1954 when both were 37. They soon became lovers and remained together for more than a decade. For half that time they lived, polyamorously, with the youthful French-Canadian novelist Marie-Claire Blaise. (Still in her twenties, Blaise had already won praise from Edmund Wilson, the eminent literary critic.) In *A Saving Remnant*, I told Mary Meigs' story up to the point where she and Blaise broke away from the triangular relationship with Deming and settled together for several years in Brittany and then Quebec. Meigs and Deming soon renewed contact and thereafter remained close friends (but no longer sexual lovers).

In *A Saving Remnant*, I was focused on Deming's life story and included only that portion of Meigs' history when it crossed hers—a few paragraphs on their life together and a few lines on their later, lifelong friendship. A full biography of Mary Meigs remains to be written, and this brief essay is meant to encourage some enterprising young scholar to undertake the project. An abundance of manuscript material exists, much of it untouched by scholarly hands. Meigs' story awaits telling in the rich detail I believe warranted. Her own papers are housed at Bryn Mawr College's Special Collections; Deming's archive is at Harvard's Schlesinger Library; and Marie-Claire Blaise's papers are divided between the Bibliothèque et Archives nationales du Québec and the Library and Archives Canada. A great admirer of *Lily Briscoe*, I've been tempted to take on the assignment myself, but have resisted. At 93, I'm still up for a new project—but not for multi-archival digging in faraway places.

What I can do here, in the hope of enticing a biographer to take up Mary Meigs for an in-depth portrait, is to expand somewhat further on the minimalist account of her life in *A Saving Remnant.* For this brief portrait, I've drawn primarily (along with a limited amount of archival material) primarily from Meigs' four richly autobiographical books. The first, *Lily Briscoe,* appeared in 1981, and is the standout, but the prose in all four is elegant and epigrammatic, and the content uncommonly self-critical. I've never seen a reference to any of Meigs' books (nor, for that matter, to Meigs herself), though they reveal a good deal of lesbian history. I have seen a few reproductions of her impressively bold and vivid paintings, but haven't tried to track down their provenance nor locate the walls on which (hopefully) they still hang. In fleshing out Meigs' story—and cognizant of the limitations of space—I'll focus on two subjects: her family background, and her self-admonishing temperament.

MARY MEIGS was a product of upper-class Philadelphia and Washington, D.C., in the late 19th and early 20th centuries—and at the same time a rebel against its confinements. She was brought up in an inbred society of narrowly defined propriety—of rules for living ("etiquette") that left little room for spontaneity or dissent. Among the strongest taboos was any discussion of sex.

Mary would later recall that she had so little knowledge of the subject that on her brother's wedding day, she asked him at breakfast "What's an orgasm?" (She would not experience one herself until age 24.) Her strong-willed and traditional-minded mother and her shy, unobtrusive father combined to produce a child reluctant to assert herself, yet quietly defiant—a time bomb hidden in a rose bush. Even as a youngster, Mary was occasionally "fresh" (defined as knowing something shouldn't be said but saying it anyway). She once even dared to refer to her mother by her first name, "Margaret"—and was immediately scolded for her "horrid" blunder.

Though Mary's mother Margaret was devoted to "good breeding," she was also known for her quick flashes of anger. Should Mary dare to say that she was "bored" or that so-and-so was "stupid," and her mother would swiftly reprimand her. Yet Margaret was, according to her daughter, more than a disciplinarian; she could be "a good listener," had "natural good sense," was "nice" (adhered to the rules), and "morally serious" (followed those rules faithfully). She also gave the requisite number of society luncheons and tea parties (which Mary, from an early age, abhorred) and went to church regularly. Mary, for her part, refused communion, then refused to go to church at all. Margaret was furious, but remarkably, Mary managed to stand her ground.

High society in Philadelphia and Washington was unwaveringly racist and anti-Semitic. Mary couldn't recall hearing either topic being openly discussed, but late in life, she came upon a cache of family letters (see her book, *The Box Closet*) that recounted in great detail how her parents and their friends banded together to discourage Jews from buying property in their neighborhood. As for Blacks, they were servants, never friends. (Yet her Quaker grandmother, Mary proudly recalled, had been involved with the Underground Railroad.) Mary herself had a quick sympathy for people in distress, abhorred racism, and vigorously applauded her mother's decision to pay the hospital bills and provide pensions for all their Black servants.

Margaret and her husband Edward were also renegades in supporting FDR and the Democratic Party, and Margaret later denounced Senator Joe McCarthy as "a demagogue." In McCarthy's case, Mary thought her parents were primarily motivated by their conviction that he and Roy Cohn were in a homosexual relationship; she thought her mother especially "was mortally afraid of homosexual-

Mary Meigs

ity." As regarded the current view of women, Margaret Meigs did at least once, in 1906, publicly advocate that women should have the right to vote, though basing that right on their "moral superiority." Her advocacy was further circumscribed by her view that a woman's "proper sphere" being the home, she could see no reason why a woman should bother going to college. On that subject Mary, often described as "shy," held her ground and was finally allowed her to enroll in Bryn Mawr—though Margaret scoffed at "how pointless" college was in comparison with learning how to manage a household staff.

Mary much preferred her father Edward and saw him as the more loving—the "weaker," as he would put it—of her parents. He not only sympathized with Mary's wish to go to college but encouraged her reading. He was a gentle, patient man, subject to disabling depression, usually content to yield to Margaret's forceful wishes, and (according to his daughter) "suffered all his life from his belief in the honesty of others, and his subsequent disappointments." Although a bit of a prig (Edward disapproved of drinking because it encouraged "a false sense of cheerfulness"), Edward was far more introspective than Margaret. In contrast to her firm refusal to explore or explain herself, he was often willing to probe his own opinions, to try and get "to the bottom of things." Margaret could be unexpectedly provocative and thought her husband was "too nice"—which may be the reason she'd delayed accepting his proposal to marry for nearly a decade. "It makes me perfectly nervous," Margaret wrote to Edward a month before their wedding: "to have you talking about getting to know each other. I feel like a specimen under the microscope and I hate it."

Mary thought her mother's "instant bristling" at her husband's occasional attempt to share intimate feelings, was the source of great sadness to him; yet Edward did love Margaret—even if his "yearning for the truth collided with" her "hatred for delving and provoked [her] defensive tactics: ready-made answers, hurt feelings, or silence." Her attitude depressed Mary, and she "tended to take [her] father's side." His fragility touched her, his preference for solitude over society, and his inability to push himself forward centrally shaped and defined her own personality.

Mary recognized that her father's lack of what we today call "sexism" was remarkable at a time when rigid gender roles of "manliness" and "helpmate" were enthroned. She admired his vulnerability, his incapacity for slugging it out for "the top spot." When her mother decided that Mary's brother Arthur was "hanging around too much with girls" and insisted that he take up the "manly" art of boxing, Edward reluctantly bowed to her wishes. It was Mary's opinion that her father's deference to Margaret was a "magical leap of understanding": he'd been able to put himself in her place, had empathetically understood her worry about Arthur and had tried to console her.

While Mary strenuously favored her father, she was able to salvage some sympathy for a mother whose temperament was centrally at odds with her own: "The prevailing pattern of womanhood," Mary later wrote, "fitted her [mother] like a glove ... she thought she was wicked if she wanted her own way, if she played cards for money" and—above all—if she won ("the worst thing I ever did"). In Mary's view, her mother's only actual "wickednesses ... were those she never thought about: the snobbism and racism typical of her class, and her undue admiration for 'pomps and vanities.'" She also thought that Margaret "guarded her children ferociously from knowledge of this 'wicked world.'" Her parents, Mary recognized, had been "shaped so differently that they could never mesh together in total understanding. ... [T]heir minds often met in a shower of sparks or a short circuit. But they struggled with the intractable idea of marriage until death parted them."

THE ADULT Mary Meigs claimed that "love has always taken a secondary position in my life, secondary, that is, to my work as an artist." She once wrote: "I need chunks of visible time and hours every day of total silence in which I can attempt to see and to learn." As for her love relationships, looking back at them as an old woman in the 1980s, she detected a definite pattern: initially she would be "carried away by a genuine and selfless passion which I believed would be eternal [but] ... the differences between me and my lovers became more and more pronounced as time went on." She surprised even herself—not to mention her lovers—by her "frequently abrupt transformation from a tender and adorable friend to an irritable person who would refuse to make love... the more [Barbara] loved and needed me, the more cranky and sullen I became." Ultimately, Mary reached a point in life where she rejected "the whole idea of the couple, with its exigencies and its absence of freedom."

Her decade-long, intense relationship with Barbara Deming, the deepest of Meigs' life, is the primary case in point. In *A Saving Remnant*, I describe the course of their relationship in considerable detail and will therefore avoid repeating it here. Suffice it to say that Meigs herself, writing in the mid-1980s, entirely absolved Deming for the breakup of the triangular relationship with Marie-Claire Blaise (who, Meigs felt, made a contribution of her own to its failure, thanks to her tendency to "exaggerate her own guilelessness"). But finally, Mary insisted, it was her own personality, with openness and unavailability abruptly alternating, that ultimately pushed Deming away. It was Barbara, Meigs felt, who "suffered most in the triangle," yet was herself "never cruel, never petty, never dishonest." My own assessment coincides with Mary's: As most of those who worked alongside Deming in various social justice movements agreed, she was something of a secular saint.

Then too, like her father, Meigs had a strong propensity for exaggerating her own character defects. They were real enough, but she seems over-emphatic about them, as if covetous of claiming the totality of blame—which, after all, can be a form of vanity. Her insistence on prime responsibility for the twists and turns of a relationship may well have derived, at least in part, from an early awareness that she was wealthy. What followed, as Mary herself saw it, was the sense that her wealth protected her from falling under the sway of anyone else—or even suffering (to quote Shakespeare) "the thousand natural shocks that flesh is heir to." The downside of omniscience, if one has a conscience—and Mary did—is to feel wholly responsible when things go wrong. It was all very well for her to feel that she was in the driver's seat, but that meant becoming answerable for every unexpected bump in the road.

And Mary was far faster than most of those born into privilege to itemize—and reiterate—her temperamental shortcomings or lapses in judgment. At one low point in her life, she drew back from "suicidal thoughts" by reminding herself "that I live an ideal life, in ideal surroundings, free from the concerns of most people"—and she managed to acknowledge that without starting up "the machinery of guilt and self-hate." More typically, and repeatedly in her books, Meigs indicts herself for personality traits that were real enough but (as we know from the testimony of others) not as pronounced or disabling as she keeps insisting.

She blamed herself for a host of character deficiencies: for having a sharp tongue, for finding cooking and housekeeping "odious," for being "stingy," "snappish," and "intractable" when she *should* have been "pliable," for feeling "slow and stupid," "literal-minded and verging on stupidity." She even blamed herself for her instinctive retreat "from every kind of excess, squeamishness about any display of extravagance, greed, sensuality or drunkenness." She lived in horror of "uncontrollable or voracious states of being and their physical signs." She located the origin of her reticence in her parents' inability to "let themselves go in any sense of the word. ... [they were] unfit for combat with people who will use any means to get what they want, people for whom lying is the most important weapon in their arsenal. *Our* weapons are silence and inaction, both of which can be forms of cowardice."

She referred to herself as "pathologically shy," yet her penchant for solitude may well have been (as it often is in creative people) essential, an inescapable prerequisite for getting any painting or writing done. She illustrated the peril of "incautious love" by summoning up the sad case of her childhood governess, a Miss Balfour, who "gave too much of herself away," lost "too much of herself by attrition."

She described her own heart as "slippery and elusive ... total love is unknown to me," but typically, blamed herself for the lack: "real" love, "confident and relaxed," she wrote, was inimical to her temperament. Still more generally, she even doubted the validity of lesbian love: "when two women try to fit together, they merge one with the other with the illusion that they are interchangeable. But one does not necessarily fall in love because of a sense of identity; at times it is more like a sickness that comes from outside, takes possession, makes havoc of our rational selves, and this kind of falling in love is an aberration which has little to do with real love." She failed to consider—or notice—that the sort of obsessive, romantic love she described was also experienced by heterosexuals (and surely *not* by *all* lesbians at *all* times). What Mary did acknowledge later in life was that she herself "functions best as a more or less independent entity and that I don't do well anymore as part of a couple."

With regard to sex, Meigs experienced it relatively late in life when, at age 24, she joined the Waves during World War II and had a lover for the first time. Up until then, as she put it: "I had no idea that there were parts of my body that could be 'aroused,' either by myself or by someone else. I had never touched or explored my body or, by accident, discovered the pleasure of masturbation." Barbara Deming, on the other hand, had been sexually active since her teens, was comfortable with her body, and not at all self-conscious or guilty about her enjoyment of sex.

Deming was also enormously kind and patient. And once she fell in love, she stayed in love. Not so Mary Meigs. After the first few years of living with Barbara, she concluded that their "two bodies were out of tune with each other, each making life difficult for the other." In fact, Meigs seems never to have been particularly interested in sex, nor consistently comfortable in her own body. In her books, she portrays herself as an unworldly "puritan" regarding sex and laments her inability "to melt my petrified sensuality." She even deplores her physical presentation: "my home-cut hair, my flat-heeled shoes, and the impertinent pallor of my toenails." Looking back late in life, she concluded that "every one of my relationships has been poisoned by my guilty sense of not having given enough"—in the case of Deming, for not having given "enough passion and fidelity."

The two women, in fact, shared much: the preference for an austere life close to nature, the importance of "speaking truth to power," an insistence in regard to politics that all action be based on the principle of nonviolence (though in politics, too, Meigs ultimately decided she was ill-suited temperamentally for total immersion, and soon backed off). The two women even looked alike: both were tall, flat-chested, and unadorned. Yet their differences remained pronounced. Deming's stubborn, unflagging political conviction was driven by a profoundly searching conscience, and she became a major figure in nonviolent struggles against social injustice that ranged from anti-war protest to Black civil rights to feminism. Meigs shared those views, but *sustained* public witness on behalf of her values fell outside her comfort zone.

She tried. She went again and again to marches and meetings, not just to please Deming but to give voice to their shared concerns. But "too much" strenuous conviction finally went against her grain. After a time, her political participation became occasional and reluctant—and was, she insisted, antithetical to her own need for solitude. As she wrote in *Lily Briscoe*: "I had begun almost immediately to doubt in the depths of my being what these wonderful people told me: that the more one acts, protests, the braver one becomes. I was becoming less brave; I had a mortal fear of going to jail." Meanwhile, Deming was risking her neck more and more—and almost getting killed in the process. Meigs decided that she, unlike Deming, was by temperament "a mere spectator."

WITH RESPECT to her painting, Meigs had mixed success, with only limited showings of her work, few sales, and no gallery willing to provide sustained support. (One highlight was a laudatory note from the highly regarded painter Alex Katz telling Meigs that her work reminded him of Edvard Munch.) For a time, she turned to drawing and sculpture, but with no greater success. Quick as always to blame herself, Mary decided that her work suffered from being the product of a "too rational" brain. Increasingly, she turned to writing and became friendly with a few other writers, most notably the poet Marianne Moore, who was described by Meigs as like "an intricate illuminated manuscript with birds and animals surrounded by the fine tendrils of flowering vines; in short, she was exactly like one of her poems about which she was so modest."

For many years, Meigs continued to spend time in Montreal with Marie-Clare Blaise, though at the same time she remained devotedly close to Deming: "My friendship with Barbara," Meigs wrote, is "permanent and unshakeable." They would take long walks in the woods, "bound together by the things that make us alike: the sense of ferns and ground pine seeming to grow in our own veins; the sense of birds as creatures of our inner kingdom." Deming, for her part, would periodically try to talk away Meigs' bursts of self-deprecation, would beg her not to become prey to her guilty conscience, insisting that she could provide "five hundred reasons why her [Barbara's] own life wasn't any less selfish" than Mary's, nor, Barbara claimed, less egocentric: "I do what I do because I like it," she insisted.

In the late 1970s, with Deming's encouragement, Meigs published two books—*Lily Briscoe* and *The Medusa Head*—and would later publish several more. One of them charmingly recounts her experience as one of the eight older women who portray themselves in the semi documentary film *The Company of Strangers*. It's filled with Mary's familiar insistence that her "instinct" was always "to make a distance, sooner or later, between myself and every being who is close to me." At the 1991 Genie Awards (a festival that honors Canadian films), *The Company of Strangers* won several prizes. Meigs even became something of a spokesperson—despite all her earlier hesitations—for lesbian liberation (though the details of her involvement have up to now been unexplored). After a series of strokes, she died in Montreal in 2002, age 85.

PART II
The Case of Robert Rauschenberg*

TWENTY YEARS AGO, at the time of his first major retrospective, a reporter asked Robert Rauschenberg what it felt like to see so much of his old work brought together. "The pain and the pleasure," he answered, "come in about equal doses. A retrospective is a real obstacle. A retrospective can kill you."

It didn't. In the years since, Mr. Rauschenberg has gone on being a one-man laboratory of showy creativity: a painter, sculptor, photographer, print and silk-screen maker, set designer and conceptual artist. Today [1997], now 72 and still working in the fevered, effervescent spirit of the newest boy in town, Mr. Rauschenberg is again the subject of a major show, this time of some 400 works of such dizzying versatility and spendthrift ambition that it will take both of New York City's Guggenheim Museums to display it. Opening on September 19, it is called simply *Robert Rauschenberg: A Retrospective.*

At this moment of coronation, I think back to that raw, garrulous, charming young misfit from Port Arthur, Texas, about whom I had heard so much when I set out, in the mid-60's, to write the history of Black Mountain College. Mr. Rauschenberg had arrived there in 1948 to study painting with Josef Albers, but the austere and dogmatic Albers had taken an almost visceral dislike to the ebullient young Texan. During a lengthy interview with me in 1967, Albers claimed to have no clear memory of Mr. Rauschenberg, though he has called Albers "the most important teacher I ever had."

Although Albers's formative influence is now a staple of the literature

---

on Mr. Rauschenberg, few additional biographical details of his time at Black Mountain are ever offered: simply that he married a student friend, Susan Weil; that he had a son with her; that the marriage collapsed in less than two years; that he returned to Black Mountain in 1951 in the company of a young artist, Cy Twombly; and that he and Twombly then took off for extended travel in Italy.

And no more is said. That is, until recently. Over the past decade, some art critics have argued that

Robert Rauschenberg
Photo: Nationaal Archief, Netherlands

Mr. Rauschenberg is a highly autobiographical artist, that the fragments of his personal history are embedded everywhere in his work and that until they are "read" in a more honest spirit, his art will never be fully intelligible. In particular, they refer to the homoerotic imagery encoded in his work from the beginning.

The advent of this new criticism was the 1986 panel "Homosexuality in the Arts," which James M. Saslow, an art historian at the City University of New York, organized for the College Art Association. The key presentation was by Kenneth E. Silver, a critic at New York University. Silver argued that Jasper Johns' 1955 *Target With Plaster Casts*—plaster casts of men's body parts in little boxes over a large target—ought to be "read" in tandem with Mr. Rauschenberg's 1955 *Bed*, a painting on a patchwork quilt, as having been created by a pair of lovers in the same year, under the same roof and representing "some approximation—maybe an inchoate and impulsive bodying forth ... of the power of their then new relationship."

Sensation! The silence had been broken, a door opened for what is now a small flood of iconographic re-readings. In a 1992 article for *Art in America*, Jill Johnston reinterpreted some of Mr. Rauschenberg's early work as subversive "meditations on received ideas of gender." She pointed to "Canyon," a stuffed American eagle in flight from the canvas, as illustrating not merely same-sex desire but homosexual abduction and rape. The art historian Jonathan Katz, in turn, has argued that Mr. Rauschenberg's use of gay signifiers—like the photograph of Judy Garland in "Bantam" of 1954 —can be seen as daringly explicit for that deeply homophobic decade.

Katz further pointed out that in Mr. Rauschenberg's 1959-60 series, "34 Drawings for Dante's Inferno," the illustration for the canto in which sodomites are described as eternally sentenced to run barefoot over hot sands includes Mr. Rauschenberg's own foot, outlined in red, at the top of the drawing.

Walter Hopps, chief curator of the Guggenheim retrospective and of the previous show, "Robert Rauschenberg: The Early 1950's," agrees that a knowledge of Mr. Rauschenberg's youthful experiences "is essential to an understanding of many aspects of his art and maturity." But apparently only some aspects of that experience are, in fact, deemed relevant. Decoding Christian symbolism in Rauschenberg's early work is acceptable; decoding homoerotic imagery is not. Critics who have done the latter go uncited in the 1993 and present Guggenheim catalogues. This can be viewed as censorship through silence or as the justifiable bypassing of a "gossipy" scholarship that invades privacy.

Which brings us to the bottom line: Is it permissible to discuss an artist's personal life? And to what degree? Who has the right to give such permission, morally and legally? The answer, it has been argued by the curatorial museum establishment, is to "follow the wishes of the artists themselves." Which means, obviously, ignoring the newly seen homoerotic iconography in Rauschenberg's work. As someone only a little younger than Rauschenberg, I, too, grew up with ingrained habits of the closet and am sympathetic to the complicated issues of "emergence." I am also aware of the underappreciated psychological compensations and pleasures that secrecy, especially when inconsistently employed, can provide.

The intricacies of the privacy debate were illuminated when Jill

Johnston, in her book *Jasper Johns*, explicitly described both Twombly and Johns as "lovers" of Rauschenberg. One result was that Johns refused to permit any reproduction of his work in Johnston's book. Its publisher, Thames and Hudson, countered with a "note to the reader" that characterized Johns' decision as "an obstacle to the free exchange of ideas, interpretation and critical response."

That sounds like a deserved rebuke. But what about the equally hallowed right to privacy? Isn't it Johns' right, at least while alive (many famous folks try to protect their images even beyond the grave, but guardians of the culture often don't go along), to control what is publicly said about his personal life? Well, yes and no. In a culture that sanctions the relentless airing of the private life of the President of the United States, on what conceivable grounds do we exempt from discussion biographical details about any other public figure? That Rauschenberg is famous is beyond dispute. But he is a "public" person in other senses as well. He displays his products for the public's gaze, response, critical commentary—and sale. And he displays them, moreover, in museums that rely, to varying degrees, on public support.

Since all of the artist's experience goes into creating art, why are only some aspects of that experience mentionable? With Rauschenberg, the matter is further complicated by his own equivocal candor. He has loaded his work with same-sex iconography. He has, Jill Johnston tells us, always been "upfront and open" with friends about his sexuality. He has even gone to the edge publicly, telling *Interview* magazine in 1990: "I'm not frightened of the affection that Jasper and I had" and he didn't "see any sin or conflict in those days when each of us was the most important person in the other's life." He added, astonishingly, "It was sort of new to the art world that the two most well-known, up-and-coming studs were affectionately involved."

No clear boundaries exist any longer between the "public" and the "private"—just watch any show like *Oprah*. Moreover, those who strive for celebrity surely now recognize that in the process they surrender a portion of their privacy. Setting aside the historic mission of scholarship to "tell the truth," we should nevertheless remember that discussing a public figure's sexual orientation is not the equivalent of revealing specifics about intimate acts.

One can argue that, on these matters, Rauschenberg has all along been in advance of the curatorial museum establishment. He has overtly affirmed nothing while implying everything; he has been resonantly silent. The establishment has been merely silent, blocking out all mention of sexuality and developing an ideology around its reticence: namely, that direct biographical discussion is the most retrograde sort of critical inquiry—a vulgar and sentimental version of what we all know is an unstable, shifting, multifaceted reality.

Susan Sontag long ago argued that to reduce art to its content was to tame it, make it manageable. I would suggest that much depends on the content. Discussions of same-sex imagery are likely to explode the manageable. Encoded messages, once revealed, rip off the masks and challenge the prescribed formulas that have tyrannized our understanding, letting all sorts of alive things breathe at last. ■

CHAPTER XI

Joe Carstairs

HER OWN AUTHORITY

Nineteen twenty-six proved a banner year for Joe Carstairs—yes, she referred to herself as Joe, not Jo—winning the Duke of York trophy, then the most prestigious in speed boat racing, indisputably marking her a champion racer. She was the only woman in a field of nine in the star-studded event, and the sporting world's excitement over the race had led tens of thousands of fans (one estimate put the figure at a million) to crowd the banks of the Thames. In short order, one contestant after another fell by the wayside, knocked out of the competition by ignition failure, an engine blowing up, collision with a buoy or another boat—or being thrown overboard by the powerful swell of the water. [1]

By the final heat, only two of the nine boats remained in contention: Herr Krueger, the German entry, and Joe Carstairs, steering her seventeen-foot hydroplane, dramatically painted black, with a white stripe running its length. Approaching the finish line, both finalists ran into trouble. The connecting rod on Krueger's boat broke, disabling it, while a tangled rope in the gears threatened to stop Carstairs' boat cold—until she somehow managed to cut it loose with a knife, and raced to victory. That same year of 1926, she won a number of other major races and was awarded the Médaille d'honneur, given annually for the "most meritorious motor-boat performance throughout the year."

For the next half-dozen years, Carstairs continued to compete, and with remarkable success. But the sport was both dangerous and expensive—both of which Joe, having driven an ambulance in France during World War I, scoffed at, telling one reporter that the so-called "dangers" involved were better seen as "discomforts." However, she did acknowledge that "floating wreckage at speed can cut a hole through the bottom of the boat like a razor cutting canvas." And in racing, she *had* been "thrown overboard at speed," leaving her with three broken ribs, though she refused rescue until her severely injured mechanic had been hoisted to safety.

Joe further acknowledged to another reporter that running into "a head sea could be nasty ... you get a jar absolutely right through you ... like a terrific electric shock." Still, she quickly added: "It's a marvelous sport. At the end of a race you're filthy, covered with oil, soaked with water most likely, and nearly deaf with the noise, but there's nothing in the world so satisfying."

If the danger didn't dissuade her, neither did the expense. Her American grandfather, Jabez A. Bostwick, was one of the nine men who in 1873 comprised the Executive Committee of Standard Oil, and its sixth largest shareholder. He had sweeping power over the affairs of several Standard Oil companies that collectively made up the monopoly. The

Joe in her speedboat "Newg"—Gwen spelled backwards—after winning the Duke of York Trophy Race on the Thames.

powerful group of nine not only drafted
general policies but controlled all deci-
sions involving the diverse types of oil and
refineries, the buying of crude, the purchase of chemicals and lumber, relations
with railroads and other shipping entities,
and price quotations.

Jabez A. Bostwick's daughter Evelyn
was Joe's mother, but a wholly disen-
gaged one. Something of a jaded, volatile
troublemaker, Evelyn married four times.

Joe Carstairs at Whale Cay, 1947.

Her first husband, Albert Carstairs, is barely mentioned in the surviving
documents and seems to have played little role in Evelyn's life and next
to none in his daughter's. Evelyn's fourth marriage, on the other hand,
was to Serge Voronoff, a surgeon briefly famous in the 1920s for trans-
planting monkey testicles into male humans as a purported treatment
for "rejuvenation." Joe rightly considered him a charlatan, and the two
were rarely in each other's company. Meanwhile, Evelyn Bostwick became
increasingly drawn to alcohol and drugs. As an adult, Joe was quoted as
saying that she'd "never been frightened of anybody except my mother."
There was no riddle to their mutual dislike. Joe herself provided the key:
"I was never a little girl. I came out of the womb queer." At age eleven,
Evelyn shipped her off to boarding school. [2]

Jabez Bostwick died in 1892, leaving most of his fortune to his widow
Nellie. Joe, meanwhile, had bounced from school to school and then from
job to dead-end job. After the outbreak of World War I, she became an
ambulance driver in France (the male drivers called her "Tommy"), and,
while still a teenager, she shared an apartment in Montparnasse with
four other young female drivers. One of her first sexual experiences was
with Dolly Wilde, the niece of Oscar. Joe sometimes tagged along with
Dolly to Natalie Barney's famous literary salon, but neither she nor the
Bohemian crowd could muster up much interest in each other. Joe loved
sex, but the book-centered and sophisticated manners of the literary set

were antithetical to her brisk, strenuous style.

Much more appealing to Joe's earthy sensibility was the taxi service she and her friends from the ambulance corps put together in London after the armistice. They called themselves the X-Garage, perhaps signaling their noncompliance with social norms, and made themselves available to transport customers as far as Ireland. Joe seems to have thoroughly enjoyed the adventuresome side of the business, but her need for cash came to a halt with the 1920 death of her grandmother, Nellie Bostwick. Knowing her daughter Evelyn's capricious ways, Nellie had already set up two separate trust funds for Joe. By 1922, they were yielding her an annual income of some $200,000—roughly 3.5 million in today's currency. She became still richer when her mother Evelyn died in 1921. After three years of complicated litigation over the will, by 1925, Joe found herself in possession of a considerable fortune.

Without pausing for breath, she immediately commissioned the celebrated boat-builders on the Isle of Wight to build her an up-to-the-minute, seventeen-foot hydroplane, and named her "Gwen" in honor of her friend and sometime lover, the cabaret star Gwen Farrar, then on the verge of fame. From 1921 to '24, in partnership with Norah Blaney, Gwen appeared regularly at leading variety theaters. Among her standout shows were *Pot Luck*, with Bea Lillie; *Rats*, with Gertrude Lawrence; and *The Punch Bowl*, with Hermione Baddeley.

HER FORTUNE legally secured by the mid-1920s, Joe closed the X-Garage, and for the next half-dozen years devoted her full—and formidable— energy to speedboat racing, to the sport that perfectly combined her physical daring with her instinctive indifference to "propriety." Between 1925 and 1931, she participated in most of the prominent powerboat races and won them often enough to cover the top of a good-sized dining room table with trophies. And she did so without apology, explanation or, seemingly, self-consciousness; she simply accepted herself. The '20s, to be sure, were a decade more tolerant of gender and sexual nonconformity than any preceding (and several that followed). Doubtless both her wealth and her manner—"this is me; take it or leave it; I couldn't care less"—played a role in her general acceptance in a decidedly male sport. Whatever the cause, during the '20s, neither her competitors nor the press mocked her, and "society" did not call for her exclusion. In the more conservative 1930s, however, there was something of an uptick of criticism in the press of her "mannish" ways.

Actress Gwen Farrar, Tallulah Bankhead, and Joe.

Occasionally, too, someone—usually a stranger—would address her as "sir" or "mister." When that happened, Joe, who couldn't have cared less about "passing," seems to have mostly reacted with detachment, choosing to regard the remark as an innocent mistake, or accepting the fact that there will always be people who take offense at any deviation from prevailing norms.

What she did not do was attempt to bring her appearance into conformity with standard gender expectations. She wore her hair in a crew cut, had tattoos running up one arm, and wore mostly working-class dungarees or trousers. Her "manly," even rakish, stride through the world—her gaze assured, her purpose commanding—was performed with apparent disregard for its effect. When in pursuit of a bed partner, she seized the initiative, appropriating her right to take control and steer the course. Yet she wasn't possessive and didn't demand (or possibly want) lifetime fidelity. Her pattern in love affairs was short-term and serial. Her many partners were invariably young and drop-dead gorgeous—and none of them, as far as is known, was accorded the privilege of actually spending the night with her in the same bed. She retained a photograph of every woman she bedded down and put them on display under the glass top of a coffee table; the total was well over a hundred.

Joe's sexual pattern was more traditionally male than female—or rather, it represented what many men, at least in their fantasies, would regard as ideal, except that Joe, unlike them, was exceedingly generous to her partners, heeding their wishes, showering them with gifts, never suggesting exclusivity. As Alex Stoll,

Marlene Dietrich on Joe's French fishing yacht, the Arkel, *in 1939.*

who knew Joe later in life, told me in our 1997 interview, Joe "was just completely open;" "I think she was a little pissed that everybody kept everything a secret, because she was the one who didn't. She was just very honest, very down to-earth, not sentimental or pretentious."

AT AGE 34 and facing tax problems in both Britain and the U.S., Joe, with typical audacity, decided to buy the barely habitable island of Whale Cay in the Bahamas, nine miles by four, for the sum of $40,000. In doing so, she became in essence the sole ruler and for a time, nearly the sole inhabitant. (At the time Joe bought Whale Cay, only a single shack existed, inhabited by a man and his wife who only occasionally tended to the lighthouse.) Covered with shrubs and weeds, the island, Joe was told, was entirely non-arable. Undeterred, Joe rolled up her legendary sleeves and embarked on an eight-year project that at its close could boast an elegant pseudo-Spanish villa complete with hand-polished mahogany, a power plant, fifteen miles of paved road, a wireless station, a schoolhouse, and an agricultural enterprise that included homes and a chapel for the several hundred Bahamians who flocked to Whale Cay's generous salary scale—and eventually produced the largest granary in the Bahamas.

During the mid-'30s, with construction crews largely in possession of Whale Cay, Joe traveled widely, and would do so even later, mostly to shop and to visit friends on the Florida mainland. But starting in the late '30s, Whale Cay became her chief residence, and remained so for the next forty years. And she made it a comfortable one: she had a private staff of four houseboys, a nurse, a male cook, and several hundred Bahamian workers to maintain the plants and crops. When guests were in residence in the villa, dinner was served formally at nine o'clock, with a dazzling, charismatic Joe descending the curved staircase into the dining area in a formal naval uniform complete with trousers.

After dinner, drinks (though Joe herself was a teetotaler) and dancing took up some evenings, but card-playing was the leading indoor sport, with Onze (a game similar to gin rummy) and poker the favorites. In attendance most of the time was a rotating parade of stunning female guests occasionally accompanied by a male—usually a famous one, such as the Duke of Windsor, who was at that time the governor of the Bahamas. The roster of visiting female celebrities was larger and included, at various times, the singer Mabel Mercer, who Joe regarded as "a very great lady ... very proper—just the opposite to me"; the actress Gwen Farrar and her current lover Tallulah Bankhead; and the international celebrity Marlene Dietrich.

And therein hang several tales. The few who have written about Joe have shaded the story variously, but as I read the limited evidence, Tallulah Bankhead and Joe did have a brief affair. However, Joe's relationship with Marlene is more difficult to characterize. That Marlene did sleep with women (including the notorious Mercedes de Acosta), and that she and Joe for a time became close friends, is indisputable. The two women—tough, down-to-earth, authentic—were something like natural soul-mates. At one point Dietrich even sought Joe's opinion on which film roles to accept, and the two cruised the Mediterranean for two seasons in the late '30s aboard Joe's French fishing yacht, *The Arkel.* In Maria Riva's impressive biography of her mother, Marlene Dietrich, she confirms that Joe "was the only one who ever called Dietrich 'Babe' and got away with it." For her part, Joe was unquestionably enamored of the bewitching Dietrich and—possessing a powerful sense of entitlement—she repetitively offered to build Dietrich a dream house on the Cay, promising that she would live like a fairy-tale princess. Still, I go with David Bret, one of the more cogent of Dietrich's biographers, who concludes that although

Joe "hoped for more than a platonic relationship," Marlene and Joe "never became sexual lovers. Marlene was only interested in ... [Joe's] personality, which was said to have been electrifying [and] ... took it all in with accustomed humor."

JOE CARSTAIRS sold Whale Cay in 1975 (it quickly fell to seed) and thereafter moved between her houses in Sag Harbor and Naples, Florida, where she died in 1993 at the age of 93. In old age she remained, as her friend, Ellen "Pucky" Violett, told me: "awfully sweet, but old school"—that is, not at all political. "Joe wouldn't talk about her own history," another of her friends added, "but she would talk about being gay." According to Alex Stoll, who knew her well, Joe was never "an old lady"; even when she had to hobble around with the aid of two canes, she maintained a boat in Sag Harbor, "a sort of small yacht, and she did everything, unroped everything ... [she] remained vigorous, mentally strong." She also remained "very down-to-earth, and very, very honest, not pretentious, grandiose, or sentimental, but sympathetic"—and, above all, "completely comfortable with herself." ▪

NOTES

1. The description of Joe Carstairs' racing career that follows relies heavily on a batch of some two dozen contemporary newspaper clippings given to me by Julie S. Sewell, a close friend of Carstairs. She gave me as well Joe's album of extraordinary photographs, including several of Marlene Dietrich and Tallulah Bankhead. I'm indebted as well to Alex Stoll: she introduced me to Julie Sewell, and provided her own recollections of Carstairs.

2. The quotation is from Kate Summerscale's *The Queen of Whale Cay*, Viking, 1998, to which I'm indebted for many details.

3. From interviews with Ellen "Pucky" Violett, Alex Stoll, and John Jessup in 1997.

CHAPTER XII

Queers
for
Justice

Here are some facts you might not know:

1. Most gay people belong to the working class, whether "class" is defined by income, educational level, or job status.

2. Class identity is an amalgam of identities: One's place within the economic structure is deeply inflected by race, ethnicity, gender, and sexual orientation.

3. Most people in this country, including many with poverty-line incomes, identity themselves as "middle-class."

4. In some states, employers can still legally fire workers simply because they are gay.

5. The workplace remains strongly defined by heterosexual norms. Most straight workers believe gender comes in two, and only two, packages: male or female. And most would claim (at least officially) that lifetime, monogamous pair-bonding is the best guarantee of a contented and moral life.

6. Within certain segments of organized labor, there's been a growing understanding of the effect of homophobia on gay workers and also a willingness to address it.

7. There has not been a comparable growth in understanding within national

gay organizations about class issues. Nor any notable concern or announced agenda to deal with the economic plight and deplorable workplace conditions of many working-class LGBTQ+ people.

Here are a few myths that commonly pass for facts among many non-working-class people, gay as well as straight:

1. The typical worker is a male in industry who heads a family.

2. Minorities are now well represented in union leadership positions.

3. The national gay movement is dominated by people holding radical social and political views.

4. Many labor union leaders are either stealing from their treasuries, in bed with the bosses, or both.

5. Organized labor's politics are strictly centered, and properly so, on issues relating to wages and working conditions.

Such "facts" are widely believed, dominate public discourse, and deeply affect the culture of the workplace, the attempt to organize unions, and the personal lives of workers. An important collection of essays, *Out at Work*, edited by Kitty Krupat and Patrick McCreery, spells out these interconnected issues and, in doing so, clarifies why progressives active in class, gender and sexual orientation politics need to recognize their linkages and combine their forces to a far greater degree that has been the case to date. The result could be a strengthened new engine of social reform.

Out at Work rightly insists that the national LGBTQ+ movement must, if it has any hope of becoming genuinely representative of the needs of most gay people, broaden its agenda to include working-class issues. And the union movement must—if it hopes to increase its numbers much beyond its enrollment of roughly twelve percent of the workforce—take far greater cognizance than it currently does of the oppressive conditions that dominate the lives of workers who are gender and sexual nonconformists.

Specifically, unions need to assume the responsibility of creating a climate in the workplace where those who are not straight white men can feel comfortable in being open about their lives and can be assured that their needs will be represented forcefully during contract negotiations with employers.

The traditional union agenda of fighting for higher pay and better working conditions needs to be broadened to include such issues as homophobic harassment at the workplace and domestic partnership benefits for LGBTQ+ employees.

Any sustainable alliance between the LGBTQ+ and union movements must be preceded or accompanied by a considerable amount of transformative work within each movement. The dominant ideology of most of the large national gay organizations, such as the Human Rights Campaign, would require a profound shift in emphasis away from their traditionalist, centrist concerns, a shift that their middle-class constituency—and this is a huge sticking point—might not support.

Political scientist Cathy J. Cohen has explained in a brilliant essay, "What is This Movement Doing to My Politics?", why such a shift is nonetheless urgent. Cohen argues that ever since the demise of Queer Nation and the refocusing of ACT UP on issues relating to global AIDS, there's no longer a radical domestic wing of any import in the national lesbian and gay movement (with the exception, I myself would add, of the transgender movement; small though it is in numbers, its challenge to binary notions of gender is of profound importance). [1]

Most of the numerically and monetarily significant national gay organizations appear insufficiently focused on a genuinely transformative politics. If we look back to 1998, for example, the Human Rights Campaign endorsed the profoundly conservative Alfonse D. Amato for the Senate; the Log Cabin Republicans honored a black politician who has worked against affirmative action in California; the National Gay and Lesbian Task Force accepted (but later returned) a sizeable contribution from Nike, which employs sweatshop labor; and the Gay and Lesbian Alliance Against Defamation accepted (and did not return) a gift from the right-wing, union-busting Coors corporation. Things have improved over the past two decades, but in my view not enough. As an example I'd point to the seeming lack of interest within the movement in national legislation that would guarantee to every adult citizen an annual income of, say, $30,000.

Cohen's disgust with the national gay movement's efforts to "sanitize, whitenize, and normalize the public and visible representations" of the gay community—to embrace and focus on mainstream assimilation—has led her to ask, with justifiable anger, "Can I have [radical] politics and be a part of this [gay] movement? I am sorry to say, I'm not sure." Cohen doesn't minimize the importance of continuing to work through traditional political channels, such as electioneering and lobbying, in order to win much-needed civil rights legislation. But she does worry, rightly in my view, that a focus on civil rights alone has thus far been of most benefit to those gay people who are comparatively privileged and has closed the door to the less conforming members of the community—people of color, say, or "cross-dressers," or S/M devotees, or those who identify as transgender.

What heightens Cohen's concern is that so little discussion seems to be taking place within the major gay political organizations about the right to a living wage and to decent working conditions. As Cohen pointedly puts it, "Without dialogue and debate about what greater good we are working for, we may in fact achieve inclusion, but inclusion in an oppressive society."

There's some ground for hope in the emergence of smaller, more radically-minded lesbian and gay organizations—for example, the Audre Lorde Project in New York, SOON in Atlanta, Esperanza in San Antonio, and the national Black Radical Congress. The hope is that they will grow in strength, influence, and resources. But as matters stand, those who control the gay community's major resources and organizations are currently, one might even say smugly, committed to assimilationist goals that have little to do with gay working-class grievances and a lot to do with making it easier for the already privileged to "join up." And the bitter truth, as gay progressives well know, is that these organizations are powerful because their assimilationist goals do accurately reflect the values and hopes of the majority of gay people.

Patrick McCreery demonstrates this point clearly in his superb essay in *Out at Work* on the politics of the federal Employment Non-Discrimination Act (ENDA). McCreery shows that the outpouring of mainstream gay support for ENDA is, on one level, understandable, since it would, if ever passed, extend needed employment protection. But those benefits would come, McCreery argues, "through an unabashed privileging of normative sexuality—meaning non-fetishistic sexual relations between two adults in a monogamous, committed relationship. And this, in the long run, would strengthen the hetero-normative environment of the workplace." [2]

If we turn to organized labor's side of a potential gay-labor alliance, we find a comparable picture: A formidable set of obstacles to cooperation, in tandem with some recent developments that provide at least limited grounds for optimism. Among the obstacles, the foremost is the still significant amount of homophobia in the workplace. A mere 30 years ago, homophobia was so fierce and endemic that only a rare homosexual would think about "coming out"—knowing that the consequences would almost certainly include being fired, verbally harassed, or physically assaulted. Today homophobia continues to run deep in the workplace, and gay-bashing remains a constant threat. But harassment is now somewhat contained by the existence of gay caucuses within some unions, as well as by the determination of various union leaders, preeminently (until his retirement) John J. Sweeney, the head of the AFL-CIO from 1995–2009.

Until Sweeney's ascension, the AFL-CIO had traditionally concentrated its efforts on protecting the rights of those union members who held down the best-paid jobs. For the fourteen years (1995-2009) he remained president, Sweeney stood that tradition on its head. He championed *low* wage workers, and crusaded above all to bring minorities, immigrants, Indigenous peoples, and women into the union fold. The attitude of these groups towards *each other*—and all of them towards LGBTQ+ people—varied in the years ahead; harmony has not reigned, the solidification of a political alliance not assured. For LGTB people, gaping holes remain in the thicket of existing protections— not even physical safety has been assured in the workplace.

Combating homophobia in the workplace remains a challenge, with progress decidedly piecemeal. Union membership itself, moreover, remains wobbly. At Sweeney's death, enrollment stood at twelve percent—down from thirteen and a half percent when he took office in 1995. In regard to homophobia, some of the worst offenders in the workplace, sadly, are members of other minorities. Their own experience with oppression hasn't automatically translated into sympathy for other oppressed groups. And especially not for those who, by their very being, offend against deeply held religious beliefs and ingrained notions of "proper" gender behavior.

The inability of minority workers to join hands in solidarity has led some activists to feel that if further inroads against homophobia in the workplace are to come, they will have to be initiated from the top, from those in union leadership positions. Yet other activists deny this; they argue that the general increase over the past few decades in public understanding about homosexuality has already, at the workplace level, changed a significant number of hearts and minds: Gays are now more willing to come out, and their straight counterparts are more supportive in their response.

Those who hold to an optimistic view can point to the emergence of such bottom-up formations as the Lesbian and Gay Issues Committee (lagic) in District Council 37 (the union of New York City employees), as well as the creation of Pride at Work, a national caucus of gay, lesbian and transgender trade unionists, which in 1998 became an official constituency group of the ALF-CIO. In a deeply researched and closely reasoned essay, Tamara Jones has illuminated the dynamics at play in these new groups. Using the formation and history of lagic as a case study, Jones demonstrates how the rules-driven bureaucratic structures of many unions thwart decentralized decision-making and power-sharing. In particular, they constrict the ability of gay and lesbian organizers to increase their numbers and leverage in the struggle to redefine "workers' rights" in a more expansive way.

Jones persuasively shows how lagic itself has adopted some of the formalistic features of its parent union, D.C. 37, and has become more traditional over time; it now largely foregoes the radical inclusivity that had marked its early days, and no longer addresses the significant variations in lifestyle and belief that exist among its highly diversified queer membership. The key lesson Jones draws from lagic's evolution is that "the existence of a lesbian and gay union caucus does not automatically pose a radical challenge to the status quo, nor is it inherently conservative."

One has to look to the specific conditions in which a particular gay caucus is operating, Jones argues, and has to recognize that "often, mobilization and organizing occur within organizational fields and institutional settings that were not designed to support transformative or collectivist politics." Jones' insights are persuasively stated and will hopefully be taken to heart. But we need to recognize, too, that—as with all social movements that are genuinely progressive—the struggle for gay rights in the workplace will inevitably pass through alternating cycles of advance and retreat.

As for the specific question of whether it's possible to create an expanded alliance between gay and non-gay workers that could serve as an important agency for social change, there's evidence available to feed both optimism and pessimism. The pessimists would emphasize the ongoing homophobia at most workplaces. As AFL-CIO head John J. Sweeney once put it, promoting the rights of gay and lesbian workers has "been a slow and painstaking process... And we still have quite a long way to go. Historically, unions have had to be challenged and prodded before opening the door to people their members view as different. For gay and lesbian workers, in particular, that remains a hard reality to this day." (Sweeney doesn't mention transgender workers, but should have, since their travails are often severe and usually go unacknowledged.)

There's additional fuel for pessimism in the way those national gay and lesbian organizations with the greatest resources and the most visible public presence continue to ignore or marginalize economic issues. Many LGBTQ+ activists and organizations remain aloof from the union movement, in deference to a politics of assimilation that ignores any radical analysis of class. Transgender organizations, moreover, stand apart from "a politics of assimilation"—or any process of normalization—yet the two largest LGBTQ+ organizations, the Human Rights Campaign and the National Gay and Lesbian Task Force, have until recently focused their time and money on assimilationist issues such as the right of gays to marry or to serve openly in the military. Those two issues now "resolved," there has been significant movement on the part of the national LGBTQ+ organizations to reset their priorities. They are not yet working for an issue as radical as a guaranteed annual income, but nor have the vast majority of merely liberal organizations like the American Civil Liberties Union.

Recent efforts on behalf of the Employment Non-Discrimination

Act illuminate the difficulties ahead in expanding *broad* protection for working-class people—straight and gay. Since 1994, the Employment Non-Discrimination Act (ENDA) prohibiting discrimination in hiring and employment failed to win passage year after year. Twice, when the Democrats had a Congressional majority, the ENDA bill did come close to passage, but in 2007, after a passionate struggle within the LGBTQ+ movement to insure transgender inclusion, the bill failed to pass the House. When inclusion was dropped—to an uproar within the gay community—the bill died in the Senate. Even if passage had been achieved, President George W. Bush had threatened to veto it. Subsequent attempts at passage in 2009, 2011, and 2013 again failed to win support in either the House or Senate.

Since 2015, LGBTQ+ activists have shifted support from ENDA to the Equality Act, a bill with more comprehensive protections—not only in employment but also in regard to housing, public accommodations, public education, federal funding, credit, and jury service. In 2020, the Supreme Court ruled in *Bostock v. Clayton County* that Title VII of the 1964 Civil Rights Act *did* protect employees from discrimination based on their sexual orientation or gender identity—but the ruling only covered employment. The struggle remains difficult, and ongoing.

As for an expanded gay-worker alliance based on a radical agenda (like that bogey man, a guaranteed annual income), those who hold to an optimistic view of the prospects, can cite a significant amount of evidence to bolster their hopes. Certain unions, particularly the American Federation of State, County and Municipal Employees (AFSCME) and the Service Employees International Union (SEIU) have taken the lead in supporting strong LGBTQ+ caucuses and in educating straight workers about the significant amounts of fear and discrimination that gay workers experience in the workplace. Increasingly, straight workers recognize the material importance and the ethical rightness of making sure that domestic partnership benefits for gay people are negotiated into contracts with employers. It's also true that an increasing number of gay and lesbian workers are casting aside their doubts about the value of unions and are beginning to recognize that organized labor, for all its shortcomings, could well become a significant force in the struggle for gay rights, benefits, and safeguards.

Not only might unions transform the workplace for gay people, but as gay workers take their place at the table, they, like women and people of color before them, could help to transform union culture. Once social identity issues join economic ones as an intrinsic part of union demands, heteronormative standards could then, over time—probably over a lot of time—give way to a far more inclusive embodiment of the exceedingly varied lives, the amalgam of identities, that unions, like it or not, do in fact represent, even if, until recently, they mostly preferred not to notice. A reconfigured working class would fully acknowledge not merely the geographical and economic dimensions of its struggle, but also its racial, gender, and sexual ones.

Think of it: an economic justice movement that included gay people, and a gay movement that concerned itself with a more equitable distribution of wealth. Emerging in tandem, they could engineer a revitalized workplace and a reinvigorated politics. With so much at stake, it's hard not to go with the optimists—and after all, how but through optimism have social justice movements ever come into being or been able to sustain themselves? ▪

NOTES

1. See the elaboration of Cohen' s argument in her 1999 book *Boundaries of Blackness.* See also Anne Balay's *Semi-Queer*, as well as *Steel Closets.*

2. In the years since writing this essay in 2001, the seemingly futile series of efforts to pass ENDA shifted after 2015 to supporting a more comprehensive Equality Act, which was designed to include more than discrimination in employment. As of 2022, though, the Equality Act has failed to pass. In June 2020, the Supreme Court ruled that the 1964 Civil Rights Act did protect against discrimination involving sexual orientation and gender identity, but not the other forms of discrimination that the Equality Act would have covered.

Coda I

OUTSIDERS AND THE SHAPING OF HISTORY

In choosing between several dozen essays for this collection, I decided to include a few ("The Two Eds," "Mary Meigs") that reveal the "ordinary" side of daily life for some of us who came of age before Stonewall. Most of the portraits in this volume, though, are of figures who may not be household names but who led distinctly, and precociously, political lives. (I knew a number of them personally.) Many of them were too radical in their views to be today claimed by the centrists who still dominate LGBTQ+ life—people who stretched the boundaries of acceptable thought and behavior. Andrea Dworkin, for one, was an in-your-face radical feminist at a time when the LGBTQ+ movement itself was in its infancy. Sylvia "Ray" Rivera was a gender nonconformist at a time when deviations from the standard roles of "male" or "female" were tantamount to announcing yourself a "borderline personality." Essex Hemphill's struggle against racism was uncompromising to the point where he literally risked his life.

A number of the essays in *The Line of Dissent* focus on political issues and strategies that through time have prominently defined the LGBTQ+ movement. I myself have sometimes been a participant in the internal struggles that have periodically divided the movement, and my own views have inevitably influenced—not always consciously—who I decided to write about and *how* I wrote about them. Historians don't usually call attention to the fact that their process is irreducibly subjective, yet there's no escaping the fact that a work of history is always based on two main components: the fragmentary evidence that has survived and the unavoidably distorted interpretation of that evidence resulting from the historian's own distinctive experience and values. "Objectivity" does and should remain the goal, but no matter how scrupulous the historian, that goal can only be approached, not achieved. As I hope is obvious, I'm no exception to the rule.

In my view, for example, too many gay people have become mere assimilationists; they want in, they claim to be "just folks." It's a view I don't share. Many of us, I've long argued, have had a set of historical experiences different from the mainstream straight world, and, as a result, have developed a unique subculture with a special set of insights and perspectives. That subculture has much to teach the mainstream—if it would only open its ears—and in regard to a host of matters: that lifetime monogamy, for example, is not the only "moral" and fulfilling path to happiness; that many of us (more men than women, I believe) would affirm the difference between love and lust, the quite different expectations and rewards of both long-term relationships and short-term adventuring, the autonomy that results from not replicating the obligatory patterns and connections of the traditional family, the periodic blessings of being single and enjoying solitude, the deep pleasure that can attend nonsexual friendship, the freedom to discard encrusted notions about standard gender roles in favor of exploring expansive versions of "maleness" and "femaleness." Politically, too, we've produced our fair share of rebels, and across the board they've challenged the authoritarian structures embedded in both the classroom and the corporation, no less than in the war-making machinery that grinds out patriotic platitudes and mangles young lives.

But our potential insurgency has been much diluted over the past several decades, sidelined as a casualty in the campaign to win mainstream acceptance. The Gay Liberation Front's post-Stonewall demands have been replaced by the clamorous claim that we're just like everyone else—exemplified by the struggle for gay marriage and for the right of gay people to serve openly in the military. In the name of assimilation, we've muted our cultural differentness and concealed our transformative struggle against mainstream definitions of what it means to be human.

It hasn't turned out the way some of us had hoped back in the years immediately following the Stonewall riots. And maybe that's okay. Maybe assimilation, not transformation, is what most of us have preferred all along. Maybe becoming flag-waving patriots is the farthest out result ever possible—in this country, at this time. The grumblers among us always were and still are a decided minority; the gay majority itself tends to view us as ingrained malcontents in danger of slowing or destroying our acceptance by mainstream America.

Maybe, as is often charged, those radicals who banded together after Stonewall to form the GLF in 1970 were simply deluded utopians. Well, maybe. But mainstream America tends to level that charge against *anyone* who advocates substantive change—and nothing less than that, many radicals still believe, is equal to the threat of survival. Most of the people you've met in *The Line of Dissent* scorned "a little diddling around the edges" as insufficient to meet the challenges our country faces. Nothing will do, they argued, but a core reformation, with special emphasis on removing the deep racial, class, and gender divides that still characterize us. But, one could counter, surely a partial expansion of freedom is better than none at all. "No," most of the people in this book would respond: the long-range result of cheering minimal concessions as if the millennium has arrived not only misrepresents their depth and tangible impact but also dissipates the demand for *real* change.

The fact is, in the LGBTQ+ community these days, I don't hear much of any authentic, transformative call—except from the vehement trans community. The radical demand for social reformation is, in anything, coming from the Right. The country is going to hell in a hand basket, and most of us are still repeating the tired mantra of asking for "a place at the table." The subliminal subtext—inadvertent one hopes—in the "just like you" slogan is that we're just as committed to a shallow, callous, dumbed-down set of values so eloquently represented by the Neanderthals of the Republican Party.

I suspect that most LGBTQ+ people celebrated Stonewall's 50th anniversary with feelings of satisfaction at what was being widely hailed as the speediest success story in our country's long history of social protest. The insurgents among us were and are a depressed minority; even the gay majority views us as professional malcontents, perfectionist dreamers, unable to savor progress even when it stares us in the face.

There's some truth in that indictment. But only some. The focus of today's national gay organizations continues to be on assimilation, a goal based on the assumption that our mainstream institutions are structurally sound and morally acceptable. Some of us reject that assumption. What we see instead is the sheer cruelty of an increasingly powerful Far Right. We see Blacks still being shot down in the streets, women still being denied the right to control their own bodies, economic oligarchs still in control of the nation's wealth, perilous changes in the climate still being largely ignored, increasing billions still being spent on weaponry able to destroy whole cities, on guns for the masses, on cars without drivers, on trips to the moon. Yes, there's a progressive opposition gathering strength—but to date it has been stalemated by a deadlocked Congress and a Supreme Court racing to return us to the 19th century.

Joining and staying with the fight against concentrated wealth and entrenched power is a tough assignment. Most of us are already dealing with too much in our lives. We're weighed down with obligations, with piecing together a living, with the struggle to stay afloat. The exhausting demands of daily life are already threatening to overwhelm us; adding just one more straw to the camel's back (so it feels) could see us splayed out on the concrete.

But here's the thing, the paradoxical thing. *Some* people—like those featured in *The Line of Dissent*—don't throw in the towel, don't succumb to the daily pressures, don't sneak away from the barricades and melt back into the mute multitude. Where do these exceptions come from? Why do they join up? Why do they stick?

Multiple studies have concluded that no matter how abysmal the circumstances in which some children grow up, no matter how steep the odds against them, some small percentage of them do manage to survive—and even to thrive, to continue doing it *their* way, to remain in struggle against the powers-that-be—and who even manage to lead satisfying lives. The one ingredient that seems present for a large majority of such children is an adult figure who cares for them unconditionally—and who *encourages* rebellion against things as they are rather than caution against over-reaching.

Clearly, there haven't been enough such caretakers to go round. And so, it becomes much easier for the youngster, yanked off a path they'd tentatively set foot on, to give up on their "differentness," to bend to authority's "truth," to surrender their own peculiar ways and melt back into the anonymous crowd. Having been punished for being "weird," they switch their energy to winning access, to "fitting in." Most of us, of course, even those who start out ignoring or defying the rules, end up succumbing to them without even being aware that we're doing so. We want—at least some of us in some moods—the comfort of being accepted as one of the gang. Very few of us want to butt heads all the time, all day long. We, too, need some comfort, need to feel appreciated and understood, however briefly. And wanting that relief is no disgrace: the pressure to fit in, after all, is prodigious and, to avoid buckling under, we seek sabbaticals from the turmoil of resistance.

Some of us go in and out of political commitment, but the trick is to use the periods of retreat to renew our energy for an eventual return to the struggle. This, of course, is no less true for rebellious heterosexuals than for homosexuals. They, too, need some solace from the stranglehold of normalcy, a chance to break away from doing their lives by the numbers. Think of the comfort that at least *some* straight men manage to take upon learning that it's okay to be less emotionally rigid, to deflate their traditional role as "head of the family," breadwinner, ultimate authority, final decision-maker. Think, too, of the comfort many women take when, conversely, they break away from the rigid confinements of homemaker, cook, bottle washer, and nursemaid.

More people every day, or so it seems to me, are uncomfortable with their role in the traditional family; many of them nonetheless stay in the traces. They seem to do so hesitantly, reluctantly, frightened of trying on new roles, of being shunned by their conforming friends and neighbors, rejected by outraged families. And so, if they stick to their nonconforming ways at all, they make sure, simultaneously, that they modulate their differentness from the horde and polish their traditional credentials at least every *other* day.

And therein lies a problem. In times of stress, economic or otherwise, desertions from any new path become commonplace. In the 1930s, the devoted union man, to save his job, votes against collective bargaining. In the '40s, the believer in One World decides instead to don a military uniform just one more time. In the '50s, a canvasser for Henry Wallace's Progressives sneaks back into meetings of the centrist Democratic Party. In the explosive '60s, large numbers of "ordinary" people join the rabble-rousers in protesting the vicious war of destruction in Vietnam, and then straight away turn their backs on further protest and rejoin the scramble to maximize their income and status, to prosper in the same unjust world they had recently denounced.

By the mid-1970s, the retreat became a rout, and that included the once radical gay movement. The agenda of the Gay Liberation Front shifted from a determination to remake the world to the Human Rights Campaign's centrist focus on winning civil liberties for the already privileged. For "sophisticates" of the Fire Island circuit, political protest of any kind wasn't considered chic. It wasn't until the outbreak of AIDS in 1981 that a multitude of new recruits to political activism surfaced.

AND TODAY? Radical local groups like SONG in Atlanta are putting forth a political agenda close to the one offered by the GLF in the immediate aftermath of the Stonewall Riots: namely, a vision of genuine social transformation. GLF back then—SONG today. It insists that we seriously address poverty and racism at home, challenges traditional sexual and gender norms, and rejects the view that the monogamous, male-dominated family unit was the most reliable path to a satisfying life. In the GLF, the struggle for rights had been a means, not an end. It had scorned the right to join the military (to kill) or to sign up for state-sponsored marriage as unworthy primary goals for a social justice movement. As we know, GLF didn't last long. Americans have a short attention span, plus a *very* limited tolerance for transformative politics.

This is not to suggest that nothing of value has been accomplished in the fifty years since Stonewall. One would be a fool, or grossly misinformed, to defend such a position. There has, in fact, been a remarkable change in attitude toward sexual and gender minorities in the U.S. From being widely denounced as sinners and criminals and all but universally pathologized, we're now largely (if not unanimously) acknowledged as a respectable minority—even though entrenched homophobia remains widespread, especially in evangelical America.

When trying to measure "progress," much depends on the measuring instrument you use—and the wish list you start with. The recent surge of progressive politics, especially among the young, provides some hope that centrism may yet cease to enchant the imprisoned multitude. But take care. The jailers, their prisons becoming ever larger, are making it all but impossible to scale the walls. ▪

WHO ARE THE PATRIOTS?

The indictment of self-declared "lefties" has long been common sport. And over time, some of the country's most admired public intellectuals, careful to avoid crude polemics, have joined the hunt. The esteemed sociologist Daniel Bell, in *The Cultural Contradictions of Capitalism*, anticipated the Christian Right's denunciation of "hyper-individualism" and the "pursuit of pleasure," arguing that the hedonistic concentration on "self-expression" came at the expense of devotion to the "common good." And that common good, in turn—as Christopher Lasch argued in his influential book, *The Culture of Narcissism*—was centrally reliant on preserving the institutions of marriage and the family, with emphasis on lifetime, monogamous, heterosexual pair-bonding.

George Will, the Pulitzer Prize-winning columnist, has been still more apocalyptic, denouncing what he's called the disastrous encouragement of the view that "all notions of moral normality are 'mere' conventions," and thunderously warning that the prospect loomed "of the repudiation of the doctrine of natural right on which Western society rests," a doctrine, according to Will, that allows us to know and encourage "some ways of living that are right because of the nature of man."

The doctrine of natural right? The nature of man? Instead of pausing to define either, Will proceeds to a still higher level of pontification. Not even a liberal society, he grandly announces, can leave certain "essential values" to chance. And which values are those? Will's answer is forthright: "surely healthy sexuality is one: the family, and hence much else, depends on it." By equating "healthy sexuality" with "the family," Will implied that only when the aim of procreation is present are sexual acts morally acceptable. This is traditional Catholicism with a vengeance. And what follows in Will's cosmology is his certainty that "homosexuality is an injury to healthy functioning [that] ... often reduces sex to the physical" (as opposed to the metaphysical?); "it is a subculture based on brief, barren assignations." George Will remains a highly respected public intellectual with millions of readers.

The dozen or so people I profile in *The Line of Dissent* devoted themselves to a wide range of social justice issues, including some—like militarism and nuclear disarmament—that in 2023 no longer resonate as fully as, say, racism and the gender binary. My guess is that Sylvia Ray Rivera's story and the trans cause she pioneered, along with Essex Hemphill's resistance to racism, will seem the most immediately relevant to present-day readers and activists. Which is not to say that, in the near future, another imperialist venture overseas or the further curtailment of civil liberties at home won't once again move to the top of the Left's agenda.

Regardless of the disparity and present-day relevance of the cause they espoused, all twelve of the people I've written about do share one quality: they were steadfast over time in their advocacy, their unflinching commitment, to social activism of one sort or another. Their detractors then and since—the Daniel Bells, the George Wills—often cite that trait as evidence of implacable rigidity, proof positive of derangement. I happen to regard their tenacious activism as a virtue and—I want to make clear—one to which I myself cannot lay claim. For some stretch of time, my writing took precedence over my direct action involvement. However, often—as when I wrote my biographies of Paul Robeson and

Andrea Dworkin or Haymarket, about the labor struggle in the late 19th century—writing itself became a form of activism.

The reactionary Reagan years, paralleled by the gay movement's shift to a centrist course, heightened my disaffection with the mainstream gay movement. Most of my energy shifted to research and writing. I was guiltily able to soothe myself with the (possibly valid) argument that gathering archival material and writing about LGBTQ+ lives was itself a crucial undertaking, and that I was providing essential evidence for demolishing stereotypes about gay life that had long fed public perceptions and hostility. To that end, along with writing my own books, I founded and for ten years chaired the Center for Lesbian and Gay Studies (CLAGS). Then, in the 1990s, I helped to found Queers for Economic Justice, which focused on addressing the largely ignored needs of poor and working-class gay people. Alas, lack of support from the middle-class gay mainstream forced us to close our doors after half a dozen years.

Throughout, the dictates of conscience have always had to struggle against my temperamental need for solitude. For a writer, of course, periods of isolation are essential—but that fact sometimes serves as well as a convenient justification. My need to write dovetailed nicely with a built-in excuse for not getting, and staying, involved in political work. Further contributing to my periodic disaffection from politics, and a convenient rationale at some points, was the gay movement's substantial and verifiable shift from a broad agenda to a narrow centrism that focused solely on assimilationist issues like gay marriage and the right to serve openly in the military. My genuine opposition to a middle-class agenda was further fueled by a perfectionist temperament. I tend to emphasize not what's been done but what yet needs doing. The sun can shine for four consecutive days but if clouds appear on the fifth, then the cry goes up about our "consistently lousy weather." It isn't that I invent the discord that characterizes all movements for social change, but I sometimes do exaggerate it. In a world full of pollyannas, I tell myself, somebody has to. None of which is to say that my complaints have been groundless. The dilution of the gay agenda accompanied a strong national shift to the right. The state of the nation—after so much activist struggle and so many promising alternatives—hardly gladdens the hearts of those on the Left. It had been hoped that with Nixon's resignation, the duplicity and guile that had been part of his administration's DNA had ended as well. As I optimistically wrote at the time in my diary: "The country seems to have been snatched back from the verge of genuine executive tyranny—and of a puritanical, corporate kind that comes close to warranting the label 'fascist' ... Nixon's power seems irrevocably diluted—and that's much to be thankful for."

It soon became clear that the country's problems went far beyond Nixon. The Watergate scandal that destroyed his administration was marked as well by a period of steadily rising inflation and a decline in real wages. By the mid-1970s, a full-scale economic recession had taken hold. What had been a wave of strikes for better working conditions now turned into a mere trickle, and for the rest of the decade, the lot of working-class people continued to deteriorate and the corporate takeover of the country to expand steadily. Millions were out of work—the unemployment rate skyrocketed toward ten percent—and an unusual combination of recession and inflation (dubbed "stagflation") ground away at the savings of millions more. Business leaders, led by guru economist Milton Friedman, blamed the economic slump on the recent "over-indulgence" in working-class salary raises and benefits, while a significant number of white workers ascribed the downturn to the "intrusion" of undeserving Blacks into the skilled labor force.

The casualties were considerable. One was the labor union movement itself, as the number of enrolled members continued to slide. With unemployment on the rise, resistance to racial desegregation—especially when mandated through busing—deepened. The Equal Rights Amendment, which had passed Congress, ran into strong resistance on the state level. What had been a rising tide of expectations and considerable confidence among "outsiders" and "dissenters" slowed dramatically. On the Left, a profound cynicism began to take hold, and public criticism of mainstream institutions to recede—along with a rise in the number of the radical young people decamping to farms and rural communes. A prime target became the "spoiled, elitist brats" who had been agitating for feminism and gay rights—as if such "pseudo-issues," it was widely said, could possibly be taken seriously in the face of lost paychecks and empty bellies. New York City councilman Matt Troy gave angry voice to that resentment when he openly equated homosexuals with lepers.

It was a national climate begging for scapegoats, ripe for a sharp turn to the right. Across-the-board bigots like Jerry Falwell and Pat Robertson soon found their platforms, as did Anita Bryant with her "Save Our Children" campaign—save them from what she called "human garbage." Bryant rose quickly to prominence and took out full-page ads denouncing gay people as recruiters, seducers, and molesters of children. The truth (not that Anita Bryant cared) was very nearly the opposite: all studies of the sexual abuse of children did and still do agree that the vast majority of such cases involve young girls and heterosexual men, often family members or family friends. The studies' aggregate conclusion is that 92 percent of the children molested are female and 97 per cent of the molesters are male—making statistical nonsense of the claim that gay men were the primary villains. At one point, Bryant announced her bottom-line revelation: "God hates homosexuals because they swallow semen—they eat life." Really? And straight women don't? And what about lesbians? Logic and truth, of course, had little to do with Anita's popularity.

The struggle for gay rights was itself going badly. The City Council of New York once again defeated a gay rights bill; the Toronto police raided the offices of Canada's leading gay publication, *The Body Politic*; Florida governor Reuben Askew, who was known as a liberal, said publicly that he would not want "a known homosexual" teaching his children; vandals ransacked the feminist Diana Press in Oakland, California; the police fired rubber bullets into a gay rights march in Barcelona; and the editor of *Gay News* was convicted on charges of blasphemy in London.

I, for one, wasn't particularly happy with some of the developments within the gay movement itself. I remember going to hear several friends who were appearing on a panel, "Where is the Gay Movement Headed?"

and made the mistake of arriving early for the gathering at the Church of the Beloved Disciple. That in itself made me grouchy—seeing the last of the lavender-gowned holy celebrants exiting from Mass. In 1970, Father Robert Clement had founded Beloved Disciple as the first church to serve the gay community in New York City. I thought the community would be best served by having no church at all—let alone a thriving one. Beloved Disciple, nondenominational, with a membership of 600 and its own religious order (the Oblate Companion of St. John), prided itself on its ancient liturgy and its "high church" tone.

It reminded me unpleasantly of the Pride parade that same day. Some of the largest contingents had advertised their religious affiliations—Gay Presbyterians, Dignity, the Gay Synagogue, etc.—and their floats had drawn pronounced enthusiasm from those watching on the side-walks. It filled me—DNA-denuded of spirituality—with dismay. "More gay imitation," I wrote in my diary, "of the worst of straight culture; pious posturings that seem increasingly to dominate the movement." As I'd come to realize, a basic conflict had been building within the movement between those who wanted to adjust our image to win greater acceptance from mid-America and those who preferred to assert the real differences that set us apart. To concentrate on the former, I felt, was to deny our unique history and culture, and thus not merely to demean ourselves but also to prevent us from utilizing the specialness of our experience as a tool for a basic critique of traditional gender and sexual norms.

The panel itself that day exemplified the growing divisions within the movement, dominated as it was by the open antagonism between a woman arguing for the ongoing necessity of lesbian separatism and a male panelist insisting that only undefined "socialist strategies" would succeed in securing our rights. The one panelist who spoke eloquently for the views I upheld was John D'Emilio. He issued an articulate, forceful plea for the gay movement to pay more attention to issues other than those relating to sexual orientation—not only because such issues (the criminal justice system, economic inequality, racial discrimination) were important in themselves, but also because reaching out to our natural (and needed) allies was a winning strategy. The audience responded to D'Emilio's thoughtful critique not with questions, but rather a barrage of set speeches from the audience that sounded rehearsed, rudely unresponsive to the panelists' remarks.

RECENTLY, I came across in my own archives an excited review I wrote way back in the mid-1960s of Howard Zinn's two books, *The Southern Mystique* and *SNCC: The New Abolitionists*. What I wrote all those years ago still resonates for me. The "New Day" that SNCC and SDS called for way back in the '60s may currently be beyond reach, but to recall their expansive vision does restore some modicum of possibility, allows us to catch a glimpse of what may still be possible. It's difficult not to romanticize the young adults of SNCC and SDS. Yet there's no need to embroider. In their depth of feeling for each other and for their cause, in their simplicity and courage, they stand out against today's feeble pessimism, showing us what might be hoped for when the barriers that artificially separate people are broken down.

Too much has been said, perhaps, about the impossibility of producing a social justice agenda that places chief priority on the needs of the least fortunate, and not enough about its feasibility. At the moment, fear is mounting on the Left of what many have come to see as the irreversible growth of a compassion-free, malevolent Right. Yet it's still possible to feel that no determinant, be it the entrenched weight of habit, tradition, or biology, mandates hopelessness—or prevents the transformative impulse from re-emerging. Back in the '60s, the young rebels of SNCC and SDS marked a zenith of confidence that may no longer be available, yet that doesn't mean that nothing can be done. We're freer to act—and thus are far more accountable—than the determinists would have us believe. Today's young radicals continue to believe passionately that the fight for social justice is still worth waging.

This determination helps to explain why I've never forgotten the impact that a public panel on social movements had on me several decades ago. The standout speaker was Henry Schwarzschild, who'd been involved in the civil rights struggle for most of his adult life. The words he spoke still speak to me, hauntingly: "The country is sick to its gut of quasi-moral demands." And yet, Schwarzschild continued, for us to stop asserting those demands would "violate the claims of social decency." He then went on to pinpoint what I felt had been the central dilemma of many activists over time: "you have to decide whether you want to focus your energies on overcoming certain grievances in your own lives"—like winning equal pay for equal work—or "whether you want to fasten on the broader agenda of changing the country as a whole." Did we, in other words, want to be liberals or radicals?

Exactly. It was as if Schwarzschild had spoken to me directly, clarifying my longstanding but sometimes obscured conviction that my distinct priority was to work broadly—not solely, that is, to win civil rights for gay people but to enlist in a coalition of the marginalized to fight for a drastic overhaul of class, gender, sexual, and racial disparities. With regard to the gay movement itself, I thought Schwarzschild captured the central issue in a single phrase: "the gay movement has to create itself against the impulses of its own constituency." It had to identify the prime oppressor, in other words, not as straight men but rather patriarchal ideology and patriarchal social institutions (which also victimized many straight men—along with all women).

Utopian dreams have a long, tenacious history, and over time have a disconcerting way of springing abruptly back to life. Dormancy is not the equivalent of extinction—the current climate being a case in point. As the Trumpian Right in the country deepens both in numbers and in meanness of spirit, resistance has risen alongside it—as epitomized by Black Lives Matter. The struggle between the two continues, with neither as yet managing to vanquish the other. Perhaps the odds might improve for those on the Left if the multiplicity of causes and the organizations that represent them prove able first to unify their own constituencies and then to create a broader alliance between currently splintered and beleaguered groups.

From way, way back in my mind, a muted phrase—Talmudic?—echoes in my ear, fit for the occasion: "It is not incumbent on you to finish the task. Neither are you free to give it up." ▪